"Philip Wylie, more than a quarter century ago, stirred up sluggish minds with *A Generation of Vipers*. Never since, even in his prickliest jabs at 'Momism' in American life, has he written anything destined to cause such fury among the dogmatically religious or those who believe that man was created to rule the earth—until *The Magic Animal.*

"This is a book which one reads not only with concentration but with that rare mental stimulation of being made to THINK, not just to absorb. Whether we agree with Wylie or belligerently disagree, we will be made to use our minds."
—*The Chicago Tribune*

THE MAGIC ANIMAL was originally published by Doubleday & Company, Inc.

Other books by Philip Wylie

The Disappearance
Essay on Morals
Generation of Vipers
Opus 21

Published by Pocket Books

 *Are there paperbound books you want
but cannot find in your retail stores?*

THE
MAGIC
ANIMAL

Philip Wylie

PUBLISHED BY POCKET BOOKS NEW YORK

THE MAGIC ANIMAL

Doubleday edition published April, 1968
A Pocket Book edition
1st printing .... March, 1969

This *Pocket Book* edition includes every word
contained in the original, higher-priced edition. It is printed
from brand-new plates made from completely reset, clear, easy-to-read
type. *Pocket Book* editions are published by Pocket Books, a division
of Simon & Schuster, Inc., 630 Fifth Avenue, New York, N.Y. 10020.
Trademarks registered in the United States and other countries.

This book is dedicated
to my wife, Frederica,
   whose faith enabled its writing,
to my daughter Karen,
to Taylor Pryor, Karen's husband,
to their children, Tedmund, Michael and Gale,
to whomsoever reads it,
to their children and grandchildren
   and to those of all other people,
forever

*Toda la vida es sueño
y los sueños sueño son*
       —PEDRO CALDERÓN DE LA BARCA
(Life is a dream
and dreaming, a dream)

Contents

AUTHOR'S NOTE

Twenty-five years ago I set down the first sentence of a book called *Generation of Vipers:*

It is time for man to make a new appraisal of himself.

The date was May 12, 1942, very early in the Second World War. The book made me such a reputation that many literary critics assume it to have been my first. Long known as *Vipers,* I understand it is now required reading in some schools.

It was never intended as a textbook or for compulsory perusal.

Vipers was a collection of criticisms of our nation and its folkways, written in a half-dozen weeks in a mood of ribaldry and rage. But that casual sampling of faults has led me to believe I owe its readers a companion-piece.

For they have asked me a hundred thousand times in letters, and thousands of times in person, two questions they feel are justified:

What are you *for?*

What do you think about the world *now?*

In a way, *Vipers* should have shown its readers what I am *for*. Simple things, after all: my species, man, and his prospects, to put the whole business in a phrase.

I am for truth. I am for reality. I am for knowledge. Learning. Reason. Insight. Hope. Art. Excitement. Dreaming.

Love, in another way of saying.

But Americans don't take criticism with much courtesy. They have not yet perceived that their dearest aim, "progress," rests on criticism. You cannot progress till some aspect of a current state is faulted. I did a great deal of faulting in *Vipers*.

Another unsound but common premise of my critics is that the man who points out a flaw must know its remedy. That is a form of semithought. As a people so largely involved in technology, we should know better. One man can discover a mistake in a theory or a product that it may take a multitude of minds and years of time to find how to mend.

But my heated criticisms in *Vipers* suggest that I am not merely against many things but that I have ideas, at least, about mending them.

I do.

Here, I attempt to set them forth.

My ideas derive from many sorts of special knowledge. To try to express them often requires prelude since even the literate American isn't much cognizant of the sources I use, those in science.

So, though I composed *Vipers* in six weeks, I've spent two years on the text that follows. And a dozen years before that, writing parts of books and entire books with the same end, which I put away in boxes as failures.

The key to all such endeavors was stated in the opening sentence I have quoted. Man desperately needed to reassess himself then.

In the past quarter-century various groups of men have found more facts about our species. The understanding they now have, collectively, is far greater than what they understood in 1942. But their new knowledge, new theory, fresh insight, and changed evaluation are to be discovered only among scientists and in fragments that often are known solely by experts in a branch of a special discipline of one field.

A limnologist is not likely to keep up with the news from marine micro-paleontologists. And a solid-state physicist probably will not know much about the latest discoveries of those two. So the materials required for "new appraisal" compound at some geometrical or logarithmic rate, and the layman, be he an industrialist, a congressman, a professional man, or any other usual sort, rarely examines the sciences and believes, almost without exception, that its knowledge is past his comprehending.

The result is one that not many of us bother even to consider: *The more a few men learn, the more ignorant most become.*

As a writer who has had the curiosity, energy, opportunity, and the time, taken, if not sensibly available, I have kept up with these presumably arcane accretions of knowledge. And here I am trying to show what I believe this wealth of information demands of all men for any useful "new appraisal."

To do so I have chosen, after all my false starts and the long but unsatisfactory efforts, to set forth a brief account of how man came to be and what the specialists now know he is.

I have also, later on, used illustrative incidents and personal experiences where I felt they might help. I have given the many bits and pieces of concept separate headings, as my transitions might otherwise be blurred.

And thereby I have said, in effect, what I think about mankind "now."

Its essence can also be put in a sentence: *Modern man is relatively the most ignorant example of his species ever to exist.*

Compared to what some men know to be true, that is, nearly all men are far more ignorant than their ancestors who, till recently, had a general and proportionately larger grasp of the then-known.

To go on believing as most of us do in concepts of God, Nature, and Man that are as mistaken and as provably mistaken as the belief in a flat earth is to live with a mind precisely that obsolete. Yet we do, almost all of us. Our laws, moreover, sustain our bankrupt dogma. Yet our very possessions are no longer comprehensible to us. And we have all but destroyed our opportunities for rediscovering, as a people, what the few know that people are, and must do. Lest they perish.

Most of my material is subject to demonstration. Some, though, is my opinion. I have tried to keep the difference evident. I am not able to do any better in this, my own new appraisal, for I am none of the things that people expect of one who makes such an attempt. I am not inspired, that is, not a great artist; not a certified intellectual; perhaps not even under a sufficient compulsion as a man; and certainly no messiah.

What the world needs, I'm sure, is a new sort of iconoclast, a man who will set about smashing all the temples, cathedrals, churches, synagogues, and holy structures, but one who will do it without the aim of his revolutionary predecessors—that of setting up on the ruin a new edifice for new gods as the sign of his new doctrine.

It is the individual human being who, alone, must find his own belief, his religion, or its equivalent. And it must be his uninfluenced attainment and his responsibility, too, not his adoption of some collective system.

Karl Marx claimed religion the opiate of the masses and then founded a religion like the others save for the trivial matter of godhead.

We don't need any more of these faith-centered beliefs. For the method of faith has been shown worthless in nearly every manner by which pious or dedicated people employ faith.

What we need is a "religion," if I may say the word again, that is founded in honesty and on truth and therefore must contain no dogmas but only a principle: one that permits every mind to change its beliefs every time a new truth or a truer truth indicates that duty.

But mankind is so far from such lofty state that he shows no understanding of its necessity, let alone any wish to remake himself in a trustworthy form.

By advocating it, then, I am probably wasting my time. I may be an incomprehensible advocate, also.

Nevertheless!

THE
MAGIC
ANIMAL

Chapter One

GENESIS REVISED

1 / The True Beginning

IN THE BEGINNING there was no Word.

The beginning was Matter. And Motion.

The beginning was a lifeless planet and a stable star.

Life arose; and we can tell you how.

Life is a property of matter that appears under suitable conditions and evolves while such conditions persist.

There is not any mystery about the origin of life, now. Today or tomorrow man will recreate life in a form like that which first occurred in the archaic waters of earth. He has already made viruses in the laboratory and viruses are near to alive.

He is so close to the final achievement that he can say the whole story, assuredly.

At the beginning, chemicals were moved, mixed, and altered by the energies of the sun, of lightning, of volcano-burst. They grew more and more complex as they were mingled. Intricate molecules combined. Cell-like forms appeared. The hundreds of millions of years passed and one day a special cell emerged in the pungent broths of the ocean or of a lake. It had being; it ate food; it divided and so re-

1

produced. It was alive and it was life. Nothing important remains secret about its origin.

The event was inevitable in the circumstances. An ocean of mingled elements and the spectrum of energies meant life had to occur, given time, just as diamonds must when the pressures and temperatures are right for the crystallization of any available carbon. Only the date was a matter of mathematical chance and chance was allowed plenty of time, eons.

Perhaps life arose many times in slightly different or even identical cell forms, and perhaps these tiny beings perished in many single forms or colonies before the first alive species managed to avoid such a fate. But a life form became established in due course.

The food of this first life was abundant: chemicals sluiced from the land by the rivers and rains, heat-mixed into a rich supply, sun-joined, or transmuted by the lightning of archaic storms in gulfs of time. The primeval creatures soon changed, as they had to, and as the forms of beings have changed ever since. But in about a thousand such changes, all but one is pointless and usually harmful.

Today, we call the changes mutations and preserve the rare, valuable alteration to breed better animals and create new strains of crops and of flowers. Today, too, we find more and more of our own imperfections arise from some alteration of a parental gene. And in people, too, that eternal incidence of valuable mutant genes is unchanged. Where these molecules, which give its pattern to every human infant, are flawed, the child is commensurately afflicted.

Each useful gene-change in each thousand random variations gave its possessor a slight superiority in the common effort to survive—the effort that involved the first alive cell and still involves each cell and all cells. Every owner of such an improvement was better at survival than its sire, since its built-in new benefit had that very value by definition. But any mutation, the harmful sort or very rare one of benefit, was itself rare.

Perhaps three billion years ago, a time span once believed unimaginable, is the approximate date of the successful rise of a chemical complex into what we call an alive state. Three billion years is not an unimaginable time interval however, and we would serve ourselves well to learn to sense such numbers as billions and the greater measures of the spans of time and the reaches in space. For those who cannot conceive of them cannot think in the only terms that enable anyone to understand reality nowadays.

The early living units, in due course, formed colonies like the algae and molds that most people think to be slime.

Such is prejudice, for the primordial slime was composed of crystals as is all living tissue still. Life substance is sharp and brilliant; it has geometric configurations like gem stones and is slime only to the ignorant mind, the mind that has had no chance for learning or the mind that rejects truth offered it.

In due course a one-celled species evolved with a new and mightily advantageous design. A design with two forms, male and female. In the female, numbers of units were formed— eggs, which were not spawned until they had been fertilized, that is, implanted with material from a male cell of the same new species.

Hitherto, life forms had increased by dividing in halves that then grew into whole beings, and divided again. But the two-sexed species enabled each pair to produce many of their kind. And each of the offspring now had, as the inherited code for its form and functions, an admixture of the genetic codes of two parent cells. So its variation was much greater than that of the halved cells of sexless beings.

2 / Why Sex?

Slowly, by those infrequent, random changes and the survival of the rare mutants with helpful differences, our ancestors evolved. The process used minute differences, but each enhanced its owner's ability to adapt to the local or some slightly foreign environment. The rise of a new species took eons and could be seen only if a motion picture of the event were made at the rate, perhaps, of one frame a century.

Joseph Wood Krutch, with whom I have the luck and honor to be acquainted, has a special name for this slow drama. Each accidental-but-helpful gene change is, in his term, a new "invention of Nature." And it can be informatively regarded by that word: invention. Of all such inventions, the next most dazzling was sex.

It was also a step-by-step achievement. The beings that reproduced by dividing in two eventually began to exchange nuclear material long before they became male and female. It was an occasional act that may be seen in some one-celled creatures, today. Ultimately, however, there emerged a class of creatures, still single-celled, but of two sorts, distinct enough to be clearly male and female. The female's eggs had to be fertilized by a male in this new species.

The benefit of that invention was twofold. In the females, the eggs were formed internally; but when fertilized and hatched, the offspring were genetically more varied than those produced by simple division. The genes that carried the pattern for their forms were combinations of the genes of two beings in the new species. The possible variations of genetic material thus resulted in much greater diversity of the young. And that obviously provided a greater selection of forms for adaptation, and for survival.

But the far more stunning result of Nature's invention of sex was that it increased the numbers of every generation. Where reproduction by division had limited each new generation to two beings, in place of the divided one, sex now made the numbers in each new generation a multitude. The early, one-celled creatures might have had twenty sons and daughters, hatched from twenty eggs formed in the female cell and fertilized by a male. Twenty for two, instead of the pre-sex limit of two from one, per generation!

As evolution proceeded and organisms became many-celled, that rate rose. Countless lowly species have thousands of fertile eggs, or as in oysters and numerous fish, millions, per generation. Innumerable insects produce such masses of offspring too. And that multiplication of a species, per generation, was the marvelous advantage of sex.

For when a generation merely adds one unit to its prior generation, that species will not be able to evolve very fast. The chance that a mutation, let alone a one-in-every-thousand valuable mutation, will occur in any one generation is remote. But a life form that, owing to sexual reproduction, can produce a million fertile eggs per pair, and perhaps do so several times in the life span of a pair in each new generation, has nearly a million times better chance per generation at that rare, priceless gene shift. The mutant individuals will be abler to survive than their traditionally formed siblings, and so likelier to meet and mate, for one thing. Genetic improvements can be passed on by like-altered pairs or by one of a pair, through the eventual mating of two of its descendants with the same beneficial gene.

So the "invention of sex" astronomically accelerated the evolutionary process. If sex had not evolved, if life on earth had continued to proceed by sexless fission, the highest forms on earth today might be jellyfish, or worms of some sort.

But, as the brilliant Dr. Krutch further observed—and was first to do so as far as I'm aware—sex involved a new liability. The very capability for producing thousands and millions of new beings per generation, if without limit, would defeat its purpose. A few unlimited species would certainly and soon populate every livable area and use up all the available food in the world. A few species, then, would spoil Nature's evolutionary process, since it has involved a production of the greatest possible numbers of species, not merely the greatest numbers in a few kinds.

With sex, then, came the need of a biologically essential limiting factor, as Krutch made clear. And as everyone can easily perceive when told.

The new invention was death.

All two-sexed creatures die.

Previously, the generations produced by the dividing of sexless, one-celled creatures did not automatically perish. Death was accidental then; statistically certain, sooner or later, but not mandatory at any point. An amoeba might divide in two, not dying, but living on as two beings. The two might divide into four, the four into eight, the eight into sixteen, without any deaths during all four generations. If our ancestors had had intelligence at that pre-sexual stage, they would have imagined themselves to be immortal, or at least potentially so, with death a risk but not a certainty for any individual. The price paid for sex was, and remains, mortality.

All two-sexed creatures die assuredly. Many kinds die immediately after they have performed the function required of them to ensure their next and abundant generation.

Krutch's insight has endless connotations, plainly. It suggests much about man that men have not considered. For example: Since death is the cost we pay for sex, and since life evolved fast enough by sex to produce us, it seems to me mankind ought to find a sufficient compensation in being male or female for having to die.

In his essay, Krutch made no such assertion. It will not be found in any scientific treatise. The thought is my own. But its truth is implied wherever life exists. How?

Nature is even-handed with all beings. Each evolved advantage of every species gives rise to a commensurate liability, for an unlimited advantage would, by definition, lead to the conquest of all, or of many other species, by the creature endowed with a capability not finite. The lethargic reptile that took wing as swift bird lost its great span of years. The dog that smells and hears so acutely pays with poor vision. The automated efficiency of the insect leaves it helpless wherever it meets unprogrammed situations. This balance occurs universally.

But to modern man, especially Western Christian man, the suggestion that human maleness and femaleness ought to be susceptible of an expression that would make us ready and willing to die will seem horrendous. For our beliefs, faith, culture, and supportive law have been arranged to make us imagine that sexuality is shameful, dirty, obscene in many innocent enjoyments, and even the essence of Original Sin. Sex is ruled by the church, sanctioned as permissible only under church-permit, and death, too, is ordained as a bearable prospect, or one of eternal damnation, according to the individual's submission to or violation of the repressive and often ugly ordinances of the church.

This usurpation of sex and death as a claimed route to ecstatic immortality (for the rule-abiding) is the instrument by which most of our minds have been corrupted—made guilty and, therefore, held in the thrall of the church.

Yet, if human sexuality be the root of man's evil, as we believe and furiously try to confirm in law, then this aspect of man represents the first violation of its eternal principles, by Nature. God, in that case, created man to cheat him and to torment him. Such is the unarguable sense of that special set of regulations we call "sex morality" and ordain as if in this area the perfect morality of Nature had become, for man, a mean and perverted repudiation of its own basic ethos.

But suppose we do note that our sex "morals" are man-made and related by man to his species only. Suppose we then assume that being a man or a woman should of itself justify the cost of our death. How then should we behave? It is a good question, I am sure, and the most important next one for man to ask and so, hopefully, to resolve. At the moment, however, I shall let it stand as a question, and no more. For, to ask it straight and expect it to be understood or even heard, a jungle of human delusions must first be cleared away.

3 / When Did Man Give Himself That Honorary Title?

Man has been here on earth a long while.

The ape he was became a non-ape at some distant point. But the recognition of manhood was not sudden, I am sure, and fossils attest to that assurance.

Yet somewhere, sometime, two million years ago or more, man began to see himself as a distinct creature and, in his view, far superior to the rest.

Then the news went round.

The news of the big title, self-applied: Man.

The Word.

Whence, then, came the Word?

Man invented the Word, and all words.

That must become understood now.

A short fifty years ago most people were skeptical even of the fact of evolution. Those few who then knew the truth believed, however, that man had arisen some twenty thousand years in the past. They quickly have learned otherwise. So must we.

Today it is known that man was not a whole, finished, and sudden-appearing creature. His primate ancestors moved from forest to prairie perhaps at least ten million years ago, some five hundred times longer than was supposed, when man's descent was first seen. Man probably appeared in about our form a million years ago. The time does not matter here. Perhaps there were even several kind of men and but one of them endured. Or possibly we are descendants of assorted proto-men. No matter.

An ape with a slightly improved brain, an animal, we would say, sired our sires.

What made one such, ultimately, a man? What was the distinctive attribute of the first creature with which we identify? Here are samples of our usual, scientific suggestions of what may differentiate man from other animals and especially from apes.

Speech.

Contemporary apes communicate but do not converse, exactly. They have, however, a wide range of hoots and grunts, calls and cries with particular meanings. Their gestures and expressions are many also, and with understood meanings.

What about *reason?*

Apes can understand symbols to some degree. They are able to learn to use tokens as money to buy food. So we may say they have brains that not only enable them to communicate, if not to converse, but brains that allow them to abstract a little—to comprehend that one object may stand for or relate to a different idea, thing, or procedure—which is imaginative and the basis of all thought, all reason.

Till just the other day, as our history goes, many scientists believed our earliest human sires took on that aspect even before they began to use true words. The dividing line between what we call animals and early man was believed by such scholars to occur with *tool-use.* The brain that could employ and modify objects for useful purposes designed by that brain is man's exclusive organ; and the earliest primate to own such a brain was a man. They used to say.

But yesterday, as real time passes, it was found that wild chimpanzees make and use tools. They strip leaves from their stems and probe with those refashioned sticks into holes to retrieve termites they then eat. Termites otherwise inaccessible. And they crush leaves to dip in puddles of water too shallow to scoop or too deep in crevices to lap. They dip their crushed leaf sponges into such water and squeeze it into their thirsty mouths. Tools, of course. And occasionally they hurl rocks or sticks as weapons.

In the deep past of primates, men lately also discovered there were certain little apes that hunted baboons with clubs and seemingly built fires to cook their prey. Tools, indeed! If toolmaking and tool-use define man, what of those archaic "fire apes" of Africa?

It is then necessary to acknowledge that such primates are not subhuman, by the "tool" definition. Not exactly mere beasts. Loren Eiseley's ape-cooks are extinct, so no semantic warp is required for them. The chimps are contemporary, however.

So, as people saw capacities they considered human in apes, some did suggest apes be upgraded. Given a qualified membership in the human line—made, say, two percent members. The other and far more logical inference didn't occur to such people—the inference that men are, still, animals. Only animals. Wholly animals. Animals who elaborated brain-use especially, and then exploited their wit to create an illusion about men: that they are not animals, or are superanimals. Which, of course, is vanity, as they ought now to realize.

In any case, our presumed distinctions between us and them are but that—presumed—and ridiculously presumptuous.

Multitudes of orders of animals use skills for further instance. Some ants pluck leaves as food for fungi they raise to eat. Birds build nests. Rodents dig complex and purposeful burrows with rooms for various functions and hidden entrances and exits. There is a fish that uses a water jet to knock insects out of the air. Gulls combine their ability to fly and the convenience of rocks below in order to drop and crack shell-enclosed sea food. Such uses of objects for adaptive purposes are numberless. Yet none of it was seen by scientists as the making or the use of skills, or the evidence of any awareness; not till very recently.

Why not?

The skills employed by the ants, birds, chipmunks, fish, gulls, and others in their countless kinds are not their conscious inventions, usually. What serves them and the way it serves generally involves no individual thought, as we define thought. These animals have inherited the program, the procedure. What they do is, therefore, called instinctual. It is innate. It is a response to a built-in mechanism. The form of each contains structured matter that produces those functions, we now say. And the pioneer in all such acts was usually a mutant, we state, one with the new trick built into his genes by purest chance. We tend to say such things, unless, of course, we still cling to home religious doctrine that is no longer tenable by any educated person. Men with even a modicum of contemporary knowledge accept the biological proof of instinct in all living beings.

Except, most still say, *for man*.

And now, to some degree, *for chimps* also.

Most of us still believe that in man an absolute change occurred. And we generally imagine the event was instant, complete, and pervasive. The Christian myth supports that notion. We are wrong if we heed such old tales though. Man emerged gradually; but instinct remained. Man merely hid the fact of it, to enhance the illusion of his own transcendence.

Man did become aware, however, in a degree that no other being is aware. He knows who he is, and what he does, and why, at least superficially. Knowing that, he could deny he had an animal's nature. He did so. He insisted he was born with a mind which, in a twinkle of time, shook off the instinctual patterns that, for some three billion years, had been the guide of all living things.

Only we now find our hitherto-assumed monopoly of awareness and individuation is shared, somewhat, by an ape. And maybe by some ancient apes of which many must have been able to communicate quite well, and which did use clubs, and even, perhaps, fire for cooking. Of these, several weren't ancestors to man or even near relations. Their high degree of humanoid qualities somehow failed to lead to that further step in evolutionary complexity that produced man. Only one line or one set of lines of similar creatures managed to sustain a certain special tendency toward evolving awareness that appears in our species. Perhaps just one final mutation, occurring in just one non-man, accomplished that.

The father of us all.

From him, we inherit our language skills, our infinite capacity to use tools, our strong sense of identity, and the general awareness that enables us to know we exist, each one as an *I*.

Our prized, so-called humanity, too, began with the him who was our first father or the her who mothered us all, if man arose by a last mutation.

Our love was born.

That all this may yet be superimposed on an instinctual matrix, many scientists might deny, and most persons now alive consider false or, at least, act as if it were false.

The idea that our awareness is still directed and driven or even influenced by the innate relationship of form and function observed in all other orders was scarcely considered until a century ago. Then, Sigmund Freud began to offer data that indicated man must be motivated in ways identical with or analogous to the innate ways of the rest of living creatures. Other psychologists have probed the matter in other ways. And their information has made our instinctual nature evident. Very recent biological findings have finally established those suppositions of psychology by tangible proof. Instinct rules man; and to deny that now is but to show an ignorance of known truth.

Instinct was always apparent in human acts, however. No other force could account even for the fury with which men hold to their beliefs, against all evidence and all reason, including the still-prevailing belief that they are not instinctual.

We remained blind to instinct only because recognition of it would deprive us of our singular arrogance, our long-time belief in ourselves as not only superior to other animals but possessed of qualities denied them. Not beasts, but divine. Not subject even to death, but individually immortal, we said. Not just flesh and blood, a body fitted with implicit and appropriate functions, but something unbound by flesh and even by time, owing to a special attribute, a soul.

How could we have blundered so? And why?

The insight needed to perceive why we contrived that massive, enduring error is not difficult for honest people to gain, I am sure. Let's try to gain it.

The first step involves only a rearrangement of man's usual description of himself.

He claims to be, in Krutch's phrase, Nature's greatest invention. Perhaps so. But he has yet to prove that, even in the sense he means.

What he is, in truth, differs even here.

Man is an animal in whom inventiveness itself evolved, the inventiveness that had been Nature's monopoly for three billion years, a monopoly seldom licensed even a little, till man was yielded the art, entirely!

Man is not the invention of a supra-animal. That is his idea. In fact he is an inventive animal, which, of course, is still quite grand. Now, let's enlarge our analogue.

The millions upon millions of ever-more-complex species, with their ever-rising ability to adapt in more varied ways to differing environs, can be seen as separate inventions of Nature. They had nothing to do, or precious little, consciously, with their changing forms, their diversifying functions, and the on-going elaboration of both.

Then, slowly, a next animal evolved, a rare type, being relatively unspecialized and so capable of immense adaptability; a species that became increasingly aware and, so, capable of conscious acts to abet its adaptation. The newly invented creature thus became an inventor.

With every deliberate invention and with every discovery useful to this species, its self-awareness grew correspondingly. Who first sharpened a stone and fitted it with a handle to make an ax for a preconceived purpose knew that he was thus acting, and acting as an individual.

He knew another thing, too, however vaguely at its beginning: He was employing past observation, in his present, for a future intent.

He had thus entered with his mind and commenced to employ another dimension besides the three of space. The new dimension was time. His unspecialized form permitted this being to sense the present as space in which to be aware of time past and of time yet to come. And as that dimension opened up for man, all that he is, which other animals are not, became accessible to him, and so led him to be, today, what he is—or thinks he is—that is different from his fellow beasts.

4 / Early Explorers in the New Territory of Time

In another book published years ago, I tried to set forth this idea, which I regard as a subjective but evident experience of our ancient forebears as they entered time's dominion.

The concept was my own. But it still seems to be justified by such understanding I have of man's present condition, his history, and what has been found about his past, together with all I understand of the life sciences, of biology, that is.

If my theory is right, or even nearer right than others concerning the same situation, it merits an attention I did not attract to it then. Oddly enough, certain aspects of human belief and behavior I described to illustrate applications of my fundamental concept seem to have been entered into general thought as if they'd long been there. Yet this principle remains unnoticed.

What follows here partly assumes that my overlooked principle is valid. But evidently it is a difficult idea for even the educated to encounter raw and perceive as to import. Yet its import is total and shattering, since it means that the way we think about man is utterly mistaken. Few want to see themselves so very much in error.

I shall here undertake again to explain my insight. And may be able to do so with more force and clarity than before owing to the advances that have subsequently occurred in the animal behavior area. Nothing, at any rate, in the scientific knowledge I had when I first wrote, or in knowledge since gained and become known to me, diminishes my sense of the truth in my concept. All, on the contrary, seems to give it support. With that I put it forward again.

Animals-not-men, including our pre-human ancestors, obviously lack (or lacked) the ability men own to employ time as if it were a space or a territory, by imagining.

Animals can learn a little and remember a little. Even cockroaches can learn a simple maze and remember the proper path for a day or so. That much time span is theirs. They use a bit of its dimension, with aim and effect.

But scientists are leery, and rightfully, of trying to guess what any animal's sense of "self" may be. I, however, do not quite need to conform to their exacting rules.

I can guess a bit about "what it's like" to be a lynx. By basing that imaginary idea on what a lynx does, and what it doesn't and cannot do, I can guess about its sensations of time. It remembers what it was taught by its parents as a youngster—about local dangers and the ways to hunt. It is able, given the luck, to learn about some new factors, such as the sudden arrival of man, the hunter, in a region where man had not been before. A lynx may, then, use his experience to invent novel ways to locate and avoid men and may even teach those skills to its offspring.

But its basic sense of being is of its present. Most of what it needs to do it knows innately. No one will have taught it to mate, for example. But sufficient motivation arises in the lynx at the suitable time to enable it, perhaps clumsily and after some ineffectual first attempts, to carry out that function. And it does that *when* it does, out of present-time impulse and without the slightest awareness of its own prior creation by that means or of the act as one that extends its kind into the future of the lynx species.

As for the lovely creature's sense of *I*—what is it? Little more than sense of *I*-right-now. An awareness, perhaps that it is one of the lynxes. A realization that it has diverse reactions to each and every other lynx when at least one or more are present. A constant identification of itself as *not* any other living species it encounters. And a sense about them of great diversity, relating to their menace and so on. A sense of lynxish *entity,* then, but only insofar as that is useful at the present moment.

Man has all that, too. But when his species, or its immediate ancestral form, began to use its imagination to enter and move about in time, a difference arose between man, lynx, and all other animals. This new creature's memory of its past was not idle, mere nightmare, or, it may be, gloat. What it remembered could be evaluated, now, for future ends such as improving techniques of predation or of escape from bigger predators. At first, of course, the present-time employment of imagination to exploit the past for future gains was a vague and occasional act. Man's ego was still much like the lynx's, "now-fast" and identified objectively.

But we do not enter time as we do the three dimensions of space—in reality. We do it by making images of past events and, from them, making new images in our present that may relate valuably to other images, those of future needs or wants. This image-making is man's "magic," in my term, here. But its probable early employment is causing speculative anthropologists and others a worry, as their image, that I find a little funny. Why?

Assume that time became a territory occupiable by human imagining.

From the day when a man began to use time as such territory to the day when he became aware that he was doing exactly that, a million years may have passed. For unmeasured ages, in other words, man used time without an abstract recognition of time as comparable to distance, bounding areas, but also as if boundless.

In the interval, however, his explorations of the dimension endowed him with an attribute almost wholly new in nature, a sense of ego. For a sense of ego like ours is possible only through an understanding of time as a dimension.

Our human ancestors, human because they had thus begun to use, or enter into, time's domain, did not soon form concepts of themselves as existing in time. They merely exploited what they could snatch and use in the region for objective aims. The practice grew and it spread. It was pragmatically fertile.

The rudiments of culture appeared. Instinctual needs had to be fulfilled, of course. Nevertheless, the ways of doing so became more varied than those of other species. The means to adapt grew to be many also—skins for clothes, fire for warmth, thorn hedge or stone barricade as a protection against predators, clubs, knives, scrapers, nut-and-seed pounders, caves for homes, rude shelters, the discovery that co-operation among men would greatly amplify the capability of any equal number acting separately—all that, and more. And ever more.

What time-use permitted, in another sense, was a space in which to contemplate causes and then deduce effects. Of course, causes were not soon really understood on any major level, and effects were therefore often ascribed to unrelated causes. That process is still nearly universal, and the right name for it is superstition.

But even in man's limited explorations of time's territory—his very early and partial but growing grasp of an ability to reason, and to do so owing to that unique property reason requires, imagination—his species developed in a new way and along a special line.

It could, a little, do what man does now a little more: *think*.

That rudimentary skill gave his species an immense advantage over all other animals. He could plan, as they could not. He could observe and reason and then act in ways no longer limited by instinct and its time-present condition, its unaware or, at most, only faintly aware perception of past lessons, its concentration on the now, its ignorance of the morrow.

The best inventions of other species do not require any great ability to use time deliberately, as man does. Instinct has only an immediate goal. Its surge and purpose need not even be known, nor even its existence, before it becomes operative in them. So an animal's instinct prevails. It cannot set aside even temporarily what it must do, even to wonder what *it* is subjectively. For what it is has already been sufficiently described by what it must do; so its detachment remains faint or nil. Much detachment, possible only in present time, would be dangerous, since it would use up a space where instinct should remain active or at least on tap.

That is still man's frequent condition, too! And his constant opportunity, usually ignored.

Abstraction is trifling in the animal mind. Symbolic employment is limited to a few species—apes, porpoises, perhaps some others, but not many, in our sense of symbol-use. And no animal save recent man is aware in its present of its infinite condition. There's our principal otherness. What is it?

No other being knows all its life that it will die.

But when man became able to employ time in his head lucidly, he discovered, in whatever primitive shape he then could, that he was not only *I,* and *I*-knowing, but that his *I* would die.

5 / The Grand and Greedy Design

The cost of sexuality is death as has been shown. Man long ago discovered the cost, but not the reason for it. Not, almost, till this moment!

When man became aware of his certain, individual doom, his then-new sense of self was affronted.

For that new and seemingly independent sense of *I* was still bound to the instinctual state of man's ancestors. They did not know about death in the sense that the knowledge pervaded or could even enter their every living moment. What they did know, what activated them, was only those present-time drives designed wholly for one end: the maintenance of their species. Each living thing has that central and transcendent design for maintaining its kind.

An individual's survival is always of far less importance, a commonplace that needs no illustrative support.

Most of the time and the energy of most birds is devoted to individual finding and defending a territory and with that, to attracting a mate, mating, and rearing its young by feeding and protecting them and by teaching them what they must learn to survive, where such instruction is needed for the species. And that is so for lions. Neither birds nor lions have to be taught how to find a territory or to mate—it is instinctual knowledge. The proper urges occur automatically at the proper age. But bird or mammal, instinct or learned behavior instinctually taught, all is designed for the perpetuation of the species and for the individual only in the degree necessary to that unknowable end. With insects and other less sophisticated beings, the drive toward species maintenance is altogether innate. Nothing need be taught (even though much can be learned, it has been found), yet every lowly creature does what it does for the continuum of its kind, exactly and exclusively.

So the fundamental purpose of life is species maintenance. It could not be otherwise. Life depends upon that one motivation, innate, learned, or the product of awareness and of inventions that such an imaginative state permits.

All life has an identical command: carry on.

In our special way, we are aware of the order as it relates to all beings but our own kind. When a female animal battles to death to protect her offspring we call that a display of mother love, though it is mother fury, in fact. But it means to us that the mother's continuum through her young is more demanding than her own survival.

As man evolved, however, a new, deceitful, but bewitching, song flooded his mind: the melody of *I*—self-enchantment, owing to self-awareness. Power diapasons rising from practical uses of time.

As man, the beast continued necessarily on the trajectory of life that all other beings have to accept and follow. His young had the same importance as all other young creatures. If his kind was to endure, they had to be procreated, reared, protected, and trained until they could continue that process. Whatever that required of this brainier primate, he had to accomplish, even as the others.

But to a being with the new sense of self, the capacity to use time, one with such inventiveness as was thitherto only Nature's, the sure knowledge of death seemed unbearable.

The first men to come by it were surely horrified. It spoiled all the fun of being men. Their time-use, which had so clearly established their supremacy among the beasts and thereby inflated them so immensely, now suddenly and treacherously revealed their individual doom. It was like a complete betrayal, I'm sure. Think why.

Underlying man's consciousness was that evolution-long drive toward species continuum. Perhaps the feel of it, in man's prehuman ancestors, was akin to a sense of immortality. No forebear had known he would die, the early man must have felt. What then had happened to the ancient confidence in present-time foreverness?

The ego of man could not by then accept the continuum of his kind as the sufficient purpose of existence and his true and only form of potential immortality. He had come to seem too valuable to himself as an individual for such sacrificial jettison.

Dilemma!

How could the new and great self be enjoyed when its very perception revealed its temporal nature?

How could I maintain my obvious superiority while knowing I was mortal and might perish in the next hour, or week, but, whenever, that I surely would?

What suffice it that my offspring continue my kind when each of them also, individuated and not-me but another self, is as surely doomed?

What escape might I design to be rid of this ego-shattering vista I have seen by exploring time to this degree?

Cast about. Put your new attribute to work, your imagination.

Invent.

Maybe, for instance, this sudden perception of my death is mistaken. Maybe I misread the evidence of corpses. Maybe there's another life even for them?

The dead aren't destroyed, just gone elsewhere? After all, everything in my mind is an invisible idea including this idea of my certain death. Obviously such a humiliating idea is a crazy error. The "self" of the dead must just go to some unseen place, being invisible as my living *I*.

So man surely began to invent that place.

I, he decided, having this knowledge of me, being therefore different from and superior to other creatures, can readily perceive my *I* is something apart from flesh. So I have an *I* of insubstantial sort, a spirit that is not flesh; it is a ghostly soul; and it will be immortal, though my body dies. It will, at that moment of death, leave my body and join the old ghosts, where they, the souls of my ancestors, abide. In the Happy Hunting Grounds, the Elysian Fields, Paradise, Nirvana, Heaven.

Or (and this, as I shall show, is an accompanying and inevitable part of any such invention) I shall go to an afterlife with two possible kingdoms—one of reward, the other of punishment. Punishment due me, if I have not here sedulously carried out the proper orders of my tribe, obeying the rituals and observing the taboos that describe the roads to my afterlife.

That came about, of course, because instinct still imposed its moral form on the invention. And till man thus corrupted it, all instinct was moral, determining right and wrong perfectly for every species. So man had to relate some right-and-wrong system even to his great delusion.

That delusion soon became his overriding, conscious concern.

He turned away from the meaning of existence as species survival, and so as the only possible likeness of immortality for his species. He switched to an effort to preserve himself first, not his posterity as always before.

He filched from his posterity that portion of their due that he required to establish his selfish lie. Man gained by stealth from instinctual morality his corrupt means to strengthen his illusion of personal eternal life. His offspring could be handed the same boon, the faked afterlife, as compensation for their loss of their due care, and love, and the parental sacrifice previously implicit in that now-abandoned devotion.

And that was the beginning of man's perpetual cycle of calamities, his failure to this hour to *be,* as being is meant.

Long, long after the Beginning, then, came *that* Word.

And the word was not God, but Fraud.

The true word was twisted into saints and demons, angels and fiends, into water gods and gods of the winds—the endless gods men clung to with that stubbornness which all other species exhibit, not for themselves as individuals, but for their pure purpose, the continuation into All Time of their species.

Man thus perverted the meaning of life owing to his dread and his vanity. He does so still, Christian or pagan, atheist, humanist, or communist.

The force supporting that act of craven arrogance was the basic life-drive of all men, all animals—now perverted. Once man invented a territory in time, beyond death, any heaven and hell, any mystique for on-being, the power of his territorial nature was available to sustain the myth.

For instinct cannot distinguish such fictitious novelties. So it became harder to abandon that artifice than any other task of the mind. The continuing expansion of man's awareness made it seem to an equal degree ever more necessary to believe the myth, his contrivance, in its soon-varying forms. Varying, because, as men migrated over this planet, distance, new environs, and new adaptations, together with fading memories, led to new arrangements of his abiding fantasy. The first religions of men, their primitive myths, thus began to differ.

Then, whenever men with conflicting myths encountered one another there occurred on both sides a repugnance, a sense of the error in the other, now seen as the heathen, the infidel, the territorial brigand.

And holy war began.

So essential to ego, to human vanity, to this assumption of a soul, was fealty to the local myth concerning the way to post-death existence, that all contrary reality, fact, or truth was denied if that could be managed. Managed in any fashion, however senseless, stupid, inhumane, brutal, or cruel. The residue of inconvenient truth was ignored or misinterpreted to fit the local dogma; that failing, it was held to be one of God's mysteries or God's paradoxes and beyond all human understanding. Maintenance of the local doctrine, whatever it might be, was more important than honesty, realism, logic, truth, plain common sense, or even sanity. The basic invention had to stand firm else its essential lie about immortality in the territory beyond death-time would founder.

The area in which man therefore allowed himself to observe reality, measure it, and understand it correctly became limited to that region in which he could do so without disturbing his design of his hereafter or the rituals and ceremonies described for his lifetime behavior by that. His laws, social codes, manners, compulsions, taboos, and all such doctrinal baggage was set outside inquiry; to doubt an established faith was made heresy, punishable by death—even now, sometimes, as in the USSR, and even though the faith there is secular.

Man's imaginative potential was thereby locked into a prison to serve his hopeless intent.

Whenever a man used imagination logically and so uncovered some new truth contrary to local dogma he was forbidden to disseminate that truth or he was killed as a fiend. Credulity prospered; the search for knowledge faltered; and learning became a discipline in ways to evade learning, save for certain practical ends.

The earth was flat because it looked flat to the priesthood. It was bounded by the sea because wherever men went they came to the sea.

It was the center of the universe and the sun went around it, or back and forth across it, because man had decreed himself the center of everything, and would not have it otherwise lest he lose his imagined hold on the immortal territory.

Was he not obviously divine, anyhow, and no beast? Proof? He could kill any living animal. Q.E.D.

In the third century before the birth of Christ a mathematician named Eratosthenes, who believed the earth to be a globe, devised a way to measure it and found by a tidy experiment a figure for its radius that was only fifty miles off from the fact.

The believers in myths forgot it, perhaps, or never heard of it, or if so, dismissed the knowledge as heresy. And when Galileo presented some similar information nearly two thousand years later the Christ-enraptured priesthood made him deny what he knew was undeniable for the sake of maintaining the holy illusion. And, of course, so as to keep the power given all priests by their managerial status in the fraud.

Man's fall was real. It occurred with his earliest invention of the territory beyond the grave.

In the beginning was Truth.

Then came man.

And in his beginning was the Word.

And the Word was a Lie.

It still is.

For even those relatively few men who have eschewed the myth in every form have not yet rejected the method by which the myth was established. They are still unwilling to relate to Nature and Truth, as men. So they have merely invented new escapes.

They have made themselves detached: uninvolved, they call it, or objective. By such schemes they have abdicated their humanity, for men are social beings and when they refuse to be involved with each other (and with Nature, also) they are not men in any proper sense, or human.

Many are alienated, nowadays. Or objective, as scientists assert themselves to be.

Others exist without a description of themselves, imagining there is none. Life is for the moment only, they aver: less, then, than worms. Sartre's existentialists. Or the Communists—whose heaven is, still, an image descried beyond present lifetimes—even though they've denied God and a private eternal life. They are atheists, who have yet placed creed above Nature like the godly folk and so use faith as their red means to believe a time-future myth one might call atheology.

The cruel faithful and the hard-nosed dissenters cling to that same method.

In one true way a fable or dream is necessary. We cannot wholly know the future or anticipate it surely. Yet if we are to have any purpose, any meaning, we must imagine one that gives value and point to the days and years beyond us.

"All men," Carl Jung said, "live by a myth."

The question that remains is how to invent or elicit or discover the "myth" that best fits our reality as human creatures.

Myths based on afterlife certainly do not relate to the true intention of instinct in other beings. They are not derived, except by burglarious transformation, from the universal command to continue the species; they do not, therefore, contain moral orders appropriate to that purpose.

Efforts to abolish death by false contrivances are thus amoral. Yet, as one man of genius has reminded us, the urge to evade death was so intense even in the Age of Reason, the eighteenth century, as to prevent the scientists of that time from being intellectually lucid. They could not arrange the geological and fossil data they possessed in its pattern of evolution.

Even that recently, Loren Eiseley pointed out, the abhorrence of death was so intense that those brilliant men clung to an idea that supported the beliefs in afterlife, the idea that no species could become extinct. The concept then was that God had created a worldwide set of living things, wiped out all of them, and created a new group, over and over.

To imagine the correct explanation of fossil creatures, no longer found alive anywhere, would be to realize that men also were liable to extinction and owing to natural acts, not God's.

Scientists of that era were so imbued with the ancient and continuing myth of man's specialness that no such extinction, such annihilation even of a single species, could be envisaged. Thought, even that recently, still supposed that whatever the truth about the origin of man and animals (of that surely lesser sort) might be, all creation had been aimed toward culmination in man. And as man was the whole purpose of God, the supreme and God-sired wonder on earth, its lord and overlord, he could not perish, being the final product of God's creative intention.

That observation, Eiseley notes, shows how scientists can be kept blind by contemporary mythology, and so may entertain prejudices of which they are not conscious. They also, he adds (far, far too casually!), have not accepted any human responsibility for their work and findings and the use others make of those. Another aspect of their prejudice, I would say.

It was in such a climate of the mind that Darwin entered his long-aborning concept of evolution. Long-aborning in other minds but not till Darwin's day proffered as the true account of all creation.

No wonder it met hostility! No wonder men still have not accepted its inference. Its inference that, since we are animals and part of nature, it behooves us all to find out what that means.

A few men can say what that means, now, in new and deeper and more real terms. But not a civilized man in a million has given their discoveries much purposeful thought.

They all should. For the new truth is not any presently accepted truth. And it is nearly too late to learn and use it, even if it be expressed as what it is, man's last hope.

Chapter
Two

OF
LEARNING

1 / My Problem: You

IN THE PREVIOUS chapter I have made several statements that will be doubted by many readers. What I must still state, to lead to a final expression of what I believe to be Truth, will require more assertions equally liable to instant rejection. My problem is to avoid being sentenced without being heard. I ask, then, why is such summary treatment likely?

First, I will be doubted simply because I am not a scientist accredited in the fields from which my information comes.

Every layman's credibility is questionable, of course. And every scientist's, too. But since this book is a serious effort, not only to outline many scientific facts and theories, but to extract from them a moral concept, I am under an obligation to indicate in some way what I have learned—where, when, and how. That evidence will be found as needed. One of my problems with my readers will thus be resolved, at least as far as seems feasible.

I also have the common right of a free man—the right to ask that anyone who would dispute him be open to changed views if his collapse. Otherwise, the man who made a knowledgeable assertion and is then told it is not so has been given the lie by the only liar in the affair.

That leads to my second problem, the giant problem of learning.

Up to this very day, the cultures of man have not dared use the only genuine method of education. Let me lead to its definition by easy steps.

A young child is born with the capacity for true learning; the openness, integrity, and the unbounded curiosity that should become his lifetime way to knowledge. He is not long allowed such authenticity. The child begins to learn by believing what he is told. But he very soon realizes that what people do fails to correspond with what they have told the child to do.

So acts, not words, become the child's gauge of truth. That method of evaluation is, of course, proper realism, in the child's world of unrealist adults.

A Christian, and all Christians, as Jesus reportedly said, is only what one does and all do. Christianity is not, then, evinced as a belief, or any mass of beliefs with that name. It is the history of what claiming Christians have done, and the news on this day's TV of what they are doing, and it is the intentions they will carry out, tomorrow and thereafter, so long as people call themselves Christian and indulge in behavior. "By their acts . . ."

The child discovers that fact at an early age. So he begins to choose what he will believe according to the acts of others, not according to their stated ideals. He selects for his examples people he likes, and likes on that same scale of primitive judgment, by behavior.

A child is born a scientist: both have an identical attitude; all that is allegedly believed is open to doubt, scrutiny, and evaluation by the test of what is really happening in that area.

Men are still too primitive to allow the child to keep so reasonable an attitude, however. For modern men have many beliefs that they feel must not be questioned, since their dead destiny and the future of their particular civilization are presumed to rest on those beliefs. They are religious beliefs; and they also appear as law; they are the basis of nationalism through patriotism; they sustain the current mores of every society, the right-wrong of its manners and customs.

What we call education, then, must imbue students with such arbitrary ideas as if they were unchangeable truths. Where various members of one culture disagree about many matters, and where each group maintains its version as absolute truth, the children are usually indoctrinated in some special creed, if that can be forced on them.

All such dogma is reinforced by acts. And acts are convincing. In this case they are near overwhelming. As religious acts they comprise the costumes of the clergy, the rites, the icons and images, and also the church, cathedral, mosque, synagogue, temple, or shrine. These are not real, but mere symbols for imaginary things. Yet they seem concrete, wherefore actual to the child, and so reinforce his faith in whatever the cement-verified belief may be. Since none of those beliefs is a true representation of man's place in nature, all will produce erroneous acts. Sinning, then, is the sure result of faith, and sin is what sustains our foolish faiths, in the main.

Schools, being secular in their majority in our nation, cannot enter into a critical examination of the dominant beliefs. Religious beliefs and derivative fiats of law, together with customs that determine values, goals, prejudices, and so on, are not open to critical study in our educational beehives.

Schools and most colleges present, in general, only the theory and data outside those immense but taboo bounds. And even that segregated information is tendered in the way that is, still, man's near-universal method: as fact.

It is easy to accept information so proffered. And it is usually accepted as no more subject to change than religious dogma, where allegedly truer truths are put forth in the same way, save that some secular data can be proven.

By the time a young person reaches adolescence, or sooner, he will not only have caught on to the adult habit of feigning a belief belied in deed, but he will have incorporated that technique. Wherever his desires conflict with an ideal, belief, or law, he will attempt to carry out the desire, while hiding the act from others, to keep the seeming of virtue.

Moreover, the young person will by then have learned a subtler technique for living with lies. He will have become aware that grownups often do not even know when their acts betray their beliefs. This seeming unawareness will initially astonish a child. He may then be the cause of much embarrassment by pointing out the truth and the discrepancy to culpable adults. But soon even children realize that grown persons can say one thing and do the other, yet not know they've betrayed themselves—and not even be able to accept any amount of proof of such hypocrisy.

So the child begins to construct his personality in the same distorted form—molding by repression, till he can split his own mind in two parts, both believed valid, though mutually exclusive, and neither allowed communication with the other. Acts are then possible that violate belief, but the violation is no longer perceivable by the conscious fraction of the mind.

In order to be able to live with and bear so odd a condition, it is evident that an extremely rigid barrier must be established between the now-contrary mind-portions. And the wall must be maintained at all costs, for the wall-maker increasingly assumes as his whole self the part not walled off. Even a glimpse of the unconscious slums would wreck the city of his Ego-land.

And that would destroy the individual. So, at least, he is certain. And even correct, in a fashion; his deluded *ego* would surely be ruined by a whole-self view.

I hardly need note that the force that maintains this schism has more power than any other of any being. Men cling to their convictions in the face of disproof, and, of course, without acting according to them; men die rather than alter dogmas; they also go out into all the earth to teach others to think and believe as they say; and if men refuse, they undertake their conversion by other means: war, that is.

Thus the Christian claim to love, and to brotherly love, established behind a wall (and seen then as righteousness) has, so far, produced a thousand or a million times as much hate, horror, slaughter, torture, deceit, internal schism, bigotry, and misery, as it has occasioned acts of love.

And secular education, even in those areas where it is allowed, uses the same means. The grade school pupil, the high school adolescent, and the college student assume that they are learning truth. That is the conviction of their teachers and professors, also. Neither group tends to see their data as probably mistaken and liable to revision or later to discard. Neither is trained to unlearn and to relearn, two necessary elements for real education.

What the adult finally comes to believe as knowledge, therefore, is taken as reliable, a territorial part of himself, a realm now very imaginary.

He has not been educated, then, but merely indoctrinated. But as all he thus believes describes the range and furniture of his mind, it, too, like spatial territory, is his, and as precious to defend as a wallet.

What one has learned and what one believes are assumed to measure what one is. Any question of a mere detail of that, let alone proof of error, is deemed assault on an inviolable territory of self.

The result of such a process is the modern, allegedly educated man.

He has an education. He has a belief. He has a morality. So he presumes. He actually believes only because *he* is doing the believing. He knows what he learned in school merely because *he* learned it. Any contrary, modifying, or other relevant knowledge is, then, taken as an insult to *him*. To yield to criticism or admit ignorance is weak, craven, a failure to defend one's borders. Our educational technique, in sum, renders most graduates uneducable. Added enlightenment imperils the little given and is seen as a personal affront.

It is also felt to be disillusioning to learn more, or differently. The act leaves a man, in his view, not better off but diminished. It causes inferior feelings, trauma, despair, and creates a void and a grief in the *amour propre*.

That being the supposed cost of enlightenment to us, who wants it?

Only very tough people will even chance such personal devastation: only very honest and very brave people, people who do not relate present knowledge to pride, a rare sort even in partial forms.

Man could and he should reverse the process of establishing belief by this method.

But think of what he would bring about!

All believers in dogma would take the view that whatever new information, knowledge, or insight revealed error in their dogma or faith must instantly be welcomed, immediately disseminated, and everywhere employed by the faithful to reform proven errors of the previously sacred doctrine.

Human education should proceed that way, of course. What is taught should always be taught as subject to revision in the light of future findings. The student should be allowed to realize that his greatest accomplishment will be the maintenance of a lifetime interest in the advances of knowledge, so as to be able to take part in man's one real adventure, by the deed that is his bravest: the constant acquisition of new knowledge and the ceaseless revision of all prior belief that such knowledge demands.

To find that what one believed to be fact or truth is now revealed as error, or must be modified, or added to, or has become untenable, is the highest feat intellectually possible if values are rearranged to fit.

It is the act for which our species is structured and the most needful use of the mind if its owner is to know self-respect. A brain is meant to learn. While learning continues, the brain is functional. When learning ceases, when it rests on any knowledge as final, that brain has shut down and its owner has declared himself mindless. Conviction that will not suffer change is, then, the evidence of a brain surrendered to emotion.

But what reader has such a mind and that kind of education? Who will reform that way? And who can add to his heart what his brain accepts?

Thus when I say we know how life originated and say the process was physical and inevitable, given the conditions obtaining at the time, I am not going to convince people who believe by faith that God did the initial deed and God made man, too, and made man something, furthermore, that other life forms are not: divine, or able to become that by usurpation for himself of the eternal time-territory of all other species.

Given the full evidence, such people would reject it on their own say-so—people who would still claim to be honest, intelligent, and well-educated.

So my problem concerns the will of civilized man, in these days, that orders such mindlessness. For if one rectification of a dogma might cause a man to give up his Christian faith, how shall such a man survive a hundred? Or a thousand? The numbers essential for him to believe truly, that is? Nothing would then be left of the believer, he believes.

Yet knowledge changes knowing in just such an ever-augmented way. Much of what was solemnly taught as fact ten years ago is now known to be in error, or utterly unsound, or of a different nature.

The question that must therefore next be asked concerns the cause of our modern willful delusion. Why is our orientation toward learning and knowledge so hostile to enlightenment, while still claiming to be knowledgeable?

How is it even possible that a being that has used its reason, its logic, its power to doubt, question and make the ensuing correction of countless given ideas—one that has created such marvels by that means—remains a being that presumes it can reject the same means at its own arbitrary will? What makes man seem different from other animals is that learning capacity; the less man uses it, the less human he is, the nearer to snake or wasp. Why does he so degrade himself?

2 / Evil and Good

To find the cause of that, our debased and dishonorable condition, we must look deeper into our beginnings and into all nature.

We shall thereby see that the very first life form, and every one that evolved since, and every living thing now on earth, plant or bird, fish or mammal, *save man,* possesses a constant knowledge of the truth, for its species.

We shall see that merely to exist requires an innate sense

of right and of wrong; and see how to determine both, for every life form.

With the Beginning, there was Ethos, then. Thought.

Thought, of that sort.

Our common, earliest ancestor, the first living being from whom we all have descended, was not itself much of a thinker, of course. It was able to eat and multiply (by dividing) and its halves, when they reached a certain size, were able to then separate into identical halves, both alive and doing those things.

One should notice that the moment the primordial chemical mix became alive, it had that new attribute. It could select the right food—and reject what was wrong. And it could replicate.

The first living thing nature composed contained all the information needed to be alive. It "knew" that much. It could make the proper choices. As evolution acted and forms grew complex, their "know-how" increased in exact amounts for their new needs.

The first living thing merely drifted about in its chemically rich ocean.

But in due course, there evolved an organism that had a tiny tail, or, perhaps, the hairlike extensions called cilia or a flagellum, something it could move in a way that enable it to travel. And when those first, self-propelled beings appeared, they immediately knew which way to go. They could now swim toward their food and also back away or turn aside from chemicals and conditions that were dangerous to them. They had ways to get out of too-hot water, for another possible example. And how to retreat from a current too cold for their survival.

Biologists call such built-in kinds of usable data *tropisms*. Tropisms, they say, are reflexes that automatically cause their owners to respond to environment in ways suitable for them. Once biologists got up a name for the marvel, they pretty much ceased to consider how marvelous such tiny bits of universal "knowledge" of right and wrong really are.

Another great discovery or invention of Nature probably preceded the ingenious idea of locomotion. That was the designing of chlorophyll. Chlorophyll, the green stuff of plants, is a chemical substance that can use the energy of the sun to change water and carbon dioxide into sugars, foods of a kind a living cell can oxidize, or consume, to get energy and to grow.

With the proliferation of cell forms that were equipped to change water and carbon dioxide into nutrient material, the earth's atmosphere began to be altered. The evolving green world, as it made food from a gas and from water, released oxygen into the earth's once oxygen-scant air. We can breathe today only because of green things and the endless ages of their oxygen contribution to their environment. We owe breath to algae in the sea, and the great masses of swamp cover, to forests and jungles, to mosses and ferns, to all the rest of verdant nature and billions of years of its metabolism.

Most of the chlorophyll-containing life forms remained stationary, They needed no means of moving themselves—with some few exceptions, of small size. And the green world is still largely static. It moves only through its spread as seeds and spores by external forces, winds and water currents and birds and beasts that carry them from the rooted parent plant. Carbon dioxide, water, and sunlight are everywhere, or they were. So plants didn't need to move about individually.

In the water, our common ancestor took forms of endless sorts. At length, there occurred a single-celled creature of a size man's naked eye could perhaps just have spotted, the size of a paramecium, for example. And those sires could move about. They could also use the primitive green plants and their by-products for food. All that long way, each species of our forebears had built-in directions for what to do and what not, to keep its own kind continuing. It is so obvious a fact that even scientists still take it for granted usually.

What causes a single-celled organism to act and react appropriately? Answer: tropisms.

But someone finally asked *why* form and function were always both congruous and correct. And what *that* implied, if anything.

Where, they next inquired, does tropism end and some

other form of knowledge arise? If, that is, "knowledge" can be used in describing tropisms, as I've done.

With such questions, arguments began.

Creatures more complex than those with tropisms still lived according to rules they somehow knew, rules that gave them the same sort of information about right and wrong for their numberless kinds. How?

Well, that fancier phenomenon could be called instinct.

People, including many scientists, began then to describe instincts. Mating instincts. Herd instincts. Hunting instincts. There were hundreds of terms. And laymen began translating the terms, often with scientific aid, into lay language: the killer instinct, for an example. "Jungle law," for another, just as wrong.

An inevitable big question followed that "answer." Do human beings have instincts?

At the turn of the century, biologists and other scholars went charging off in all directions on that.

Laymen, however, didn't like to think about it. Not many of them, then, had even accepted evolution as proven. Scientists themselves were still disputing its method. Did new species arise when individuals were obliged to improve old characteristics, which were then transmitted by inheritance? Or did accidental mutations of endless and random sorts result in the occasional survival of a usefully mutated creature and the transmission of that genetic capability to its off-spring?

In a strange and new way, which is not relevant here, there may yet be found evidence to support the former idea to some modest degree. But it became certain that evolution moved ahead largely by that awesome and waste-ful-seeming process of accidental gene change in individu-als, of which roughly one in a thousand would be useful and so, perhaps, handed on to offspring. The other nine hundred and ninety-nine, by definition, would be useless or even harmful. So evolution is wholly, or at least mainly, ac-complished by a process that only rarely provides a change of a helpful sort. Species therefore arise slowly and by minute steps, for no mutant will likely be so different from its kind as to be an avoided freak.

That is an observation to keep in mind.

Meanwhile, the matter of possible human instinct became a battle of scientists and laymen.

It had not previously occurred to people that they, too, might be in some fashion dominated by instincts as animals were now seen to be. The thought was simply impossible to all who believed in a concept of man as *not* animal.

If it were true that instinct controlled mankind, people had reasoned, supposing it even thinkable, *how* did it do so? Where was the evidence? Wasn't man's capacity for reason sufficient proof that man had no instincts? Wasn't his special creation by God the certificate of man's separation from instinctuality? Didn't his power to kill all animals show he was not like them?

Sigmund Freud's concept of human instinct appeared at about the time some few people had accepted the theory of evolution as truth. Freud held instinct to be essentially the drive of sex. Sexual taboos so common in that era of pan-Victorianism, produced the varied neuroses of the day, so Freud said. Mental ill-health was seen as negative evidence of repressed instinct. Our species, by that hypothesis, defines us as basically sexual.

But instinct, Freud theorized, was hard to discern because man had developed two kinds of mind. He was only partly aware even though he believed himself to be wholly so. Instead, his repression (of sex-linked urges) had set up a second, or unconscious, mind where unacceptable realities were stored in the locked dark. Here, however, his hidden instinct still acted.

Consciously unable to carry out his repressed and so unknowable desire, he was obliged by its existence to give it some other function or expression.

Lust for a forbidden mother could surface as a different lust, or it could revenge itself for being chained up, by paralyzing its jailor, physically. The conflict of conscious beliefs and unconscious desires could produce all manner of symbolic phenomena. Man's ego, or *I*-self, would not and could not acknowledge forbidden doings in that man-made dark self, or id; and the invisible confusion made him take sick action as compensation.

Freudian theory was more complicated than that, of course. And it had great impact. For it presented a logical picture of common human behavior hitherto impossible to understand.

Other psychologists soon suggested modifications and revisions of Freud's theories. Adler held that a power drive, not sex, was man's overriding instinct, and added the term "inferiority" to the language. Jung outlined a galaxy of archetypes and their opposites as the components of what he called the collective unconscious, a concept somewhat similar to one that had been called racial memory, but not actually the same.

The important fact here, however, isn't the debating that soon arose amongst psychologists. What is cogent is the emerging agreement on man's conscious-unconscious psychology, on man as instinctual, and on human instinct as having an innate right-wrong structure—a potential not even noted till recently.

Eventually, biology was to demonstrate human instinct directly. Its nature, as defined by that science, did not entirely resemble instinct as it had been postulated by Freud, Adler, Jung, and the others. But the proof of instinct in man, derived from animal studies by biologists, is very new. It has, however, put instinct on an unarguable, if altered base: that of territorial demand, for illustration, as a primary human imperative and an innate pattern.

3 / The Dinner-Bell Boys

In the meantime, another theory about human behavior rose to challenge theories of instinct and the unconscious mind. It arrived at a welcome time for multitudes of people, including multitudes of scientists, who were outraged by Freud and the rest. It was called behaviorism and stemmed from some work of a Russian scientist named Pavlov.

What Pavlov found, and what his finding then did to thinking in our century, particularly to our thinking about education, is scarcely credible and certainly proof that man is mixed up about himself somehow.

Pavlov's classical and revealing experiment was simple.

He rang a bell before feeding a group of hungry dogs. He set out food. The dogs began to salivate when the food appeared, of course. But in time and after many repetitions of bell-ringing and food-offering, the dogs would salivate when the bell rang even though no food was offered to them. That behavior was described as the working of a conditioned reflex.

Hundreds of experimental psychologists and biologists then began to condition the reflexes of all sorts of animals.

A philosophy was developed to embody the new finding. It was called behaviorism and John Dewey, in the United States, was a principal founder.

Behaviorism began to seem to many people, most scientists included, the basic explanation of living acts. At least, the behavior of higher animals was explained that way. And the explainers set out to prove their dogma. They even proved it, to their own satisfaction. Their motive was potent.

For when they applied the theory to man, it relieved many of the anxieties occasioned by the concept of instinct and an unconscious mind. Such concepts were disturbing because they implied that logic and reason, even when used by scientists, might not be so rationally employed as scientists liked to presume.

The behaviorists stated that man was born a completely blank state and that all he learned and knew and came to believe, after birth, was the result of conditioning.

That made sense of a sort even to religious people. If a child was born a blank, it behooved each and every convinced believer to make sure all possible children were conditioned to accept the absolute truth, as that believer knew it to be owing to his faith. Behaviorism did nothing to untangle the snarl of contrary dogmas in religions. But it did allow religious people to imagine their own ideology was right and its promulgation a holy duty.

It also, of course, caused behaviorists to imagine their one concept was the final word about the process of learning, since education was seen merely as the conditioning of reflexes, a process that depended entirely on environment, or external circumstance.

Environment made all the differences in people.

Of course, that broad application of a special phenomenon was unwarranted. Today, the deed seems literally insane. Why insane?

If behaviorists had examined even Pavlov's work more closely, they would have seen a point at which its wide applicability vanished.

For Pavlov made a further observation about his dogs. When they were not hungry, they wouldn't salivate, no matter how long and hard he rang the bell.

Reflexes, then, could be conditioned only within certain very obvious and easily measured bounds.

The behaviorists overlooked that.

Let us see the result, since most of us are still somewhat its victims and need the insight for salvation, if we would, indeed, be saved.

Chapter
Three

THE FIFTY-YEAR
FOLLY

1 / Onslaught of the Oafs

BEHAVIORISM NOT only seemed a refutation of all theories of human instinct, but it had yet another connotation that appealed to nearly all biologists at that period.

By 1900, the great leap forward of science was well under way. Its methodology had been established: be objective; count, test, conclude, doubt anew—and continue, ad infinitum. Freud's unproven, vague, and often-revised monologue had left the laboratory people without anything they could count, measure, or test objectively. Biology was, in any event, still engaged in classification, in anatomical survey, and in recording the gross behavior of animals. Organisms were, therefore, being studied as if they were machines and the most-favored terms then were mechanism and mechanistic.

Observers bent backward to avoid projecting human values on animals. This attitude perhaps came from and surely heightened the powerful, prescientific sense of a gulf between men and beasts. To report a mink as ingenious, a moose as curious, an otter as playful, was held to be anthropomorphic

40

—an unwarranted attribution of human qualities to a machine-animal that could not possess them.

The experimental evidence provided by Pavlov was the key to all behavior. All was learned. All, then, was mechanical.

Scientists went to fantastic lengths to justify their corrupt version of Pavlovian gospel. Newborn infants were tested for innate characteristics—and found to possess two: a fear of being dropped and a fear of sudden, loud noise. That those two simple yet intrinsic responses could be demonstrated in newborn human beings ought to have shown the investigators that not all behavior, not quite all, at least, is learned by environmental conditioning.

It didn't. On the contrary, the lack of any further or other evidence of innate responses in infants was regarded as if proof they had none at all. None, so to speak, worth a scientist's consideration.

Experiments with birds and other animals, showing that patterns of behavior are innate and persist for generations, even where learning by conditioning has been made impossible, were also largely ignored. If forced into consideration of that kind of evidence, behaviorists would insist that the experiments had been performed in some unscientific way, or wrongly interpreted, or that the experimenters were unreliable if not dishonest.

When it was pointed out to them that no animals revealed their full life-pattern of behavior at birth, a pattern, which, however, showed up at a suitable age, the behaviorists even had answers for that. A fawn does not know how to copulate or have any drive to do so. At maturity, the urge and know-how appear without any teaching, that is, conditioning. But the visible mass of such information was not a sign of instinct to behaviorists. It simply revealed auto-conditioning, learning by trial and error, they stated. What prompted such trials and their continuation after error, to the point of success, the self-styled Pavlovians did not tell anybody.

So dogmatic was the general biological view in such matters, and especially in the matter of anthropomorphic interpretation of observed animal acts, that the mere mass of rationalization needed to support the doctrine should have overtoppled its excesses. But no.

To point out that, no matter how hard you tried to condition it, you could never get a crab even to try to fly, was regarded as merely facetious. The fact that form plainly defined and limited function, in sum, did not seem to be pertinent to those "rational" behaviorist fanatics. Genetics, at that early part of the century, had not yet advanced far enough to undo their absurd dogma.

And near half the century would pass before a new discipline for the study of animal behavior would start to dislodge the general fixation on behaviorism. This approach is called ethology; by demonstrating, for all time, the reality of instinct, it returned behavioristic concepts to their proper and special place.

But the applications made by the people enchanted with reflex conditioning as the be-all, went marching on in our land, a plague that is epidemic to this day.

2 / Personal Reminiscence

I came into collision, as a young man, with behavioristic dogma; and I have been in a head-on and sometimes shocking smash with it ever since.

Much of my boyhood was spent in the woods, in the Adirondacks and in Canada. I was often there alone and I saw many things.

One of my naturalist mentors, Dr. Frederick King Vreeland, was, however, a passionate opponent of anthropomorphism. And I soon found he regarded various reports of my experiences with wild animals as projections of my feelings, not true observations. It became impossible for me to convince him of things I'd seen with my own eyes. So, resentfully, I began keeping to myself matters I knew Dr. Vreeland, and others like him, would reject as misinterpretations or fancies, if not lies.

All claim of humanlike behavior by wild animals, or by domestic animals and pets, for that matter, was labeled nature-faking by the scientific community—and Dr. Vreeland was a scientist. Such men as Ernest Thompson Seton, popular author of wildlife tales, were regarded as unspeakable examples. It took the ethologists to reveal that some of those writers, Seton among them, were exceedingly shrewd and accurate animal observers. The behaviorists were the ones who had lost acuity.

I was fortunate, however, in that Vreeland and other naturalists enabled me to make many of my deepest journeys into the forest and also fortunate in that I enjoyed leaving our main camps to thread the wilderness on foot, alone, and to explore remote lakes and creeks in a canoe, alone.

For I began, early, to come to conclusions about wild animals that were very different from the sort scientifically allowable in those days. I was sure that the mandate against anthropomorphic ideas was not a valid absolute.

And I kept to such opinions even though contrary ideas ruled biological belief for many years more. It was my private doubt of the mechanists and their views, I now believe, which caused me to take an interest, years later, in depth psychology and, especially, at first, in the theories of Carl G. Jung. Behavior, I knew from boyhood, needed a different interpretation from that allowed by behaviorist fiat.

I come from a stubborn line, and I tend to believe my own eyes rather than anybody's theory, where there's a difference. I ought to, and hope I someday shall, set down some of the experiences with wild animals that were mine. One experience, particularly.

At eighteen, on an expedition Dr. Vreeland led, I spent months in a part of Quebec where it was certain that no one had ever been before us. Not many men have ever done that.

Most so-called wilderness opened up by explorers is not wilderness. There will be natives in it, and natives will probably have lived there or at least hunted there for thousands of years. Our idea of discovery, as in the "discovery" of America, is absurd. Somebody discovered America perhaps fifty thousand years ahead of Columbus and there were a million or two people in the place when the Catholic sailor made his mistaken landfall.

That idea of "discovery" is analogous to many other errors. When a European first entered a dark reach of Africa, or ventured west in this land, he was deemed a discoverer and what he found was hailed as new to man. In a parallel way, man sees himself as no animal, but his own different and new discovery. So we eternally fool ourselves.

My main point here, however, is that few men have ever entered a wilderness where the inhabitants have never smelled man, or felt his arrow, or seen their kin cooking on his fires. I have been in such a place. And my adventures with many animals were so different from the scientifically acceptable sorts that I realized, even at the time, and however inarticulately, the ruling views of men on animals were idiotic.

Man had so distorted and evil a belief about wilderness and the creatures in it that he was beyond learning the truth, even then. Today, half the people in America don't know one tree; their image of the wild state of being is maniacal and, I am sure, the cause of man's ever-greater reaching toward a happiness that outdistances him increasingly with his every next effort. His orientation toward nature is wrong and his awareness addled.

Fifty years ago man's science was as anthropocentric as his deism; and the behaviorists made that position a religion, in effect.

In 1920, when I entered Princeton University, their gospel was rampant. Every freshman was obliged to take a course in psychology and philosophy. What was called psychology embraced that area from James through Thorndike and Watson to a grand conclusion in Dewey's behaviorism. Philosophy took off with Socrates, Plato, and Aristotle, proceeded through the route of Kant, Leibnitz, Spinoza, Descartes and the others, to culminate in Dewey's philosophy of behaviorism.

Not a few freshmen, including myself, had by then begun to read Freud. When our psychology-philosophy professor was asked about psychoanalysis, he annoyedly shrugged it away. Freudianism was merely hypothesis, he said, not bothering to admit that all of his psychology was merely hypothetical, too. Freud's ideas, he went on, related only to medicine. Freud's field was morbid psychology, if, indeed, he had any field of real value. Nothing for Princeton freshmen to bother their heads with, he assured us. Smutty-minded, as well, in his view.

During my Princeton years I took a course in evolution under a Professor Scott. He was an old man, then. Much later I learned, from my friend Bill Gregory, long Director of the American Museum of Natural History in New York, that Professor Scott had been the first American scientist to defend Darwinism in the United States. That little time had passed since Darwin's blow to man's belief in his non-animal and divine essence! I studied under the first professor to take up Darwin's cause in America.

It is not, then, very difficult to understand why, even though so much more has been learned since Darwin's great idea reached this land, that evolution has not been really assimilated by the American people—and the later concepts aren't even known to exist.

Not difficult to understand but painful to live with. For the refusal of most human beings to revise their beliefs when new truth has emptied them of worth is no cause for pride in our species, but a sure reason for pain and humiliation.

Pigs, wart hogs, and camels are immeasurably more honest, realistic, and morally courageous than these reluctant men if all are judged ethologically.

For a millennium and a half the ideas that we lump under the name of Christianity prevailed in the Western world. And then, in a century and a half, less than a tenth of that long and dark age of faith, something called science began to destroy, one by one, every single fundamentalist tenet. But the faithful carry on—the willful faithless, now.

Evolution, for instance, was not just rejected during some short spell. It is still evaded by the majority of Americans, either outright or in their unconscious minds, because they retain the inferences of the ancient and exploded myth about man's separation from animals, and so, from nature.

Psychologists like Freud were tracing man's religious myths to causes so near to animal (and so close to truth) as to set the clergy and their benumbed hordes into spasms of repudiation.

But with the coming of behaviorism, all such resentful and credulous people had a reprieve, they thought. Ironically, the new finding left them with no actual support for any religious ideology; however, it was used to justify every kind.

3 / The Crackpot Crusade

Fathered by John Dewey and fostered by Irwin Edman, the new faith soon absorbed the attention of the most influential professors of pedagogy in America, those in Teachers College at Columbia University. They had seen the light! Teaching was but reflex conditioning. Learning was exposure to the technique. Unfortunately, the nation's normal schools believed Columbia Teachers to be the godhead of educational method and means. Many of the pedagogical concepts now fledged were not justified by John Dewey's philosophy. But Dewey was evidently unable to prevent such distortions.

Out of that seminal group at Columbia came, for example, the crazed idea of the schools' responsibility for the nurture and conditioning of the whole child. In turn, that led to another unearthly postulate: the whole child must not be traumatized or made to feel inferior at school. The creed is now called democracy-education. And it is responsible for our custom of holding brighter pupils to the pace that the dullest can maintain, for one grim example.

If environmental causes were the full explanation of human quality and capacity, as behaviorists believed, then paradise was at hand. All evil and crime and wrong could be wiped out by making man's environment and his education suitable, and equal.

This, of course, is the thesis of Marxism. Man is there defined as an economic creature exclusively, another commodity, in effect.

The American mania for reflex conditioning led also to the see-say method of teaching reading. It was used in most schools for more than a generation before anybody called attention to its result: Johnny couldn't read.

So devastating was the effect of see-say that most colleges

and universities are still obliged to provide classes in remedial reading for entering students. Many universities find
such instruction necessary for more than half of their ma-
triculants. And the majority of university graduates today are
inferior at reading compared to graduates from the days
when it was taught in the pre-Columbia, or phonetic, manner.

Behaviorism had suggested to its devotees that the phonetic
step in learning to read could be omitted and so reading
could be taught by direct reflex conditioning, for example,
by drill in sight recognition of combinations of letters that
actually represent sounds. Such a method might have been
proper for instruction in reading Chinese characters or Egyptian hieroglyphics; but it did not even relate to the reading
of symbols for sounds. Scores of millions were casualties in
consequence: mentally crippled for life.

Much of the present decline of values and loss of direction
in America may be attributed to that folly at Columbia and
its servile adoption by the nation's schoolteachers.

For almost half a century they have failed to teach Americans to read with ease. The ever-more difficult language of
our technological age has thus become utterly inscrutable
to most people. Schools have even ceased offering instruction in grammar and attempted to replace that hard, necessary discipline with the fantasy that grammar could be
learned by aural conditioning. But reading by the eye only!

So America is now populated with adults who are ignorant because there is no way to inform them. That adult
and still-emerging mass of school-retarded persons is become
the audience for the candied pap of TV, and nothing more.
The few literate survivors, alone, are aware of the degree
of that degradation, while the hundred million verbal casualties of behaviorism, the quadraplegics of recent pedagogy,
don't even know they've been maimed.

Twelve years of schooling and, in scores of millions of
cases, another four of college failed to lift them to a reading
level above that required by comic books. And the adult
comic book is TV, of course.

Yet that is only a second catastrophic effect of the cult of
reflex conditioning.

4 / Saint Ivan: the Pavlovian Apotheosis

American liberals and intellectuals flocked into the behaviorist fold. The doctrine explained everything, which is the function of all doctrine, of course.

Doctrine has one common premise: that there is an intrinsic, homogeneous aspect of man.

Christianity holds that all men own a soul, which, then, is susceptible to salvation by, of course, Christianity.

Democracy holds that all men deserve equal opportunity, hardly a doctrinal statement. But a dogma is easily elicited from it by those who reject logic: that all men are potentially equal.

Behaviorism carried the premise one step further, by asserting that all men would become equal if given equal external conditions.

Psychology has shown that the postulate of a soul is mythical.

Biology has proven that men are not equal, identical, similar, or anything of the sort, from the instant of conception. Common sense ought to have made all that evident to Java Man. It didn't and still doesn't, since common sense is what men most passionately wish to evade.

Its absence in the leading liberals and intellectuals of the twenties and thirties used to baffle me. And I knew many of them.

My first job after I left college was with Edward L. Bernays, the public relations pioneer. That was in 1923. In 1925, I was the fifth person hired by Harold Ross for his *New Yorker,* which appeared the next year, and on which I would work for two years. The members of the Hotel Algonquin Round Table were known to me, at one remove, through Bernays. They became the people around the *New Yorker* office. I was subsequently the publicity and advertising manager for a book publisher. When my first novel appeared, in 1927, Alfred Knopf used an enthusiastic letter about it, written by my friend Theodore Dreiser. My third novel was chosen by a book club in 1930. And by that time

I knew many of the illustrious intellectuals and liberals in Manhattan, and not a few very well.

But they always puzzled me.

Those who called themselves "liberals" seemed bent on imposing some rigid scheme, social, economic, or both, on everybody, willed or no. That appeared anything but liberal to me.

The "intellectuals" and the members of a brief subdivision called "cognoscenti" had virtually no awareness of the body of knowledge mightily accruing in the twenties and thirties in the realms of physics, chemistry, and biology. To be scientifically so ignorant at that period seemed to me, again, hardly intellectual.

Investigations into the nature of reality, however, had little attraction for those folks. What enraptured them was the promulgation of unsupported notions about art, man, and society, including especially certain derivative notions of the behaviorists.

For if man was what they said, a product of his surroundings entirely, then an egalitarian environ was the ideal aim. That drift of their uncritical minds led many to become interested in, and even advocates of, Marxism.

They were to pay dearly for that fascination in the end. Yet such people established main currents of social, political, artistic, and intellectual thought in the twenties and thirties. Other people as ill-oriented, whether in education, politics, sociology, art, letters, nowadays still set main currents in other terms, but terms as specious. The root of their theories also lies in propositions as uninformed, speculative, and superficial.

Liberal or conservative, right or left, extreme or moderate, aesthetic or uninvolved, they act from what they imagine to be scholarly disciplines, but which become, on examination, pretentious fakes. Higher education devised such woolgathering when the method of the physical scientists proved shatteringly effective. Scholars tried to apply it to all realms of knowledge and to impose its technique on everyone. Wherever, in any such area, the existing material was not solid enough to warrant that application, the masters of higher education nevertheless dreamed up "disciplines" that aped the scientific method in the approach, the form, the invention of fresh terms, and by counting, measuring, and the like, thereby giving a scientific look to subjects too ambiguous for the attempt.

What is called "economics" is proffered, professed, and practiced as if a real discipline, for example. It is merely a great body of organized guessing. The so-called "social sciences," like "political science," are no more sciences than astrology or numerology. It is possible to pretend they are amenable to scholarly approach only by assuming that man is adequately known, which, of course, is the behaviorist assumption.

But if any such premise is mistaken in any way, or in any way inadequate, all scholarly "disciplines" built upon it will be, to the same degree, themselves in error.

And that is the very common situation. Intellectual leaders of our nation have often been mere fans of sundry economists and their varied theses. Art has swung from one aesthetic fad to another. Politics is no more a science than theology; and the application of such a primitive discipline as counting shows that to be true: the most scientifically sampled opinion polls disclose the invalidity of all political premise and hypothesis, merely by revealing that political opinion switches about like the jet stream and for causes as little understood.

Man's economics, his politics, indeed his entire behavior, are governed by his psychobiology; and that was beginning to be evident in the first decades of the century. But our colleges, universities, and graduate schools keep churning out myriads of M.A.s and Ph.D.s who are sure they understand society, sociology, political science, and economics, yet remain unaware of already known aspects of genus *homo* that reveal their learning to be ridiculous and irrelevant.

In the twenties and thirties, those people were sure that war was forever a thing of the past. I disagreed; and by the early thirties I was writing, in such magazines as *Liberty*, to advocate the preparation of our nation for "total war" including all-out air war. That was regarded by my betters as sin then. I was also sure that the people who believed Communism was the new, right way of life were batty. They went to Russia and came back, often confirmed in that view. In 1936, I went and came back a witness to the horrible errors of Marxism.

I was learning about physics and chemistry and biology in those years and writing about what I learned. They dismissed that as trivial: mere "science fiction." They did not realize how dated they were till Hiroshima. Too late to catch up, even intellectually.

What they revered and expounded in the area of art was an early version of what their opposite numbers are proclaiming as art these days: op, bop, pop, and a recent thing that merits the name of slop, along with the vogue for hop, too.

They were and are phonys.

Underneath the now-giant error of the educational and cultural processes that gives them false confidence was the enabling doctrine of behaviorism, still current in many applications. Their piety is of a fundamentalist sort.

My absorption in the psychology of instinct began in the mid-thirties. I investigated the theories of the late Carl Gustav Jung, then; and later, those of Freud.

A single experience I had at that time gave me a sense that my long and overt quarrel with the behaviorist liberals and intellectuals was as justified as I had always felt, but merely felt, till then.

A book of mine was published that included an effort to explain in lay terms some of Jung's concepts, and added a few of my own. Those additions now embarrass me; but the rest of the attempt seems adequate. Pre-publication copies of the work, which was called *An Essay on Morals*, went to Jung, and also, though I did not know it, to the then high priest of behaviorism who was a professor at Columbia, of course.

But he reviewed the book on its publication day for a major Manhattan newspaper and here is the conclusion of his appraisal:

"Philip Wylie knows less about psychology than a college sophomore and nothing whatever about the psychology of Jung."

The same day that criticism appeared, a letter from Jung

reached me and in it Jung wrote of my book, ". . . you understand [my theories] better than all the others." I keep that letter.

Who, then, was right about my exposition of Jungian psychology? Jung, himself? Or the overlord of behaviorism?

To him, I mailed a photostat of Jung's letter, which contained more praise than I've quoted here. The man's reply was among the sickliest of the kind I've ever seen.

". . . All of us get a bit off the beam. . . . we perhaps exaggerate. . . . come up and have a beer with me to talk it over. . . ."

That sort of reply.

It stood in my mind for many years as perfect proof of the dishonesty of all behaviorists.

Which, of course, it was, and is.

But I cite it here for a further purpose. It does more than reveal, by all it so clearly implies, the sand on which much of our present "knowledge" and "scholarship" rests; it stands for a greater infirmity.

The lord and master of behaviorism who gave me the lie, in print, and so, forever, on the record, did more than just expose himself as a hypocrite. He subtly indicated how, in his own opinion, he was *not* in error and not guilty of baseless slur.

That may be hard for the reader to see, in man's usual way of looking. But let me try to aid vision.

To my critic, behaviorism was the psychological be-all and the final word. To know what a "college sophomore" knew about psychology, in that great oaf's mind, was to know behaviorism only. He made his utter ignorance of Jung evident by claiming it was mine. But to him even that seemed allowable, since, as a convinced behaviorist, he felt he didn't need to know anything about Jung to be sure Jung was a psychological imbecile.

That conviction trapped him when he employed it to dismiss my book so peremptorily. But he could not guess, as he used his dogmatic posture to damn both Jung and me, that Jung would come to my support. The man felt perfectly safe in implying that he knew enough Jungian psychology to claim I knew nothing, simply because, from his viewpoint, he didn't need to know a thing about Jungian concepts to be warranted in dismissing them, out of hand, and unexamined.

His intellectual position, then, was not just peculiarly hypocritical, pontifical, ignorant, and so a blind path to self-exposing acts of sabotage; it is the position of every dogmatic believer.

And that is the important insight.

The man with the doctrinal belief isn't teachable and does not even realize that fact.

A convinced behaviorist is like a convinced deist or a convinced Keynesian or Communist or Birchite.

To be a theologist, for another example, demands the assumption of God as a premise and one not debatable.

God can then be a Trinity, or include Mary, or be seen as an abstraction, and even, as lately, be presumed dead.

Theology is seemingly real under such conditions, down to the absurdity of "Christian atheism." Any acknowledgment of deity, unitary or multiform, humanoid or galacto-mystic, admits a position to theology.

All "scholarship" that then ensues from both the general theory and the innumerable special theories of theology (which still hold most of mankind in thrall) has the same effect (to the degree it is held) that all conviction, including behaviorism, as here shown, must have on believers: total paralysis of the brain at whatever boundary conviction describes.

No dogma, in another view of this, is open-ended.

Where a man says, "I know," he cannot learn, even if what he thinks he knows is plainly kook.

And this is the crisis point of our species.

It is here that the ancient "method of faith" as a means toward learning "truth" has collapsed before the scientific method.

The latter is open-ended, ideally.

It holds all present fact and truth as tentative and subject to revision, eternally.

Its premises are, all, tentative. It can postulate "ether," for instance, and then abandon the idea, but still be astronomy; or it can change to astrophysics, yet stand steadfast as a true discipline and the same one.

Theology cannot do that. Nor can sociology, economics, and other such academic hoaxes.

Scientists as men, and as groups of men, can and do, of course, subvert the principle and take premises as convictions.

The act is, indeed, still commonplace; and the behaviorists are but one group of such people, though unfortunately a most persuasive example.

A few men, at least, are beginning to see that the central problem of knowledge, and of man, lies in our false identification of the individual self with dogma and the dogmatic process.

To enlarge the psyche's territory some part of it must first be yielded up. That is the crux.

A question that will be asked about it then becomes pertinent:

If scientists can be and often are precisely as dogmatic as religious fundamentalists, even about science, how can any man reach a reliable position on anything? In one way, nobody can. No final or eternal truth is man's.

Since knowledge is certain to increase, what we hold as knowledge at any time is certain to be changed in ways we cannot predict, ways that may show some aspect of current knowledge to be mistaken.

That being the case, the only tenable intellectual position is one in which a readiness for change is the constant state.

In the simplest form this can be seen as a realization of the certainty that our offspring will be able to know many truths we do not, and will perhaps find that many of our postulates have been unsound. And they should have the same awareness about their next generation, too.

However, no such approach to belief, conviction, and knowledge is presently evident. Is it?

We want our children, most of us, to believe as we did, and we devote immense effort, time, and treasure to that patently sinister end.

Which, I think, is only a sign of the continuing mistake man made when first he entered the infinite territory of time with his mind and tried to usurp it. Only that one aspect of his being makes the entry. Only the mind can. Imagination, that is, man's unique capacity to envisage the past in any present, and from that to imagine time-future.

All that he has seized there for himself, he but imagines. All he is, as mind, is imagined.

What dimension the beast could not occupy, man imagined he could. What belongs to the species of birds and worms and elephants and apes, man imagined was his immortal and private land. The territorial need that began with early life and was perhaps three billion years old when men evolved had always been three-dimensional in form, and but a present moment of time, valuable solely for acts related to the extension into future time of the posterity of each breed. All spatial imperatives were for the sake of such ends, and not any individual's save as the individual served those ends.

Man changed the law.

That is, man *imagined* he had changed it.

And he has not been sane since that day.

He has been lost to nature and lost in nature. Lost in time. Lost in knowledge and conviction. Because he then became lost to morality.

His aim was to transcend his animal by that invented abdication of natural law.

It has cost man his nature and exiled him from purpose.

Yet if the new method by which man is slowly learning some degree of truth, the method of science, leads men, still, into dogmas, into seizures of imaginary areas in time, how shall any man use even that potentially sound way to become moral again—that is, to recover true natural law?

There is an answer to that.

5 / All Knowing's Not Knowing

To judge science there is the method of science itself. One must know how to apply it and the steps leading to any concept under consideration. That, in turn, implies an understanding of the principal theories and findings in the field under scrutiny. And it further connotes some capacity to appraise the attitude of the people offering whatever is under study. Are such persons special pleaders? Victims of the narrowness of their field? Moved by emotion rather than reason? Devoted to an overruling and particular viewpoint or doctrine? Above all, have their claims been checked by the disinterested experiments of others?

To decide what scientific claim or concept one will accept, even tentatively, is thus a matter of one's own, final choice.

Of my own opinion, here, often, if the reader wishes.

But that does not set me and my opinion in a democratically equal position to other people and their opinions. To judge my choices, another person will need my information as a first requirement. Given that, and still disagreeing with me, he will have to follow the lines of logic and the scrutiny I've used to reach my position.

Both my selected facts and my particular uses of reason will then be open to his criticism, though not before then.

It is that method of science in which I have confidence and which I attempt to employ. And as my material, I attempt to select the data I believe science has established firmly enough to credit in this way.

Most men tend to do otherwise.

Their authorities are cited without critical assessment. Their alleged facts are set forth as established by those authorities and are unexamined. If faith is their means to conviction, they are not morally eligible even to argue in the honest way outlined here. Yet most men still form their certainties in that deceptive way.

Few take any personal responsibility for their convictions.

They hold to them because the Bible allegedly supports them, or the Vatican and its Pope, or a politician they admire and so, trust, or because they were given those eternal marketing verities by their economics prof in 1934, or because it is simple common sense, they say, an obvious, a historic fact—or anything else they can cite as their source of asserted truth, their arbitrary source.

That condition is so near to universal as to make it impossible for most human beings to face its central truth: that, whatever they believe, think, or claim to know, it is they, alone, as solitary individuals, who are responsible for its worth.

Environment, educational opportunity (or its absence), home influence, a thousand factors, admittedly enter into what they believe or doubt, know or do not. Yet the utterly ignorant will offend here as viciously as the gulled dogmatists.

A mind so vacant, or one so rigid as to be wholly unaware there is anything of value it hasn't learned, does not even merit the name of a mind. Yet how many people are able to acknowledge, even to themselves, that what they believe rests on outside authority, which they have never questioned? And how many will openly admit they don't know, and never tried to learn, beyond any given, alleged, but never-pondered "truth"?

How many of us, then, are our own authorities to the extent we claim authority? How many of us have examined what we believe and made comparisons of that with the beliefs and the knowledge of others?

How very few!

Yet every living person remains his own final source of belief, be it founded in his best effort to know and to think or in his acceptance of somebody else's ideology without attempt at evaluation.

In that way, almost every man is an island.

And most of these island minds don't realize that the continents of knowledge lie over a far horizon, beyond an ocean of ignorance that they insist is solid ground and part of a "main" they cannot even point to. For their sea of faith and dogma is not substantial but myth and if they had courage enough to step out on it, they'd sink.

To join the continent the sea must be bridged or the island moved.

And for that end the man within must do the work. No improvements of his outer environs will be enough. Such benefits at best may only abet his chance to see where he isn't.

Chapter
Four

TERRITORY

1 / A New Vista

WHILE THE behavioristic educators were stalling American education, some scientists continued to experiment in areas the behaviorists insisted were non-existent. Among them was an Austrian named Konrad Lorenz. His early work disclosed that some species can be strangely molded at the very start of their existence.

New-hatched ducklings, for example, regard the first animate being they encounter as their parent. Lorenz demonstrated that odd phenomenon in America by hatching out ducklings on a lecture platform where they saw him, first—squatting and quacking like a mother duck. Upon that, the little birds began to waddle along behind Lorenz.

This phenomenon was called imprinting.

I suppose the behaviorists at first imagined imprinting to be more evidence for their special theory since it was, plainly, an example of conditioning. But it was also an example of a special conditioning of an aspect of animal essence that occurred immediately on egg emergence and was not reversible afterward. That was a point against behaviorist assumptions since it indicated that animal personality, or something like it, was programmed at the start of existence, for ducks, at least; and for many other creatures, it was shown. So, certain major tenets of behaviorism were proven false. What about man?

The whole child, as both Catholics and Freudians have claimed, is very "whole" before school age, and so impervious to school conditioning in a degree. But people are not ducks.

The imprint psychologists did not stop, at that early finding. What happens, they asked, to cause the hatched bird to accept any first-seen being for its parent? What is the innate state allowing that?

Led by Lorenz, such investigations soon disclosed data embarrassing to the behaviorists. For example, in one batch, brood, hatch, or litter, an immense difference among siblings was found, although their environment was identical. As among men, so in all the life forms, individuals were seen not to be born alike and blanks. There are genius pigs and pig morons in effect. Every capability appears at every possible degree of diversification for each species—and environment is not the first cause of that.

Heredity makes the difference, a datum on which domestic animal breeders had based their efforts for thousands of years. (How could the behaviorists have ignored that?)

At this point an absurd situation occurred. In Soviet Russia, the foremost biologist, Lysenko, insisted that environment was the be-all of living things, a mandatory position since Marxist dialectic rests on it. But Lysenko's efforts to prove the assertion (and his claims to have done so) shortly became unstuck. He wasn't able to condition even wheat to environs where wheat had not thitherto managed to grow.

The non-Communist geneticists, certain that characteristics of plants, and of people too, were inherited (not acquired from environs and then handed down to offspring), watched Lysenko's hopeless efforts with open contempt and, finally, public mirth.

Stalin supported Lysenko as long as that was possible.

Stalin was obliged to. If Lysenko was wrong, so was
Stalin. So was Lenin. Lysenko was wrong. The steam went
out of Lysenkoism. One more behaviorist dogma was dead.
And the Reds ought to have revised their ideology accordingly then—though they appear not to have done it,
even now, insofar as heredity, environment, and man conditioning are concerned.

Lorenz and his colleagues asked other questions the
behaviorists had shied away from.

What is it in living creatures that is susceptible of imprinting?

Conversely, why can't animals be imprinted beyond or
outside their form and function as nature has set these?

What is it that can be variably motivated within those
limits?

And what about wild animals? Animals in no way
affected by man, not even aware of man? Are they the
same as animals men have hunted, nearly all animals and
nearly everywhere for tens or hundreds of thousands of
years? Are the animals that know men as killers identical
to those that do not? And how do domestic animals differ
from their wild relations? What about pets and what about
wild animals men have made friends with? New answers
poured in.

Classical biology dropped dead. It remains in that healthful state, although today the very much changed "classical
biologists" are locked in debate with "molecular biologists."
The classicists doubt their opponents can or ever will
create life in the lab. But such battles are proof of progress;
truce in a science is always a sign of imminent explosion,
not of certainty assured.

Men in the new science rediscovered and interpreted in
a correct way data that the behaviorists had arbitrarily
rejected, explained by rationalization, or ignored. One clue
long available was that ill-considered observation that the
song of birds is not a bird-equivalent of music, but a
public notice that the singer owns the territory from which
it sings and thereabouts, for a distance specific to that
bird's kind.

Here, then, was another "innate" attribute.

2 / Wonders and Words

But before I carry this report any farther, I'd like to issue sort of a hurricane warning, one intended to prevent damage—to me, anyhow—by a storm that would otherwise be pure hell.

The ethologists at this point had to return to a concept of "instinct," the word most abhorrent to their long-dominant colleagues. But every time an unaccredited author uses the word "instinct" he is liable to furious rebuff by professionals. They rebuff each other for the same cause, too. For there is no agreement about that word and some biologists would like to forget it. Such definitions as are made, however, may border on the fantastic.

As an example, I offer a marginal note entered by a friend on an earlier version of this treatise.

"The animal behavior you describe as 'instinct toward species continuation' is more accurately the absence of any instinct opposed to a cause for phenomenon."

Since my friend is a world-famous anthropologist, an equally renowned psychologist, an author, and a great guy, I bowed appreciatively.

But the refinement seems tiny. Animals may, indeed, be able to behave in certain ways owing to lack of any inhibition and without actual "drive" of positive instinct. So what? But such distinctions make me hope any scientists or overinformed laymen who chance to read these words will forgive me for my way of using language. And I trust those acute editors (who have put questions about usage on my margins) will do so, too. The only means I can find for trying to say what I am, here, is to use the terms that seem to me to "do," trusting that their particular meaning at the particular point can be discovered from the context.

That method has disadvantages, of course. It is not precise. But my thesis will finally be found precise only as a whole, an idea, that I believe is new and will be useful. The mere "problem of knowledge" and of its expression in language is one reason I have had to verbalize an essentially non-verbal theory, the concept of our human way of "thinking and knowing." And it is the reason this book is both reiterative and rather long.

With that, I return to the "instincts" recently described by the ethologists.

They relate to territory.

Not all, but perhaps most species of living beings are "territorial." A group of one such kind will have a range-need of fairly precise compass. Before it can even breed it must establish and hold its particular "turf." Within that region, innumerable other, different species can live and establish their own, different-sized territories. But no outside group of the same species is allowed to enter the country held by its fellows.

A great deal of time and energy goes into the act of acquiring and holding territory. One need only consider the amount of singing a bird may do to appreciate the fact.

And it was soon apparent to ethologists that man is a territorial animal.

Unfortunately, I believe, the first popular book on this subject, Robert Ardrey's *The Territorial Imperative*, dealt only with part of the complex phenomenon. Ardrey quoted a multitude of authorities and cited innumerable experiments, always, insofar as I could tell, correctly. Data and experiments he ignored, or slighted, made his book misleading, in my view.

To Ardrey, territorial instinct explained in a new way a great deal of man's behavior. It does. But it explains more than such matters as our long record of nationalism and war, matters Ardrey made clear. More, too, than his demonstration of the fact that groups of territorial animals, man included, not only set up tribes and nations with boundaries defended against all comers of like sorts, but that such animals (and men) have a second territorial drive and law within the owned region of each group.

That had been partly seen and for some time was known as the establishment of "pecking orders"—an act that can be observed in any chicken yard. Each member of any such group engages in an all-around pecking contest by which relative status is determined. The rooster that can outpeck all other roosters or the hen that defeats all hen contestants becomes what biologists now call an "alpha animal." "Beta" is Number Two . . . and so on.

But it was my feeling, after reading Ardrey's book, that he was so entranced with those two insights that he concentrated on them as if they explained, and in a way excused, man's fanatic nationalism and ruthless struggle within competing groups for individual status. I closed the volume with a sense that most of its readers, whether American or Japanese, would feel that their belligerence toward other nations and races, and their frenzied intramural battles for status, had been proven and as inalterable. Ardrey himself may not have that sense of ethology, but the inferences of his book gave rise to that belief in many people I know.

Shortly after it came out, however, another best-selling work appeared by Konrad Lorenz. It was called, *On Aggression*. And it was concerned with a part of territorial "imperative" that Ardrey had neglected.

Lorenz noted that territorial species do not defend their boundaries or battle within them in a way like that of men. Territorial animals, except men, are limited in their aggressions. When one group threatens the boundaries of another, what happens is not war. Threat and its counter are ritualized. Such engagements are more like shouting contests than battles. Physical contact occurs in many species but does not lead to slaughter. Any territorial creature killed in border quarrels is the victim of accident.

The same is true of inner territorial strife. Two stags may lock horns to determine which one can possess the females in the territory of either one. But neither will fight to the death. One will yield. The alpha-beta status will stand, or be altered, accordingly. If two such creatures lock horns so they cannot separate, they will perish by ill chance, not because they had fought to kill. And if one dies from being gored, that, too, is not the intent of its adversary.

Lorenz' anguished questions, therefore, were: What is it about men that is not true of any other territorial species?

What causes men to murder one another by war and in masses? Why do men strive within their own countries so viciously that human pecking orders condemn multitudes to a bottom-of-the-heap position where life may be impossible and will surely be inadequate in ways not observable among other animals?

The group aggressions of our one species may be, at first, shouting matches. But these often lead to invasion or to so-called defensive war.

Ritual combat becomes homicidal. That is a biological novelty. Again, the omega hen, as I suppose she is called, is allowed adequate access to the necessities of life. She is not starved. Her abode is no slum. She is not a certain, first victim of chicken diseases or even the easiest and first quarry for predators. Indeed, the flock may defend its omega hen against predation as valiantly as it will an alpha animal.

Those two taboos of all territorial animals but ourselves are important. Why men evolved with acquisitive instincts but without the otherwise universal restraints is the subject of investigation and theory in the pages ahead.

Yet another aspect of instinctual behavior among territorial animals has been scientifically established and it, too, has been presented in "popular" forms. This phenomenon is another I feel Ardrey failed to define and evaluate —one essential, however, for any adequate presentation of the territorial phenomenon. It is the reaction of territorial animals to overcrowding.

When the numbers of individuals in a group holding a certain region becomes too great for its area, the entire population suffers and even collapses.

Examples of that response will be found in Sally Carrighar's *Wild Heritage,* a book published prior to those by Ardrey and Lorenz.

What it discusses (to simplify an elaborate and varied reaction amongst diverse species) is "overcrowding" reaction. Territorial animals have a third restrictive "imperative" almost psychological in seeming. Each individual within a territory must have certain, sufficient room. If its fellows become so numerous that the individual and personal "area" is diminished, all members, being equally deprived, will react in one of many destructive ways.

This seems strange because the response will be made though all other requirements of every individual in such an overcrowded territory are present and even abundant. Overcrowded rats may go mad and even become cannibals. Lemmings in that situation resolve it by massive migrations, largely of the young, who rush away, not necessarily to find an empty territory, but often, as has long been wonderingly noted, till they encounter a body of water too broad to swim, where they then drown. Overcrowded deer of one species suffered endocrine atrophy, dropped dwarfed fawns, deteriorated as if genetically, and so, died below their acceptable level for no other cause than their lack of private space.

Both scientific and popular authors—those I've noted and a great many more—have called attention to a fourth difference between man and all other territorial creatures.

The others have what is perhaps best understood as a "built-in morality." For each such species there is an innate code of right-wrong that it obeys on peril of destruction. And, in effect, the purpose (or certainly the result) of this right-wrong imperative is seen in the fact that its commands and its taboos relate to one transcendent necessity, the continuation of its species.

What each such animal principally does, and what it does not do, express a code ideal for maintaining its posterity. So it can be said, at least as analogue, that all beings except our one kind are moral and near perfectly moral for their breed and its maintenance.

Before the reader puts in objection, let me continue a little farther. Individual animals do "disobey" such codes. For wild kinds that is costly. Many domesticated animals cannot perform even the basic acts for species maintenance. They are domesticated and not moral for that reason: perversion by man. Whole species perish when their code fails owing to such causes as environmental change. Evolution is slow. All species do evolve, however. But as they do, a new "code" emerges that they do not know but sedulously follow, one suiting their altered forms.

Again, the self-destructive response (of all observed groups of territorial animals) to overcrowding may seem a violation of what I have called morality.

Even were an overcrowded group of a species the last of its kind on earth, it would react in its particular self-defeating or self-endangering way. The species might vanish. Here, however, another and greater "moral equivalent" may be involved.

In each territory of such a species there will be, doubt-less, many non-competitive life forms and perhaps even hundreds of them. These will obviously conduct their af-fairs satisfactorily so long as the non-competing holders of the same territory are in numerical balance. Such is the evident status quo of the area. However, if one species that "owns" the area becomes too numerous, it is ecolog-ically obvious that the surplus will be harmful, or will threaten others who share the same real estate.

In the trial-and-error process of evolution, it long ago appeared as fact that the greater the numbers of *kinds* of life forms, the greater the chance for form-shifts and adaptations. Variety is paramount. Death, as Krutch noted, and I've said here, was the "price" of sex paid for the gain of accelerated evolution through vast increase of individuals per generation. Death tended to prevent any one sexual species from multiplying till it displaced or overwhelmed all other sorts, or even many other sorts.

So it is at least conceivable that the response to over-crowding of territorial animals is a parallel process. "Death" of such groups, or, if not total demise, self-damage to the point of reducing the overcrowded population below its "safe" numbers, or to a far poorer state than its pre-cramped condition, is possibly for a similar "purpose." The existence of any single species is not nearly so "important" as the continuum of many, even though the "self-sacrificed" one may be deer, the "saved" insects, birds, and snakes.

So there might be that intrinsic aim in the grim reaction of overcrowded, territorial animals. The vital and minimal space mysteriously required by each such individual may be for the sake of other species, not its own one. Should that be found true, man, as a territorial animal, has something very alarming to ponder and much more damaging than H-bombs.

The "moral" qualities ethologists find in animal behavior are, of course, not perceived. No lemming, rat, or deer is aware that it lives as it does in order to keep its kind going. It has no idea, even, that its mating activities will produce young. And if it requires a minimal spatial territory for itself and responds in automatic but fearful ways when denied that, it remains unaware of why it "mutinies" and, certainly, that it may have become as-if mad, actually suicidal, or a cannibal to save other species in the same place, the very existence of which it may not know. I have heard no better explanation of the space-per-unit need, in any event.

Animal "morality," though innate, or instinctual, is un-conscious insofar as any end is concerned. Yet, for a period of perhaps three billion years, this morality of instinct has perfectly served and persisted as absolute, changing only in function to match evolutionary changes in form—or vice versa, if you wish.

Man, however, has been able to perceive that he must maintain at least the babies and children of his tribe to persist as a tribe. And he has known for many thousands of years in his "progressive" cultures that he reproduces by the sex act. Some primitives have been studied that were not aware of that. But it is sure it *was* understood by the time the Old Testament took shape!

Man, however, as I shall show in more detail, did not take over consciously the prior morality that was based on species continuum—whether an instinct, the absence of opposed instinct, or whatever name you prefer for the exact congruence of form and function with the end of species perpetuation. Man began to enter the dimension of time with his imagination—and only that way—and from them on, he was man; and natural law, morals, or ethics became perverted or nil. Man didn't want to die. I've noted his efforts to pretend he would not die. He thought to conquer nature by reason and thought he *had* reason—with the result, for one example, of our techno-logical, self-limiting civilized way of life. And man, as a territorial being, long ago abandoned the rituals of inhibition at his borders bravura and in his status strife behind his borders. He couldn't imagine he was too lowly for murder.

He used his imagination, in short, to pretend he could opt out of nature and its moral law. Since the day he came by his power to imagine in time, he never again believed honestly, reasoned truly, or acted morally, in the sense characterizing morality in his "lesser" co-inhabitants of earth—and the only real sense.

The vision of nature as it is, has been withheld from man's eyes by hundreds of thousands of years of desperate effort to be and stay that unseeing, in support of his imagined importance.

Modern man may say he respects his planet and finds nature splendid. That he cherishes life, all life. And that he also lives for posterity: his own children, at least. But he dwells in a city that has its streets and edifices standing on rock, on scraped-away life. Nature is remote from him. Life isn't known by him, really. Law unguessed.

Whenever man wants to build, his claim of life respect is shown a fraud. To build, he first uproots the life on his site. So he does not contemplate anything as it is—not even himself. His vision is only of his face in his hand-altered mirror. Nothing nature created is allowed to stand in the way of any artifact of man, however slow and marvelous was the former in becoming, however quick and rude the latter.

Recently, I bought a new car. When I drove it to my summer home, the people in the village came to look and called it beautiful.

Everywhere, that day, were trees in the color climax of fall, a surrounding of painted exclamation. The people noticed that, too, sometimes, and called it pretty. But it was my new car that peaked their aesthetic responses.

How crazy they were!

For a car is a banal object.

Cars can be called beautiful only by persons whose sense of beauty is degraded. Cars are laughable. They are bug-eyed monstrosities. Ugly things. The uglier, for our admiration of them as having beauty.

A million Jackson Pollocks could not put on canvas the effect of the old sugar maples on our street, that day. And all the cars General Motors ever shook off its assembly lines cannot match for exquisiteness of design and intricacy of function—for beauty, then—one shrub. All cars on earth are not that remarkable a creation.

The things men have made—engineers, builders, industrial designers, and applied scientists—amount to very little by that scale, the only correct one. The sum total of human works, the artifacts of savages, barbarians, medieval men, and modern—all cities and towns, every hut, hovel, skyscraper, and temple, all steel bridges, everything man has made to use since the first stone tool or wooden club— does not equal, in all parts put together, the achievement of the life forms of plant and insect in a square foot of grass. Add a mouse, or even a frog, and you will more than balance off whatever men can do for centuries to come.

Yet what civilized person is aware of that? Who, aware, sees the implication?

Who will then see what it means about man's sense of values and their preposterous exaggeration?

How quickly the graduate ape came to imagine his piddling artifacts were all-important just because they could alter the appearance of nature to his immediate benefit! How soon he became wholly devoted to that new ability! And what eons were then to pass before he even looked once again at reality and discovered something of its elegant construction! Yet what a fool he remained by continuing to dote on the triviality of his fabrications, as compared to those of nature!

What, for instance, is the entirety of Greater New York City compared to one sequoia? Even, to a small range of inanimate mountains? Or to a cubic mile of sea water with its living content? Not comparable, this mere city. A congress of rude buildings, thick wires, and big ducts, put together in disharmony and so unworkable its very air cannot be comfortably breathed.

Where, among civilizations, are the checks and balances, by which, alone, an environment can be maintained in a habitable condition? They do not exist. Or they exist as

miscellaneous worries in a few minds. We have ignored
nature, learned nothing from it, and now we face the cost
of that abdication of our trust. How gross, how irresponsible we are!

Man lays a brick. Nature sets in an atom. Man installs
a component, an electric ventilating fan, let us say. Nature
puts in a molecule. Man builds a shopping center. The
equivalent in nature would be one element of a simple
cell. And with each additions, nature arranges a balance
in the whole. Man pays no attention to that necessity, is
ignorant of its existence.

What millionaire in his Manhattan penthouse knows where
his electrically ground garbage goes, or what happens to the
trash he drops into his chute. Knows . . . or cares? And
whoever wonders, as he buys a car he considers pure splendor,
how much its manufacture and use adds to the permanent
poisoning of the earth's air or dissipates from the earth's finite
resources?

It merely vexes him if he is told these ugly aspects of his
auto.

It vexes him. Perhaps it worries him slightly. But mostly
he reacts by fretting over the added taxes he might be
required to pay even for an inadequate, niggling, and so
hopeless attempt, not to end but just slightly to reduce
even one such hazard, among the hundreds occasioned by
his daily abuses of his planet, his individual additions of
nastiness, his subtractions of all value.

A few billions, earmarked in the next ten years, to
modify this self-assassination for alleged progress? More
likely, a trillion dollars spent in that period would not suffice
for maintaining life enough on earth to let that man persist
much longer.

So, before you ever again call an automobile beautiful
(or jump with joy over any other such engineered product),
ask what beauty means and how lovely a car is, when
properly contemplated.

If you will not do that, or cannot—or if you find such
comparisons irrelevant, unfair, extreme, absurd, or lunatic
—think again.

For it is you who are guilty of obliviousness to those

sins. You, who have not yet noticed how you depend on all other life. You, who have no idea what life is.

Many geophysicists believe that if American progress continues at the intended rate, if the other civilized nations keep parallel pace, and if underdeveloped peoples on the earth succeed in their planned industrialization, in fifty years, or in thirty, the earth's atmosphere will have become too toxic for man's existence.

Suppose those geophysicists are mistaken? Suppose the day when too many species of green plants wither to extinction for man's survival, or for that of the plants and animals man eats, is sixty years away? Or even a hundred? Take that generous estimate of a century. Then, if you have young children, ask why they also should have children, since these will be doomed. And this is only one damage we do of thousands, known or not.

Such is our self-infatuation.

Such has been man's endless, stupid delight in all he could do.

How great he is!

He could add to himself machines that gave his muscles the power of steam, then of electricity, and now of the atom. He could develop mechanisms that let his eye see not just more stars but stars down light-years, the billions of light-years. He could hear radio noises across such awesome spaces, too. And he could see with electron beams objects smaller than the wave length of visible light.

He could do what he is doing right now; and he probably can do all he is hopeful (or fearful) of achieving in the future. For some brief further time, that is.

At his beginning he had only a capacity to do such wondrous things. Still, even in his million-year-old form, he was like man now; he had the same brain; and lacked only the knowledge since gained.

And he had instincts, of course.

To guide everything he has ever done, and is doing, and will foreseeably do, he had an inner state common to all living beings: the necessity to seem right to himself. But note! The others had to *be* right; man, only to seem so. He presumed.

Like the one-celled protozoan, like his pre-sexual ancestor and his ape sire, man had two opposite but fundamental directions for his drives, and only two. He was driven toward this and away from that. He did not perceive the reason for the arrangement, however. And men still do not perceive it.

Yet each pair of tropisms produces that dual effect. That just-alive, simplest cell-being is drawn toward what benefits it and repelled by what would harm it.

It says to itself, always, one of two things: Yes and no. *Si et non,* as, my friend René Spitz has put it.

Approach, its tropisms order, or retreat.

Swim up toward the light—or down from it.

Just the two. Only two.

And man?

Man is never neutral toward anything he knows or even imagines as having importance to him, whether it be deemed good or bad, helpful or hazardous, enjoyable or hurtful.

Man evaluates—just as do all other living things.

And that is all man does most of his living hours.

But he is the unspecialized animal; and so he is the most adaptable of all. His evaluations are therefore subject to as much variation as the range of environs to which he can adapt and the reach of his imagination, his image-making ability. With the unseen corollary, however, that when his values err, he pays, soon—or someday.

What an equatorial African native will desire and what he will wish to avoid differs from what an Eskimo seeks, and seeks to escape.

Both, however, will have the same two-way responses toward all external matters known or assumed to be of consequence. And both, of course, will have internal responses—values that correspond to their different environs and to the customs of their kind, in their regions. But those cultural values will be superimposed on the deeper, immutable value system common to all mankind and all life.

Whatever men do not put a price on is trash, neither good nor bad. They won't notice it, won't know it exists, perhaps, and if they know, will care nothing for it.

But if men come to imagine some irrelevant thing or

idea has a relationship with their existence, they will, of course, give it an imagined and a mistaken value. They cannot do anything with or about stars, for example, African or Eskimo. But watching stars, they may realize the sky's changing aspect is regular and relates to changing seasons, or to migration of game, or to plant development. So they will see stars as magically connected with phenomena upon which stars have no bearing whatsoever. Then they will invent a mythical relationship. Thus men came to imagine the stars affect themselves; and astrology was born out of unreason that seems like reason for those who cannot use logic any better.

To this day most people make the same error. They misinterpret cause and effect. They have their fortunes told. Their newspapers print astrological tables that millions consult and follow, with what idiocies of result any rational person can guess.

Men are still superstitious. Spilled salt means a quarrel. Don't cross the path of a black cat, walk under a ladder, or break a mirror. This man owns a lucky necktie. That young lass has a penny in her shoe. Every bit of it is nonsense. Yet it was the beginning of religion and it remains the core of such faiths. It is the motive of all pious ritual. *Magic*.

How can any man still be so ignorant, so stupid?

Because his arrogance outweighs all reason. If I believe so-and-so, he thinks, it is true because it is I who believe. We must, like all animals, seem right to ourselves, remember. They must also *be* right or perish. We, too. But men have forgotten about that.

In man, the opposite drives of his deeds, ideas, and imaginings can be given two simple names:

Love.

And Fear.

All that appeals to man as desirable, enjoyable, necessary, possible, and worthy, he somewhat loves. He is attracted to it. And it may be to objects; or may be subjective, attracting him to ideas handed down from ancient barbarians as correct, and so worthy of love, reverence, adoration.

What repels him (and whatever is supposed to, according to local belief) causes in man some degree or kind of fear. This fear may seem to be hate, jealousy, "righteous" anger, loathing, and so on, but no man can hate or be negatively moved by any cause save one related to his beliefs that is also fear arousing. The opposite of love is not hate. For hate is merely secondary and a sign that he who hates was first afraid.

A man may love women, money, learning, or all three. But whatever threatens to harm his beloved woman or to estrange her, he fears, no matter how he describes his reaction. Even if he denies that his feeling rises from fear and convinces himself that fear is not in him, if he fears, it will be expressed by a symbolic act or act-refusal —some charade to show what biologists call displacement, and psychologists, conversion hysteria.

To the degree he cherishes money, a man seeks money; in the amount he obtains it, he enjoys his gain; if it is not enough, he strives for more; and in all such conditions he is liable to fear also: to anxiety about the possible loss of his money-paying job, or of his saved money, through unwise investment, market failures, inflation, and the rest of money risks: theft, swindle, all.

If he prizes learning he will learn. Then he will defend what he has learned and so he may come to believe perpetually in that bit, rigidly standing against any later and more accurate knowledge. Such a man may nevertheless believe he is objective and without prejudice in his now-discredited learning. For such a man imagines he must only *seem* right—and only to *himself*, remember, remember.

He is a man of science, let us imagine. He can show he has been open-minded. In his field, he will have disclosed a love of learning and even changed his scientific theories many times, without distress or any other evidence of fear. Since he chose to be a scientist, a theoretical physicist, let us assume, his life choice of a career represented a very great attraction toward physics, a desire like a love. And his fear may therefore relate to people who are unscientific and to their power to exploit insanely, or to ignore, or to oppose, his scientific truths.

In any case, whatever mental flexibility he may have gained in his field will not likely carry much into the rest of his life. His use of reason and of logic and of creative thinking, his proper employment of the human mind, will have caused him to use the love-fear motivation of living things as the means to truths in physics. But he will have managed that loftiest attainment of humanity only in a special locus, a branch of science.

His *fears* may then emerge as compensatory acts elsewhere, so that his very fealty for pure theory causes him in the rest of his person to be a shy man, an oddball, antisocial, or irrational about any other area of knowing and being, or about many others. What man, indeed, is able to employ the universal love-fear situation of living beings with realism in every way, and thus to become honest and logical as a whole person, in all relationships, all acts, all feelings and all imagining?

Yet that is the ideal for man and his potential, which a few men now and then seem to have come near to attaining.

Such men love and know what they love: truth and honesty, that is, love itself. Such men also are aware of fear, for that they have this love. Aware, then, of fear's sources and causes, too; so they face them and overcome them by dealing consciously with them as fears, not as fears dressed up to seem hate, in order to hide real terror under that costume of righteousness. They are great men. Yet, they remain human. Their experience of love and its consequent opposite, fear—which engenders anger or grief or hate or repression in others—is accepted by them as part of being, with a sorrow that is like their love—universal and intense but borne with conscious courage.

Moral courage, we call that kind.

Here, then, is the heart of being: love-fear.

Attraction. Repulsion.

There is no more to it but elaboration.

But it is the elaboration that blinds most of us to its simplicity of source.

The paired tropisms that were congruent with the very first living things are as germane to man. But if we think a little way beyond that point, we will see the circumstances that led men into persistent error. For concerning this situation, man did err, from the first and till this day. How? Recall how:

With fire, with weapons, with cunning, early men found they could vanquish all the lesser breeds. Even the woolly mammoths could be trapped in pits or driven into pens and slain. And even the elements against which other creatures were helpless frequently could be tempered by human craft. Fires defeated cold. So did clothing made of skins.

The new imagination that men possessed also enabled them to exploit the instincts of beasts. Men learned their right-wrong patterns and used the knowledge to trick the relative puppets of such systems. Men baited them, lured them into deadfalls, and set snares in their runs.

Such genuine superiorities led early men to think of themselves as "other," which we do now without even questioning our presumptuousness.

Any sense of superiority of the self is a heady affair, valid or not. And so men commenced to imagine they were more than superior; they were entirely different from their animal relations—which weren't "human." And when they found out about death and then invented the afterworld, the difference appeared to be as infinite. For then it actually involved infinity—as eternity, in stolen dreaming.

But the companion error, man's new concept of himself as overlord of nature, was as lethal. He no longer viewed himself as in nature and of it, a part of nature and forever bound to be no more than that. He thought to own it, rule it, consume it.

Nature still represented his whole good. But to man, the good was now seen undependable. The harm nature did him was often violent and dreadful. Lightning struck him. Floods drowned him in his cave-homes. Prairie and forest fires exterminated his family. Earthquakes destroyed his works. Tsunamis overwhelmed them. Lava burst upon him from volcanoes. And when he domesticated animals, or planted crops, diseases destroyed both. And diseases destroyed him.

This superbeing, this pretender to animal transcendence, this time-using novelty which had the power of imagination

inherent in that, the whizz which soon could hand on knowledge, generation after generation, was still, however, largely
powerless before nature.

Hence, nature came to seem to men less as a benison and
more an incomprehensible menace. In one sense, that was
correct. To adapt with increasing effectiveness to his world,
man was obliged to make a long series of what he deemed
conquests over nature. He came to use and work the materials nature supplied with the aim of protecting himself
and his posterity against natural menaces. It was and is
his main activity—a proper one, when conducted with consideration for all the costs and consequences of each success.

But man studied only those aspects of nature that yielded
short-term protection against its hazards, that is, immediately
advantageous techniques for trapping, killing, collecting, and
reworking the products he required for his ever-more-complex life ways. What seemed beyond his control he did not
try to study, for an implied reason. It was hostile and it also
seemed inscrutable, since he could not manage it by reason.
An evil realm, nature, full of unpredictable calamity that
he believed rationally intractable.

But he also felt, since he was so punished in this realm,
that it was for guilt of some sort. His new arrogance demanded that order of counterweight. If he, the nature-con-
queror, had not somehow sinned he would not have been
struck by fire, flood, quake. So he began to relate himself
as cause to such catastrophic effects. More magic had to be
invented. That is, more religion.

Man's very power of imagination, his ability to employ
so much of nature to his advantage, was his motive for
pretending to cope, by magic, where he had no other means,
and to explain ensuing failures by magic too. No other
creature was anything like him, or remotely comparable to
him: Man could plainly see that. Why see more? Why accept
any defeat by nature as beyond his wonderful control, at
least potentially?

And so, while he exploited every seeming good in nature,
nature itself remained unknown. And what is unknown to
man or beast has intrinsically the power to arouse fear:
love's opposite and its other half, the source of hate and

rage and all negative sensations. His capacity for fear was equal, of course, to his potential for love. And now he had become very loving—of himself.

He was the first wise guy in evolution. So great, so advanced, so other, so wondrous! A being able to defeat even death, he convinced himself. For which cause, of arrogance that had no precedent and was a supreme sin against all that is true and real, his dreads were rendered as mighty, in perfect proportion.

For his magical invention of an eternal life, his giant lie, he tried to compensate with magic inevitably.

His religions were at first what religious people now call primitive and animistic. Having fabricated for himself a spirit, man assumed all things would own a similar, immaterial soul. The assumption was another fiction arising from the first but thereafter seeming to support it. That is, of course, the logical method imposed on all illogic.

Primitive religions were more exactly related to the animal morality than the ancient belief that led to our currently dominant faith. There were good and evil spirits in the beginning. With their personification in the gods, and with the legends of gods and men invented as parables for the many peoples who used such systems, a god or goddess of beneficence, or of enmity, was assigned an archetypal position in hierarchies and legends.

Right-wrong and do-don't thus were maintained by simple fables and personified images. As the gods grew more human, the demons began to form in the unconscious, taking on man's perverted idea of animal attributes. So man moved farther away from his real state, making his religious figures of good like himself, but those of evil part hawk, lion, goat, and so on.

Hebrew or Old Testament religion made the leap to what is still, incredibly, called monotheism. It had one Jehovah. But it had Satan, too, its demon-god, forked tail and cloven hoof. Still, the right-wrong, good-evil balance held. And where Satan was given lesser status, God himself was seen both as loving and terrible, all-good and all-punitive, merciful and wrathful, generous and jealous.

It was only with Jesus, and his pitiful endeavor to promulgate a faith of love without fear and a God appropriate to such an impossible condition, that man widely adopted what is still the general illusion of our time. The Christian illusion, I mean, that love need have no opposite.

Christian love, brother love, love of all humanity, a loving God, and loving Jesus so exalted believers as to drive the opposite truths into the unconscious mind. Fear, usually greater than love among men in primitive and ancient cultures, was, of course, the attraction to Christian love, the first, perhaps the only, major example. People accepted avowedly the new faith to love, to be loved, and so to gain immortal souls of equal dignity and importance. Actually, most sought escape from the cost of any and all love—escape from fear in the degree that all attachment, affection, loving, passion, care, and cherishing make mandatory as potential. To cherish is to risk that much anguish, as fear of harm to, or loss of, what is cherished.

Christian love, accepted as reality, with no other and opposite risk, caused believers to lose sight of fear.

That was essentially the promise of Jesus. So Christian fear had to be translated from its essence into displaced forms. Forms the conscious could accept, not as fearful, but righteous: hate, prejudice, violent opposition to alien doctrine, missionary efforts often preceded by armed force, Crusades, Inquisitions—the terrible rest of the presumed love bit exhibited by the least loving people ever to exist: people who could no longer see their "love" led to acts that were and are the most terrible treason to morality in human time.

From the first, man also presumed he might manage his gods by the means he had used to invent them—sorcery. Magic alone can converse with and influence magical inventions. That is plain. So the necromancies proliferated.

Man's ghosts and gods and ancestral shades were propitiated; his most precious objects were offered as sacrifices to his gods in efforts to manipulate his fate. But his real animal knew his false-conceived self was lying here. He felt the guilt and called it Original Sin. The bigger he built the lie after that, the more fanatic his witchcraft became.

He did not, of course, weigh the effectiveness of his mummery. He does not. And dares not. If a burnt goat staved off an impending storm once, that showed the value of goat sacrifice. The same gambit might then fail fifty successive times. But if it once again proved successful, on a fifty-first attempt, man was convinced of its potency. The fifty failures were explained away by magic. They were not attributed to the impropriety of goat burning as a storm avoider, but to some other alleged cause—the worshiper's errors in the ritual, or in his conduct when the rite had been tried and had failed those fifty consecutive times. Or he imagined that perhaps somebody in the group had been sinful and so ruined the effect. No matter. Properly behaving people could count on driving off storms by goat sacrifice and had done so twice.

Prevention of floods could be managed by the annual drowning of six maidens, always provided the people engaged in the drowning wore the six right kinds of leaves, uttered the fixed incantation without mistakes, and did not blink. If hail threatened crops, it could be diverted by stoning seven young boys to death. If, when the boys were dead, the hail hit anyhow, that was because one of the stone flingers had picked up a wooden missile. Punish the sinner, then.

Priests took charge here—specialists, who claimed they could detect a person guilty of the error when a magic rite failed. Whereupon the wrongdoer paid. That way a tribe with the hail-ruined crops was revenged for the fact that its otherwise reliable magic had not worked. Thus the priesthood rose to such power it will never yield while its monopoly of magic holds faithful masses in its grasp. Nowadays, holy men are not widely allowed the direct methods of ancient enforcement. When the cant fails, priests explain that the ways of God are beyond all understanding, but that the rites must not be doubted.

The foregoing is, of course, what man does in prayer and in every religious act meant to please God or to request God's special attention, blessing, healing, gift, or extra cash, forgiveness, vengeance upon foes, and the like. It is the implicit statement of the very architecture of religious buildings and pious costumery. All this is magic and nothing else.

And as long as men put faith in such trumpery, they will be alienated from their true meaning, their hope, all sanity, and any goodness.

As long as man imagines his mind, spirit, soul, or whatever he calls it, has these mystic powers he will remain incapable of realism, that is, of honest vision and true relationship with nature. For the acknowledgment of human instinct by a religious man is not possible.

It is not possible because such acknowledgment automatically exposes the delusion about what he had hitherto seen as religion. Restored to a perception of his innate morality, his yes-no, do-don't instinct, man would appreciate the primitive blunder his forebears made in assigning to themselves a status above nature and the power to manage nature by magic. That is something they cannot do, however many candles they burn, altars they erect, hosannahs they raise, beads they tell, prayer wheels they spin, or however high they build their pagoda roofs, stupas, and steeples. Designed as a way to transcend instinct, religion became its unconscious expression.

Magic thinking! Magic doing! Magical beliefs! Faith in miracles! The interminable folly of our species!

Yet man could be magical. But true magic is not witchcraft or demonology, or Christology, either. Man's imagination is his enchanted possession, but it is not meant for self-enchantment by the glorification of his invented gods.

It is not enough, however, to cleanse the self of one religion. Such a purged person will still cling to the religious method, and so keep his instinctual nature hidden. To purge the mind of its indecent, species-old habit of magical self-delusion, a human being must set aside not only all dogma and its faith-supported counterfeits of truth but also that inner process that mankind has endlessly corrupted to serve and to service the colossal fraud, the idea he is other than the rest of living things on this planet.

Then, and only then, a man can own the genuine marvel of magic. For then, and only then, will he be able to begin to imagine reality as it is.

To say, merely, "There is no God," or, as recently (and funnily), "God is dead," is not to be delivered from the clamp of faith. And even to say, "Man is an animal," and believe that, does not resolve the problem of self-infatuation. For a man can believe he is an animal and still continue to behave in the way we call human, the way, that is, of supererogation toward nature.

To make the true identification, one must accept one's animality and with that, the knowledge of the lost fact that animals are exactly moral, and men are not. For the lowliest creature is man's ethical superior; and its morality is the only kind man actually could own. All else is but noise of the loud, lying mouth.

"Good" is a *deed*. "Goodness" is *behavior*. And whether a man be good or not is shown in that one way. Only the doing of the man will define his virtue, if he has any, whether he subscribe to some Christian belief or pagan, to disbelief or agnosticism. Evil, in like manner, is a deed, not a word on the hideous index of any priestly caste. False teaching (as of the soul's eternal nature) doubly shoves the believer into acts of evil—directly, by the lie—and thereafter, by his uses of a diagram of virtue that is erroneous. The conscious listener hears the allegation of all such "virtue"; but his unconscious mind hears very clearly that it is but allegation and draws the obvious conclusions.

If this were not so, it would be hard for a man with a true religion to err deliberately. Besides, were good and evil, virtue and sin, honestly defined by any religion, then, only one religion could lead to humanity and decency. Only one Faith and only one sect of that Faith could then know the True Gospel—were it correct to assent, as do the believers, that truth cannot be found where faith is absent.

Such magical self-deceptions can be seen in many ways. Consider the arrogant and fatuous circus:

There are, many Christians say, no atheists in fire fights. Who the rational man must then ask, who, in a battle, filthy, under enemy guns, afraid and often hurt, experiencing the worst in man, could possibly believe in a god of mercy, compassion, love, or justice? In battle there are but these two: atheists and dupes.

Yet one sees, every day, and if one associates with religious people, a hundred times a day—that smugness.

Smugness that has served down the rolling ages to make men think they can control nature, being elect, the chosen associates of this God, or those gods, wherefore, not instinct-dominated as the other, lesser beings.

"God is not dead," some Billy Graham therefore boasts, "I talked with Him this morning."

Did you, Billy-boy? In this modern era? Then, where's your tape recording of what you both said?

Again, as I like to tell, there is General Max Weigand's visit to Lourdes, the biggest miracle heap on earth. He looked about, it's said, and murmured, "All those crutches! But not one wooden leg!"

How long, how interminably long, will man put up with such holy self-abuse? How can he do so at all these days?

Only, it is sure, because his instinct is involved in the deception, and so his reason is diminished to such a degree it cannot extricate him.

But *what* instinct?

The territorial imperative, plainly. That whelming and ubiquitous drive of living beings that lends its slowly evolved force to sustain the morals of animals but which can also be perverted to support man's faith in his dreamland.

Dreamland is territory, even if it be claimed as beyond all definition, by a faith or religion. Such a territory is owned in the present by believers, and so all they can grasp, for self, for family, for group, or for nation. Yet men without any such dream are worse off than the godly, since they live in absolute contempt of time-future. It has no value to these men, does not exist, and is not their responsibility, even as practical concept. The territorial imperative makes them the complete and willful predators of the posterity of all life forms, man's included, for their magic has been slain.

Superficially, it might seem the greatest irony that this myth men designed (and then claimed true of themselves) in order to look down some enormous distance on all other life should turn them into the lowest life form of all.

But it is not ironic. Nor is it one of those mystic paradoxes that the religious create to show what they cannot resolve. No one need examine them. Man's ignominy is the psychologically predictable result of every self-deception. The more man clings to gods (or, as he says, to God, without noticing that God is many gods) in order to seem the imagined superman, the more he becomes an inferior sample of what he imagines he had transcended, his animal.

Men have often somewhat recognized this sort of dualism, or bipolarity, this yang-yin situation, this up-down, in-out "dance of life." But never, in those perceptions, have enough men seen the psychomechanism behind the puzzle, or that it concerns but two halves of one law of nature.

Instinct, man keeps telling himself, is not in him. He has to say that, otherwise man is not divine; no anthropomorphic divinity could be postulated—no being like enough to man to support man's triumphant calamity of self-worship.

Yet there remains within him one clear effect of instinct, a compulsion to have some sort of right-wrong ideology. His adaptability has enabled him to set up and sedulously to follow almost any right-wrong system he could invent. The only limitations upon it were those described by his body and brain. Fancied systems of morality could not long persist if, for example, they demanded of him some custom, ritual, or life way that, soon or late, would lead to the undoing of mankind, or if they demanded performances beyond his capability. Short of such limits, however, *any* dualistic morality will suffice—for a while, at least.

Lesser creatures needed their morality only for their bare-handed continuum within nature. But man soon needed a set of do-don't rules related to his material artifacts. And when he created the self-serving artifact of a perverted ego, he needed synthetic sets of substitute tropisms to support his new notion that he was lord of creation, or would not really die but live forever, and a million more. With each subsequent invention of an ethos related, not to earthly existence and human posterity, but to the notion that nature is subordinate, or that man lived beyond his grave, he therefore added to his pragmatic code, his magical rules.

So arose numberless moralities and ideologies—customs and laws that did not relate to nature as reality, but to man's false fancy of his sublime otherness.

3 / The Trap of Tradition

The more facts man found, the more man had to make his images of deity and demon abstract, in order that his willful estrangement from reality could be maintained.

As Jehovah lost his white beard and purple robes and Beelzebub shed his horns, hoofs, and tail—as heaven's eternal pantry of milk and honey was dumped and hell's everlasting sulphur pits were banked—devout persons assumed their shifting belief was becoming more rational, by thus growing more vague.

On the contrary. The farther men moved away from a visualization of themselves as physical (and so, of their good and evil as related to the flesh), the farther they moved off from the mere opportunity to comprehend the truth about themselves.

Abstraction, however, made such beliefs as those of the modified (and splintered) faith called modern Christianity at least seem less repugnant to persons with some knowledge of modern science. The astronauts, so to speak, had failed to encounter any heroic-scale old boy up there. It is also doubtful that, if the Mohole is ever drilled, its final penetration of the earth's upper crust will spud in on hell.

Nowadays only persons who are relatively ignorant, obdurate, or stupid, or all three, would reject astronomer Harlow Shapley's declaration: "I cannot believe in a one-planet God."

The fact remains that the majority of the citizens of the United States do believe in a one-planet God. And the majority at least claim membership in religious sects that insist, as a condition of belonging, on yet other articles of faith even more medieval. It was not long ago, for example, that I heard Bishop Fulton J. Sheen insist, on a national TV hookup, that Satan was an actual being.

Such facts about Christian pretension, such details, to be gleaned from any almanac listing the membership of Christian sects, make me marvel at the incessant assertion of liberals, intellectuals, and academicians that religion is fading out in

America and has no great force. The truth is that deism of the most slavish and obsolete sorts still dominates American ideology.

If you cannot believe in a one-planet God—and who now can while claiming to be in touch with reality?—you cannot believe Jesus was God's son. You then cannot, unless you believe that, for every habitable planet, the super-deity arranged with a Mary-equivalent for another son with an aspect, form, and functions germane to those of each local, presumptively reigning species. That would involve, at least hypothetically, the magical birthing (or hatching) of some hundreds of millions, if not hundreds of billions of God-surrogates—an idea very hard to accept even for people who can and do accept the galaxies of greater twaddle required of a good Catholic, good Covenanter, good Hindu, Moslem, astrological believer, or devotee of Bug-Bug.

If that seems rude to pious readers, it is because their piety has kept them from doing their next, science-necessitated chore. The existence of innumerable planets similar to our own, and hosts to life, also, will perhaps be established when the moon-mad men of NASA quit Russia-racing and get a decent telescope in space. Then, granting even a hundred million or so planets appear as likely to have intelligent inhabitants, the believers will be faced with the problem of their redemption by Saviors appropriate to their unimaginable but surely diverse forms. Indeed, honorable Christians who believe in flying saucers ought already be praying that their operators have been or can be saved. That, or else they must acknowledge an inconsistency both in their Christian love and their logic.

Such an observation ought at the very least to serve as witness to the anthropocentric silliness of most religious belief. If so, the question about it then becomes: Why do men continue to cling to such various and manifestly crazed balls of spiritual wax, even in the face of inarguable truth, let alone in the bright presence of hypotheses to which their own ideas must rationally give rise?

The answer lies largely in tradition.

To examine human tradition, therefore, we must, once

more, return to our fair font of revealed and proven truth: biology.

For tradition, which men see as their exclusive store-house of ideals and so a veritable laser of moral light—vector, intensity, squirt-volume, and all—is animal, in etiology, essence, and effect. It is, again, like religious doctrines, evidence of instinct, inverted by man, the fool, who uses everything he has to convince himself he is not the very thing such possessions and uses certify him to be.

Until biology reached its present state, however, there was no perfect way to see that flaw in human tradition, for, to pre-human life forms, tradition was equivalent to their whole truth.

Pre-human forms evolved, remember, but only by minute mutations with correspondingly small alterations of form and so of traditional tropisms or, later, of instincts. Thus even though animal traditions changed, there was not change enough at any point to give rise to a sense of changing. The plasticity of their forms and functions was beyond discernment even if they could have discerned themselves.

For some billions of years, then, tradition appeared as inalterable to every living thing.

That circumstance is understandable. And with the evolution of man, it continued to prevail.

His traditions, however, soon concerned matters that animals couldn't conceive of. He had, now, his superior beliefs. But man's animal heritage of fealty to tradition still compelled him to resist conceptual change and to sustain old ways and old ideas. Why not? His self-esteem precluded the idea. He did not question the variety of moralities he soon invented, either, and see that they indicated his basic self-deceit in the matter.

What he said about the plain prospect was: They are wrong; I am right. Even the minor evidence of his own evolution that he was able to see, his slow racial differentiations, he also said showed him superior.

He said it, because tradition ruled him, not reason.

And so he feared others because of their difference in faith and hue. Fearing, he hated. Hating, he often destroyed them, or tried to. Lesser measures were not very effective:

The "others" were difficult to convert, that is, to enlighten, in his misuse of that word.

He could no longer see other creatures as moral, not even other men. The presence of morality in lesser species had become unthinkable owing to man's "thinking," his bastard use of imagination.

Yet, like any beast, he had his special conviction to give him guarantee for whatever tribal customs, religious procedures, magic, and myth he had been taught as truth by his people.

His need to know some means of judging what was right, what wrong, what was virtuous, what evil, remained as innate as any other creature's. But now that need bound him to any tradition into which he was born. He then worshiped tradition as an animal would, could it worship. But such an animal would be right in its reverence, or near enough right not to matter. Not so, man.

He ripped up the innate truth.

The truth that nature is moral.

He became, then, a lost being.

He still is.

And he will not find himself, or learn what man is, or even guess what he could and should become, till he recants and obliterates within his total being—both conscious and unconscious—the false concepts by which he has thus far directed himself and ordered his ways. The human ways that have periodically been revised, inflamed man's hopes anew, and so led to his serial civilizations, each of which, at last, has collapsed and vanished for the same cause.

Recorded history is evidence of that error and of its repetition: It shows that man has not yet become a successful species; and I think it can show why he has not.

He has never developed a universal belief: He has not yet accepted the only one that would furnish him with a morality all men can understand and should accept. He has not created an ideology that fits him into nature as he is truly situated. And so he has never managed, in his perpetual servitude to his creeds, to persist as a society by following whatever creed he has espoused, for more than a little while.

He could not expect to find himself or any purpose, his true nature, a valid ethos, or even a secure state in relation to nature, nor any other basis for continued association until he first uncovered his fundamental blunder.

That had happened . . . in his yesterday.

Now, man no longer has an excuse for his blind clutch of traditions—or for any more inventions of the ancient sorts.

Now, man has the information whereby he can reorient himself correctly.

He has access to instinct in its human, true form. The sufficient knowledge of nature. The requisite comprehension of his evolution and his state as an animal with imagination and so with the potential for logic.

There is no cause for him to err any longer.

And if he continues, his fate is evident.

If his now-willful errors are of the magnitude that his technology permits, his disaster will be in proportion.

Of course, many people are at least vaguely aware that civilized, Western men possess one means to cause a holocaust that would leave the earth's North Temperate Zone a burnt-out, radioactive slagland, a deathbelt where once the great majority of white men had dwelt, but then, their toppled and denuded monument, a region less habitable, for decades, than the moon.

But modern men do not perceive that such a catastrophe would be the consequence of their own errors, errors now magnified on the incredible scale of our so-called progress. They say, instead, that someone else who has the bomb would start the havoc, or have the accident that would initiate it. And they rarely even suspect that there are now many possible disasters, not of war, but of human behavior, rising from the long and ferocious effort men have made to validate their illusions about reality. Most no longer own a sense of what is real, or means to gain a perception of reality.

Doom has often come fortuitously to individuals and groups. But the doom of nations has generally been mere payment for dishonesty and dishonor, the price for false beliefs and false assumptions, finally collected.

Man was not evolved to be a walking horror; yet he has

not been other, save individually, till this day; and he is growing more grisly down our days, wherefore, less likely to persist as a species. For it is the law of nature that no species, no group, and no nation shall misjudge its own nature, or the purposes of that essence without penalty of a like degree, that is, extinction.

Chapter
Five

WHAT IS
A MIND?

1 / Other Categories

IN THE PERIOD at California Institute of Technology now called its "great days," some of the physicists had an amusing reaction to new findings. Of each they'd bemusedly murmur, "Why didn't we think of it?"

I used to spend a good deal of time as a learning guest and spellbound observer at Cal Tech in those early thirties. And ever since I have thought of that response to news that a bit of new knowledge had been suddenly added to our store. For the problem of learning is, in a sense, neatly implied by their little question:

Why didn't we think of it?

Why didn't we? For, when somebody else did so, the new truth seemed obvious.

One long-ago afternoon while walking on the campus with a pair of the atomic pioneers, I asked a question of my own about the atom, then believed to have three parts only: protons, orbiting electrons, and sometimes in its nucleus with the protons, a neutron or so.

"What will you do," I inquired, "if you find those three, fundamental particles are made of many littler bits?"

Both my companions groaned. Both looked at me with something between annoyance and pain.

One said, "God forbid!"

The other, "No theoretical evidence—!"

No prophetic vision caused me to ask that question. Anybody could have asked it right then, when the neutron had so recently been added to the atomic portrait. It was even an idle question in a way. But I never forgot it. Of course, new and smaller pieces in the atom were soon found and now there are so many that a layman cannot keep track of them and the scientists cannot yet account for them.

The reason I remembered my question was the reaction of my friends, who had taken part in the initial work on splitting atoms and had just been obliged to add to their electron-proton concept a third, that of the neutron.

So they felt, I am sure, that they and their colleagues had come up with a final answer about atomic structure. Generations of research had preceded my friends' prodigious endeavors in the high-tension lab at Cal Tech. And the equally keen work in Italy, Germany, England, and Russia. From a human point of view, then, it seemed to them that their resolution of the three-part atom had to be complete and final if only to justify both the effort and the achievement.

Every man who takes or helps to take such a step is inclined to imagine it is the ultimate, merely because he, or he and his associates, did it.

This process is related to the one discussed in the previous chapter. But it represents a next form of traditionalism. Even when a tradition is shattered and a new, authentic concept, law, theory, or what-not replaces it, those who accept the new finding tend to turn it into a next tradition.

Scientists are not in any way exceptions. They are people. And though they try to avoid being tradition-bound they are generally unable to do so, save in individual instances, now and again. At Cal Tech in those great days, however, they used to be aware of that situation in at least one fashion.

They often pointed out that most mathematical breakthroughs had been the work of young men and often very young men. Men who were able to think in different categories owing to the fact they had not yet become frozen intellectually in the existing or traditional systems of mathematics.

It is not, however, physics and math that I propose to discuss in this chapter.

It is man and animals and territory. New categories have appeared here recently.

The discovery that many animals, man among them, are territorial is very new. On the other hand, it has that look I noted above. Our territorial nature so recently became manifest that we might very likely ask, "Why didn't we think of it?"

Why didn't we see the situation long, long ago? Why have nations interminably embarked on wars of conquest? What was Hitler, for a recent example, promising to Germans that so exalted them? *Lebensraum.* Living space. Even that despicable idea of "Poland without Poles." What, then, of America without Indians?

Why didn't naturalists of the past century note the characteristic in lower life forms? Why did it take so many decades of scientific birdwatching for a man to perceive that birdcalls are not love songs or outbursts of bliss but assertions of property ownership?

Why didn't men see, long ago, that thousands of species have staked out their needed territories and defended them against all comers of their own and of hostile sorts, as if the essential provinces of each were as clearly defined as squares on a checkerboard? Why, when that was noted for some birds, did our world-ranging thousands of professional naturalists fail to scrutinize other animals at once to see if the same situation applied?

Any attempt to answer that question must be speculative. But two or three speculations are suggestive, at least.

The first one, of course, is that naturalists already believed they understood animal range. Ecologists, scientists who study the interrelationships and interdependencies of all the life forms in areas called "niches," had provided a great deal of true but different information about life ways in them. Each species, they learned, bred up or died back according to the availability of its material requirements in each niche.

Nature keeps an ecological balance. Let rabbits, rats, woodchucks, or grouse become very abundant and, unless man, or some physical accident, interferes, local predators will multiply: hawks and owls, wolves and coyotes, bobcats or others. The added number of predators would then reduce the prey horde to a low, or at least normal, level, whereupon the incidence of predatory creatures would drop back owing to that self-managed leveling-off of food supply.

It is a true observation so far as it goes, and it became our traditional way of thinking about species range. The above description is, of course, greatly oversimplified; but it will suffice to express that early ecological idea. And it seemed sound enough to divert scientific attention from the much subtler evidence of territorial behavior. Nobody had "thought of that," yet. Nobody had wondered why herds of one species behaved toward their members or toward like herds in ways that bear no relation to the palpable resources in a given ecological domain.

Another reason for the delay was, perhaps, man's traditional reluctance to find, in the conduct of lower animals, behavior that parallels his own. Partly to prevent that sort of finding, I believe, scientists had long, though unconsciously, clung to their one-way view, their insistence that no human traits should be attributed to "lower" animals.

That rule was useful, at first. It enabled scientists to do a great deal of observing with detachment. And animals are not people. Not quite. The moods, thoughts, motives, and ideas people may attribute to a precious kitty, for instance, can be exceedingly anthropomorphic and, if so, will have nothing to do with whatever the cat was feeling or thinking. Animal observers had to avoid that.

Behaviorism was another blinding factor here. It precluded even the search for such attributes as territorial instinct since all acts were believed by behaviorists to represent learned or self-taught processes, and not innate.

Such positions of science had to be set aside before any one scientist, and then increasing numbers of investigators, would be able to discern territorial compulsions in animals, let alone in men.

It has taken half of this century to reveal that scientific opposition to anthropomorphic concepts was partly caused by an anthropocentric tradition of scientists. It is easy to learn what is known. To learn more, the known must be experimentally set aside, or doubted. And that is hard.

Why didn't they think of it—when "it" refers to territorial command and "they" to scientists?

Why, again, haven't they seen *time* to be another territory where men can voyage in their minds only? Because of tradition.

Relativistic thinking has, of course, given even laymen at least a verbal idea of time as a dimension. We speak of the time-space continuum with some presumed awareness of its meaning though we may lack the proper, mathematical understanding of relativity.

Man anticipates. And he uses time as if backward, too (in Korzybski's sense of man as a time-binding animal). He can pin time down mentally, almost as he can stake out an area, physically.

But in discussing time as a territorial dimension accessible to man I shall here consider it only in the nonrelativistic sense. What it may imply in an Einsteinian sense about our identity in relation to reality and the universe, to life and its meaning, and to our current blunders in perception, I shall leave to others, or if not to them, to . . . a later time.

It's difficult enough just to envision ordinary time as territory.

The perception involves an act recommended by Ouspenski, a pre-Soviet Russian mystic who tried in a drugged state to write down the road to his strange experiences. He found, on coming to, that he had scribbled only, "Think in other categories."

To see time as territory involves that undertaking.

It is, by comparison, easy to imagine space as the agent of territorial imperative for animals, and then, for men.

We can envisage the male bird or antelope as obliged by instinct to seek out a place of a size congruent with its built-in demand, to occupy it, and to chase out all competitors of its own kind as well as all dangerous species. We can accept that as a mandatory precondition for attracting a mate and rearing young. We know it's true, now. Through the kingdom of animals we see that law in effect.

The group rule is evident, too. We do not need to accompany ethologists into jungles to know how one band of monkeys has its "states' rights" and defends those borders against neighbor bands: relations, but relations kept out of their cousins' "state"—often by a daily ritual of border-badgering that stimulates both groups of states' righters but never leads to reciprocal mayhem owing to the limits instinct places on that exercise.

The evidence is now so overpowering that we can accept it by merely reading it.

To leap from the animal category to the category of man is a bit more taxing. Yet, if we Americans will consider the fantastic fealty of ourselves to "our own" states and their claimed "rights," the truth may begin to come clear. We hold these fifty regions to be possessed by ourselves and consider them as real spaces, though state boundaries are imaginary: man's arbitrary division only. State "patriotism" is thus an illusion compared to a bird's idea it owns part of your back yard. And where such local fealty stands in the path of national good it is a very vicious territorial "loyalty." But what local zealot can see that?

Regional identification of that sort also exhibits our human instinct for territorial possession. So does all national excess. And that, too, can be a liability if one nation's homeland instinct causes it to oppose fiercely the good of all humanity.

Yet, when our own nation is involved, how do we react?

Not with the immediacy attributed by Mr. Ardrey, in *The Territorial Imperative,* to America after Pearl Harbor. Following that territorial onslaught, we remained, in scores of millions, apathetic for many months. America did not, as Ardrey states, spring to arms as one man, and overnight. I know, having spent some of those months in Washington trying to help overcome the then-frightening failure to react.

Many of our citizens did not then and still do not extend in their minds a concept of American territory that reaches faraway places. Their instinctual sense of America is culturally modified, localized, and limited to the degree that in 1942 made them for a time indifferent to happenings in Hawaii. It did so toward events in Korea, too. And it does at this moment of writing to the commitment in Vietnam. The territorial imperative may not be operational where the disputed area lies in supposedly foreign or remote regions. Not, that is, for many Americans, the sort, for further instance, who tremble at their fantasied menace of Communism within our nation but cannot be concerned with the real and appalling threat of Communist aims and deeds abroad.

When one adds time as territory to that spatial concept, another category of awareness is demanded. In man, the comprehension lag may be for generations.

And to ask a reader to perceive how he, most likely, and how most men before him have seized for their groups, their nations, or their individual selves some block of property imagined in time is to ask him to do here and now what used to take ages merely to occur.

Nations have a "manifest destiny" they assume to be like a territory they must hold and must also extend for the benefit of others. Hitler's proposed "thousand-year Reich" illustrates such a territorial idea, one dreamed to exist in time-future. The Communist aim of an all-Red world that then, and then only, will reveal the truth of Marxist postulate is that same thing, the not-now paradise. A dream of territory for the believers that no living believer can inhabit—or even verify by any method but Marxist faith.

How and why man first invented his imaginary territories of time to come, I hope I have made plain. But the final category of otherness in the whole concept may not be possible for most to embrace. It involves taking the step that sets forth all the mind's contents as imaginings that can be enforced and reinforced by the same instinct that makes a man see his house as his castle, his state as real, not as recent, arbitrary survey lines, his white neighborhood as by-Christ-not-going-to-be-blockbusted-by-niggers, his town as not to be engulfed by the adjacent city, and his *every* conviction, physical in source or merely an idea, as an automatic cause for all-out defense against any threat whatever, actual or fantasied.

Yet, how is it even possible to understand the excesses with which men have always defended (and promulgated) purely imaginary possessions unless by this understanding of the territorial instinct? How else can we see why we have used ideas with the same sense of righteousness displayed by the least and the mightiest of territorial animals —and men—where their physical property is in peril?

No past description of instinct has made man's long and terrible defense of his beliefs even a little understandable. Freud's attempt to associate our invented territories (and their fanatic defenses) with sex did not suffice. Territory is a prerequisite of sexual behavior or repression, of course. But the aim of war is not to gain room for intercourse. And the Freudian suggestion of God as an extension of a father-image, wherefore essentially an oedipal figure, is not good enough, either, to explain religious history. But this wider theory of territorial instinct serves perfectly for comprehension.

It serves, that is, when it is seen as intrinsic to human motivation. What a man believes is defended, as is his property, and to attack it seems an invasion.

There is, however, a clear difference between time boundaries and spatial borders. A man can enter a plot of land, anywhere, and cross it. He can then turn around and go back the way he came. If there is a hill on it, he can climb that. And he can then descend. If there is a valley, he can walk down into it and come up out of it.

Motion in our three dimensions of space is reversible.

Motion in time is not.

All we now know of cosmos certifies that. Every celestial body began, and is, and will become. But none is regressing in time toward us yesterday or last year or the just-passed instant. Men have wondered, always, about that fact.

2 / The Perpetual Now

Now is the only real point in time.

It is possible, of course, to imagine time-travel. Science fiction tales tediously ape Wells's *Time Machine* to take their heroes on a backward trip that no man ever made. Mathematical games can also be invented that set up logical equations for reversed motion in time. There may even be more dimensions than our three, and time as our fourth, and even a way to travel in time, along some other trajectory than the one that seems inexorable, today.

But unless and until our imagination conceives of a logic to support that idea and means, also, for the proof, we are and will be confined to our monodirectional concept of movement in time, as all things warrant.

The fact that man finally developed brain enough to give him sufficient imagination to invent a spirit able to seem to travel in time among dream realms cut man off from the honest time-use of his animal ancestors.

The further fact that man moves inexorably toward the future and cannot retrace an instant had much to do with his inventions of territory in time beyond his days and with the one-way value he gives such inventions. A man can be convinced that Jesus Christ has saved him and therefore he will join the Supreme Being in an eternity beyond the tomb. This ideology will then become his timeless territory. He will defend it (his belief) as the animal defends its rightful space. Yet that one-way extension of his imagination involves a curious act of rejection by his mind. He does not use time in the two directions that he ought, if he so uses one.

I have met few believers in an afterlife, however, who were distressed (or *jubilant,* for that matter) concerning the territory in which they must have existed before birth, by their own logic. Those I met were Hindus. To imagine he has a soul destined for eternal future life, one should, by the definition, give that soul an eternal past, or future, as a human soul, not as bug, bird, or cow. And all believers in life beyond should be as deeply concerned with the past, before birth, as with their expectations at the other end of time.

But an acceptance of existence before birth is absent in him, which was always one clue to the falsity of his big dream of eternal life in the other direction. A man is, I think, bound to "go" whence he "came," back to limbo, to non-being, as a scattered batch of energy-matter that was not alive in past eternity and at death cannot erupt a soul, to abide forever in a place the man doesn't even accord prior existence.

If, then, we cannot move in time save on the one course, where all the galaxies and quasars and dark stars and titanic clouds of dust are moving, only the present is any man's real period of time. So it is with all other animals. How man uses his eternity-of-now (which apparently should be its conscious seeming) should thus reveal his degree of orientation or aberration about all time.

This problem of reality, as present-time-only, has led to many so-called philosophies and some useful insights, as Jesus' "By their acts ye shall know them."

However, the modern man, stripped of all illusions of afterlife, nevertheless has a delusion like that of his fundamentalist fellows. His time sense now relates, in his opinion, solely to his life span. And in his effort to give meaning, or even definition, to the state, he is at any present moment busy reviewing past events or events ahead. So he is not actively experiencing himself.

Yet, think how differently nature places all other living beings in the time trajectory.

The now of animals other than ourselves is largely the whole time they know. Save for a little memory, some learning got in the past, and some short-term planning, their territory in time is forever the present. Yet their very being is related to a time-future they cannot imagine: a time territory their offspring will inhabit, for which all or nearly all their present behavior is intended. Nature runs them through time, by means of their posterity. In due time distance, every time occupant will be wholly altered. But the sea-swimming sires of man had no idea their distant heirs would wade ashore, become reptiles and mammals and us. Yet their imperative was part of the sequence. And where that sequence involved taking and holding some definite, three-dimensional area of space, the heirs of the old fish did it with absolute morality, for each new kind.

So it is not very surprising that when men could foresee their certain death as no prior form could, they erred. Three billion years of pre-human life in a seemingly endless present must have given every being the impression that eternity was real, existence, immortal.

To be alive was to be forever in now. Death was not foreseeable. The meaning of being, the end of species continuation, the ruling drive, was as unknowable as evolution itself. In the long eons of pre-sexual life, no sure mortality was even obtained for any one being. Thus the tradition of man, in my sense of the word, had as its biological basis that single heritage of present time as all time, or near to it, together with the instinctual tradition of future intent in all present acts, indiscernible to the first men, surely.

Perhaps the reader will find that assumption of such animal awareness, or such sensation, scientifically absurd. Who, then, is anthropomorphic—he or I? Has that, or any like objection, evidence to sustain it that is not the human objector's say-so?

I think we can do better than that and I shall shortly make a specific effort.

Meanwhile, it will be more orderly to preface the attempt with some consideration of the ways in which others have tried to deal with our now and its sole time reality. Here we must set aside (of necessity, for such inspection) the just-made observations about the possible sense of forever surely having carried into early man's perception. That made him interpret his new self wrongly. Driven toward the future for unguessable cause and in unseeable ways, he realized, yet still pervaded with the haunted sense of life as immortal, his primitive mind balked.

Such biological thoughts do not enter the heads of modern priests, however, so we shall set them aside for a bit.

A man like Sartre can proclaim human existence is a random thing, and assert that morality (save what seems expedient in the moment of now) is synthetic and invalid. This concept is even admired by people plainly as blind to nature, to biology, to the rock-proven story of evolution as any blind beast antecedent to Sartre. Even blinder, since such postulates imply that species continuum, itself, is pointless. The territorial instinct these existentialists use to reject the fantasies of the convinced godly are not recognized as used. Their full force thus acts as the mythical pillar supporting the vacant (or meaningless) territory and their identically unreal doctrine.

Many philosophers and religious thinkers are trying nowadays to examine present-being. Existentialism is the name for their effort too. Jean-Paul Sartre's brand is merely the leader. And, I think, the least fruitful. For I am sure no man has ever looked more intently, for longer, into his own head, and found less.

Introspection has its uses and so has intuition. But to use either without reference to what is already known is an act of faith, of arrogance, in sum. Sartre found his "instant morality" that way, the way of the theologies he discarded. To say existence is meaningless is like saying it means what Presbyterians or Catholics claim. And by that method, even the Communist inversion of all ethics to promulgate a Red hereafter is acceptable . . . to Sartre, himself.

His logos, carried into time, vanishes. Evolution itself, the long and irregular, yet ceaseless, complication of life forms, which proceeded from an inanimate jelly to man was not possible in Sartre's ideology. The "ethos" of each species cannot be, either. No purpose, or even direction, is discernible to Sartre. Man himself can give but a temporal purpose to his acts. (Except the Communist purpose, somehow, which does fit that French schoolboy's non-design, perhaps, by being amoral.)

Other existentialist ideas, however, have differed from those of Sartre.

The "new morality" of Dean Joseph Fletcher, offering so-called "situation ethics" for which "love" sets criteria, is one.

The late Paul Tillich (another of the extraordinary men I have had the fortune to know) developed what he defined as an existential concept that still baffles, as well as delights, sundry clergymen and theologists. They hotly debate what Tillich "meant." His personality and behavior, as a man—his acts—gave Tillich his splendid meaning, an existential verity that his expositors usually ignore, defenders and defacers alike.

Tillich's view, if I may take a little liberty with it, corresponded to an early, oriental one. And since that can better be illustrated than abstractly defined, I shall give an experimental version of the phenomenon. It involved something to do, not just to conceive, an act that I long essayed and finally managed.

I can now repeat it at will. The act is simple:

I select a place where man-made distractions will be minimal—a garden, a room in a quiet house, a forest dell. I sit there, alone, endeavoring by conscious effort to discipline my mind till I can drive from it all past and all future contents—all memories, regrets, every iota of yesterday, last week, a year ago, and a moment ago. Also, I undertake to reject all forward-oriented perception, any hope, fear, plan, expectation, or the like. My object is to become aware only of what remains of me in the present. To sense the present as that of which I then will be exclusively aware.

My reason for such effort is this:

So long as my ego is being bombarded with past and future material, whatever it is that I call *I* will be incomplete in present time. But, if I can, by practice and willful choice, ultimately school myself to blot out all nonpresent information, then, whatever of me remains that is aware is the whole of my *I*. It is all there really is of me. The rest of me is unreal, made up of time-departed images and visions in time-not-yet-arrived. They "exist" only as I imagine by memory and by guessing ahead.

I am convinced from those efforts, and they gain support from the testimony of countless others, that I do have a present-time *I*. And it is a very astonishing experience to meet a self not part of a self-designed past and/or future. The sudden intensification of sensory perceptions that then occurs is like the heightened experiences reported by persons taking LSD and other drugs. These vivid perceptions of *I*-now also reminded me of experiences I had when a very young child, as, for example, upon first beholding some particular shade and intensity of color. Sounds have a similar mnemonic quality and a strange, timeless poignancy.

Perceptions of that sort furnish a baseline for understanding what Tillich means by his existentialist concepts.

That sense of self is, for one thing, as-if eternal. One's self lasts, in any case, while one lasts. And the self, stripped of past and future, is keener and far more alive than the daily I-was-and-will-be-but-am-not person with whom we identify, all, or most all, of our waking hours.

The counsel of Jesus, "Take no thought for the morrow," may represent an effort to explain the need for present-time being. And that state, to recall the Pauline phrase, is a matter of acts, of doing. "What's happening" is the one true measure of actor and act.

Tillich put his existential version of that idea succinctly in a book title, *The Courage to Be*. Unlike Sartre-de Beauvoir & Co., he was thoroughly versed in the natural, physical, and psychological sciences. Tillich's existentialism could incorporate any scientific finding in his "religious" theory— which many theologists now argue was not religion at all.

Paul Tillich, however, would not play the theology-versus-science game in the old way, as played by men like De Chardin: the classical way of every Jesuit, by which one starts with the premise that God is, and uses science in an attempt to support that a priori postulate.

Most theology is just such gamesmanship, a use of one-upmanship in which the player declares himself winner before entering the game. God is, the player says, and if my opponents seem to prove otherwise, why, God still is, and they will learn so in Hell. As a way of thinking and talking about humanity and Nature, or even God, that ploy is beneath a decent man's notice.

Some readers will presume the above discussion of existentialist ideas is superficial or naïve. Of course. For all I am attempting, here, is to say: skip the paraphilosophy; try the action.

See if you have the "courage to be." See if you can repeat my experiment and so meet your existential self. You'll fail, I think, if you think it naïve.

Among the many persons I've challenged to try that experiment, few have taken me up. Of those who did, not one in a dozen has been able merely to be alone, with no diversion, long enough even to begin any adequate effort to rule from his (and her) awareness the fictitious ingredients of past and present. It takes a solitary hour or two to start trying, for modern man.

Most never got that far. They quit. Why?

Modern man cannot stand himself.

Modern men have built up defenses to hide that dreadful fact, however. Americans nowadays even believe a desire for solitude is abnormal and its voluntary employment is deranged. Young people study with a radio blasting. Adults afflicted by an unscheduled moment switch on the TV. Most of us prefer even the contemptible company of a commercial to our own selves, and even a minute of our own selves. Right-now is *that* unbearable!

3 / The Doers

The just-noted attitude characterizes our nation more completely than any other trait or custom. We are doers, not dreamers, *we say*—as if the act of awareness were mad and as if thinking must not be allowed. As if doing anything else were better than the deed of getting to know one's self by being one's self. Even our national goals are expressed in terms of manipulation of materials. A New Deal, New Frontier, or a Great Society is something to be done outside men to change everything inside—never a way to give more value to ourselves now, or to the selves of our posterity. When we look back at our history and ahead to our hopes, we look in ways bent to fit our new self-description. Americans will be terrific. They used to be, when Washington cut that cherry tree. But now? Let's use now to make next year wonderful. As doers, then, we are nothing *but* dreamers!

Our evasion of now is also evident and grim as massive, present anxiety. Since anxiety is a fear form we can see, for example, in this state of rejected present, the source of our big, raging load of American hate. It is displaced guilt, a self-hate turned outward in some then-imaginary form, such as Negro hate, Jew dread, or a fearful suspicion of the federal government as ogre.

In such false shapes, fear seems tolerable to the hater. Actually, he thereby drives his self-hate farther from any hope of mere identification and so he redoubles his now-utterly-unconscious self-loathing. The feedback is constant and no amount of rationalization will or can diminish it. Backlash is as the square of self-lash; and the final victim is the lasher, together with those who may perish with him, innocent sacrifices to false acts, meant for expiation that but becomes a compound sin.

If these pictures of the self in present time have been incomprehensible to the reader, it is only because I have failed to paint in colors visible to him, or to hang out words in a direction along which he can look, or is willing to look.

The all but universal inability of my fellow Americans to experience the self in its present is my handicap. And theirs.

Asians, Orientals, and students of Eastern philosophies may smile at this attempt. I smile back, then. For I am not engaged in an exposition of their mysticism but with the hard reality of territorial time. My effort relates only to the tragedy of those people who will not, or at least do not, have any present existence they can enjoy. Why? Why?

Does the prevalence of the Christian idea of time-beyond-death, as infinite, make time-now seem too trivial for Christians to notice? Do our dreamed hereafters destroy our now, making it appear temporal, trivial? Is that the trouble?

There can be no doubt it is one source of this trouble. But Eastern and Western traditions are both of that same troublesome sort, in psychological effect.

For the destruction of a sense of value for present time is one indirect result of traditional convictions concerning eternal life. Since they are convictions through which posterity is robbed of its biological rights, those who have usurped the rights endure a hideous biological guilt. People brought up in such traditions will, by that definition, be unable to face themselves in their present. For each such person would then be face to face with the time-thief.

Readers who understand that much may enter a demurrer still. They may agree that the godly are not so, but ask about those who have no god, or, at least, no expectation of survival after death. It will then probably be claimed that such persons, not afflicted with the old invented lies, are not liable to those anxieties and guilts I have suggested.

That is true in theory.

But people are not reoriented properly by a mere discard of the ancient time myths. They will probably do what most of my irreligious fellow Americans have done: They will, in Jung's phrase, "go into the opposites." "Forever" will become my time in my days, but now and always, seen only as past and future, in my present.

In such a time-view the self is as great a biological burglar as any that lives to make its way to heaven and/or evade hell. Both are irresponsible for territorial time as nature ordains it. Their definitions differ but not the result. The nonbelievers have plots of time just as empty of biological meaning as the believers. They call it by many names, of which perhaps the funniest is enlightened self-interest. That's a key term for all self-centered acts—the ironic apologia for time-greed, pious or secular.

If, again, a reader claims my time-now recommendation gives undue value to what is, actually, an animal or prehuman time-sense, I couldn't agree more—save for one detail. I am concerned with what I call the human variety of my hypothesized animal sensation. The animal experience of time, though not within a provable compass, may here be usefully imagined. Let us try:

Zebras come upon the partly eaten carcass of a herd-member brought down, say, by a lion. Assume that the fed predator has gone away. The herd knows the dead beast was a zebra. Knows it is dead, or, at least, that it cannot move, is not whole, and does not rejoin them. Something has happened to it, they see. But whatever that may have been, the herd is undismayed. It grazes about its dead companion, uninterested, unmoved, unaware that what it beholds is death and that an identical death will be the destiny of every individual in the herd. Zebras cannot use time enough to understand that implication of their dead comrade. It was something that happened to him. Not to them.

The time to worry about lions is when they stalk you or charge you. Then, the thought is to get away, or, perhaps, lure the cat away from your young, however dangerously for you. But your death isn't foreseen in such unforeseen straits. Indeed, even if the gorged lion reappears, the herd will know it is without hunger. So it will continue to graze, untroubled by the company of the former, but not-now, killer, hence, a non-deathmaker.

When man saw a dead man and knew, There I, too, shall be, his heritage of the zebra's sort, of a deep-scored sense of the seeming of immortality evinced by all other species, was stripped away.

It seemed impossible, his death and everybody's.

But there it was. What to do? Invent. Invent what? A spirit.

Perhaps that zebra picture will help to make my point.

Today, a man may not think he is religious. He may not believe in life after death, or any God, either. But that degree of enlightenment is negative. It says what he isn't, not what he is. To try to do that, now, man still imagines himself as a being with a sort of spirit: a spark, ideals, an intellect, or some such possession that puts him far above the beasts. He will try to prove to you he has such a property in any fashion that seems logical to him. To define man, he will tell you, perhaps, of some slum child who ran away from home and followed the sea, learned to read, got himself admitted to a school and a college, worked his way there under circumstances of the utmost difficulty, and so finally, after tireless endeavors, managed to become a bank president, a physicist, a violinist.

The teller thus implies that he has this spirit, too, this specialty of man's, which sets him so far above animals that it is ridiculous to consider they have any comparable characteristic.

What such expositors of man's spirit do not realize is this: intrepidity and valor, used to achieve some precious end, tell of acts so rare that we make heroes of those displaying the spectacular behavior. And we thereby claim to share the mystical essence implied. But the same orders of behavior are not absent in lesser creatures, or uncommon. Rather, they are the constant and necessary deeds of every deer, wolf, mouse, and caterpillar every day!

They all have that heroic "spirit" and use the same passionate drives to realize the "ideals" of their kind. They constantly display the nobility that the spirit advocates attribute solely to mankind and find there only rarely. The virtues of animals are transcendent. To try to transcend animals, however, man abandoned virtue so near to completely that he now enshrines its occasional display. One man carried a message to García. One died on a cross. Robins do both, every afternoon.

Self-sacrifice, the noblest action claimed for spirit, is the mechanism of evolution. In religions, it becomes hand-hammered into horrid forms that no longer bear any necessary relation to the reason for self-sacrifice: the continuum, not of me, but of us, on earth, not beyond the grave, but the unborn generations.

Religious believers sacrifice their own children, not themselves for the children. And not just as offerings to be burnt alive in the iron guts of Moloch. But they do it by the ruin of their children's minds, indoctrinating them so terribly in the parental faith as to deny them an independent self. Such children will not be able to shake off the imposed ideology, or to grow in the head, or to think, perceive, and recover a true perspective or any honesty, for they now must go through their days of life as special bigots, parent-warped and helpless as the babies burned alive in Baal. Surely, mind-twisting is the crueler, for its torment is lifelong and affects others.

Believer-parents obey the particular rules imposed on them for heavenly ascent, and in their obedience they still bear children they know they cannot feed. But birth control is wicked in their code for attaining the infinite territory. And sex is wicked, too; wherefore a whole civilization of believers grows up with a neurosis so overwhelming its cause seems, like one of Hitler's big lies, to be true because it is so pervasive.

Or these will be, as in our land, statesmen and leaders, rich and bright, and fathers of a dozen children they can support and educate. But religious: told that the control of birth is murder and believing that. How can such men even say "population explosion"—or advocate, for other humanity-encumbered lands, any policy that will reduce their oppressive numbers? What American, whose very piety makes his massive reproduction a necessary act and a virtue, can acknowledge his example in public while he aids other nations in population control? Who's fooled by this doer? For it is example, not spoken precept, or free loops, pills, and pessaries, that humanity perceives as real, and follows. Acts, in the now-time.

What excessive hordes of children are birthed here also, in slums and on eroded hills and amidst the swamps of Dixie, as the God of their mothers and fathers ordained! Or as private "rights" guarantee, others say. The people-epidemic is swamping America, too.

I cannot endure setting down more examples of the havoc men work in the name of spirit and self-sacrifice. It is too awful. Too egocentric, vain, and arrogant. Too merciless. Too perverse.

Self-sacrifice is the implicit principle underlying all life for the sublime purpose of maintaining life and thus enabling evolution to proceed on its way. It is an absolute cost to individuals. But the self-serving or heaven-aimed sacrifices of man, in all their variations, rob him of touch with the universal design and the earth is littered with ashes left by such peoples.

Piety is guilt, here; but opposite-seeming impiety is exactly as evil. For there, too, man denigrates beasts to augment his notion of himself. And it is man who then eternally becomes what he imputes to beasts that they never were.

Even those who admire, cherish and respect "nature," or who, in some other fashion, perceive the truth that nature is man's entire and only habitat, hold toward it an unconscious superiority. I cannot say so often enough or in ways enough.

If we loved nature, if we even took the trouble to learn what nature is, and where man truly stands amid its truths, we would (were we also sane) take steps to reveal our wisdom. We might evacuate half of each of our fifty states, say. If we did so, there would then be a possibility that nature might recover, freed of man's presence sufficiently to give a good hope of restored habitat. Preposterous? Yes. But the scale is proper to show the idiocy of our current belief that we have any chance of a long future, as we now act.

Nature cannot be salvaged from the few live museums still reserved by our most spirited nature lovers. Saving the wood ibis and green turtle will not salvage the necessary ecology. Here, we are like men cast into pits of venomous snakes who become engrossed in swatting occasional bees. Our attention is out of focus.

Nature lovers? We? Ecologists? What a joke! We conserve ducks so we'll have ducks to shoot. We hate animals!

How sick and sentimental our self-styled animal lovers are! They form societies to prevent cruelty to beasts. And if they come upon a man-tormented cat or dog, they scream for police and take the inhumane lout before a judge.

But which one in the horde of these self-styled humanitarians halts a bulldozer before it brings anguish and death to a thousand little mammals, and to a million lesser life forms capable of suffering, like dogs and cats, in their scale? Who hesitates, amongst these absolute hypocrites, to let engineers wreck living landscapes as a supposed protection from the mere possibility of flooding? Who, of these meager lovers, even mentions acts that take ten trillion lives as real as any dog's, and as valuable to those beings as freedom from torture to a pussy—the brutal misery for profit or progress? How many birds and rabbits and chipmunks do these kindly folks save from mangling by backhoes and power saws and road scrapers? From dynamite? Bulldozers?

What is a living tree to them? Less than those animals, nothing. The trees were pared away by our sires from the Atlantic coast to the Mississippi, and the deed made men feel more important, more virtuous, more bloated by this thing they call their unique spirit. Pioneering spirit. A tree is an obstacle, like a wild animal. It occupies what could be a parking space in front of a store; and its leaves, in summer, hide the store's sign or its window display. Down with it.

And so, down with the birds that nested in it, the squirrels, the place where butterflies used to affix cocoons, the shade it gave and its roots that helped to keep the near brook flowing in dry weather. Get a machine and snarl the damned thing flat. Improve my territory for me, because I am a man, and territorial improvement shows how magnificent that state is. All those that die as my weapon against nature cuts through a tree trunk are forfeit to my customer, who will park in their place, and to my artistic show of patented remedies for constipation, in further token of my grandeur and yours.

This is the humanist.

The now-fellow, who thinks earth's territory is man's and who is today suicidally bathed in the stink of his spirit, his self-importance, and his power—as ecstatic in that as the mad boy who burnt the cat alive.

I do not want ever to hear about mercy from such people; and those are almost all the best people in my country, they say.

The territory of time is in trust for our days and no more. So, also, is the territory of earth.

In it, we must live so as to leave, for our ensuing generations, a territory untouched, or, if touched, either made more valuable for them or minimally reduced. To abandon duty, there, for the sake of a coward's dream of eternal heaven, or a materialist heaven foreseen on earth (calling that end "progress") is treason to man and, were there one, it would be to God, also.

For this earth is our tentative holding and not ours to own.

No man can possess property. He can have it as a tenant while he lives, but no more. To sabotage it, to strip it of life and minerals for his private enrichment, is but to impoverish his heirs, not even proportionately but forever. To hold property in low value, as temporal, owing to a delusion of timeless territory in the sky, or the barbaric dream of man as innately the lord of nature, is the measure of man's viciousness.

The time he has to use is only his time here. His sole immortality is the potential of his species; his wealth, what hope for a continuing posterity he accrues. There lies the true account of our significance, and of any, in all life.

That can be seen in many ways.

Suppose humanity, overnight, became sterile and we then lived in the knowledge that when the last of us had died there would never be another human being? Under such circumstances, it would not be entirely irrational to exploit, wreck, rape, ruin, and consume everything for whatever pastimes, luxuries, or thing-orgies that might then serve us as brief surcease, or faint nepenthe, for diversion or forgetfulness. Not irrational, merely selfish. Greedy. Pointless.

That is what we are now doing with our planet. Yet we assume, or at least hope, we shall continue to reproduce for unmeasurable generations, all richer in things than we.

Thus the people who have moved their idea of territory into time beyond the grave, where it is asserted to be infinite, and the people who live in a now, but feel superior to animals, wherefore without any timeless obligation to Nature, are making a dump heap of earth in the only time they will own for an opportunity, as human creatures, to *be* human.

No wonder, then, that we have invented and stockpiled instruments which, if used, will wreck the already self-limiting contraption we call civilization. No wonder that this current ability of some next step in weaponeering (for territorial defense, whether physical or ideological, of course) has or will likely have the capability of wiping out mankind. That, too, would then but obey a law of Nature, a very old law, which has ordained the eradication of millions of species when they proved too destructive for the other life forms in their region.

We may be next.

Many fear we shall be.

But even of them, how many perceive that if we are to endure and so give meaning to our present lives, we must do it according to natural law: by attending, before all else, to the requirements of our posterity as far as we can foresee them? A very long distance, that, but one we could perceive with our scientific knowledge. We do not much use any knowledge for such a purpose, though.

Chapter
Six

THE MORAL
MANDATE

1 / Extensional Ethics

IS IT TOO simple to say that the true human ethics rises from the needs of posterity?

Is that way of measurement, for man, too obvious?

I am afraid so.

I am afraid so, because I know that people assume they already accept it.

I live by that standard, they will state.

My children, they will say, have always been the primary reason for what I do: They are my embodied purpose, my meaning as mother, father. I have sacrificed for them constantly. Their good has been greater than my good; and their advantage a goal beyond mine, the sole intention of my life.

Of course, of course!

And when they say such a thing, they will have lost my sense of ethos.

For I am not talking about their brats.

I am talking about all the children of mankind.

Posterity, as a moral criterion, must include all the people of our species in all the future men can foresee.

The biological imperative for each species is that.

To think you are acting upon it when you relate it to your offspring, and theirs, or to the children of white, Anglo-Saxon Protestant slobs, or to American children and those they may bear, is not to have any morals but to be, instead, a biological fiend.

To think morally of man one must consider mankind.

To evaluate a culture correctly, one must balance its gains and deficits in relation to the future generations of all human beings.

That, and only that, is the proper application of natural law.

To use "natural law" otherwise is infamous. For natural law was and is constant with every form of being. It is the way of continuation. It dominates man as absolutely as it does fish and insects. And when man distorts it he merely arranges a special path for his own ruin, ruin that to this day has been the serial fate of his every attempt to create a stable and adjusted life way on this earth by his perverse efforts to manipulate nature through cheating its rule.

What men have learned (so recently!) about truth and reality supports the common hope that each added insight will be as simple. However complex the way to it, we expect a completed scientific statement will be of an almost child-like sort.

God is love, say they, for instance.

Love is God, then?

If only men had acted on *that!*

Again, $E = mc^2$.

How right! How concise! And yet, what a tangled path led to the particular truth. How vast is that "other category" into which the mind had to find its way from all prior belief to that mass-energy relationship shown by the constant of light's speed squared.

How, then, shall I make clear the "other categories" I've learned, and those I've inferred and sometimes recorded in a long life of study and reflection?

How shall I offer those many realms to minds stuck in categories beyond which I have journeyed to a thousand new regions? And then, how shall I continue, on my own, to tell where that has taken me?

How to tell *you?*

You, imprisoned in your theology and its perverted ethos?

You, locked up in some local territory of time: the morality of your offspring's opportunism, say. You, with the crazed dream that what is good for General Motors, or for America, or for Western, Christian (wherefore *not* "free") man, is good for mankind.

You, in minor territory where a Great Society is seen in terms of money, where every effort you make or plan to that American end-in-the-future starts with a fiscal appropriation for better housing, slum clearance, socialized highways, Medicare, more schoolhouses, and more teachers to teach, presumably, that same crackpot creed.

Can you think, at all, then?

You had better try, believe me!

To assist you in that, I shall in some following words compare what we are doing (believing) with our biological (and so, our psychological, or moral) necessity.

But perhaps it would help you if I first reviewed the steps I've already tried to cut into your stone brain that show why what's really good for you is what is good for man's future, and only that.

2 / The Established Facts

A. It has been shown that life arose from the combinations of matter stirred together by energy.

B. That, at some early moment each life form obeyed paired "tropisms," built-in directions about what to do and what not.

C. As evolution produced ever-more-complex life forms, their more elaborate rules became what we call instincts.

D. Each additional step in complication had as its possible result a gain in adaptation.

E. Each such step resulted from accidental mutations of which biologists calculate about one in a thousand provided a potential advantage.

F. The more complex the life forms grew, the more they

also tended to gain in some individual capacity for adaptation.

Over billions of years, beings evolved in many lines, or species, which exhibited instinct in a new way. They were able to take charge as individuals or in pairs of a part of the instinctual imperatives. They had a built-in code of which they were obliged to reveal some elements, by teaching, to their offspring.

But that instruction was not done consciously. What lesson these beings—birds, mammals, all vertebrates—needed to teach was still innate in them.

G. As some of them evolved farther they achieved an at-first small but eventually considerable capacity to invent additional adaptive devices, as individuals, and to teach those new techniques to ensuing generations. Here a new wonder appeared.

It can be seen from almost any suburban window.

One can there watch life forms for which men have no use—or none they are aware of—"wild" beings, then, such as songbirds, as they adapt to man's so-called civilized environment.

This pre-human development was an enormous step forward in the long story.

Let me give an example.

Until recently and for fifteen years my wife and I owned a home on a four-acre tract of South Florida land. There, the live oaks, Caribbean pines, cabbage palms, palmettos, and other forms of indigenous vegetation were allowed to grow as they had grown before man came to Florida. To that jungle-like space many birds and animals returned, or moved.

Among them, in time, was a pair of foxes. Before the foxes arrived, our property had been invaded by common rats. They multiplied in part because we supplied the birds in our area with very considerable amounts of food: grain, suet, stale bread, and sunflower seeds. Most of this material we kept in an open carport in G.I. cans from which it was carried, daily, year-round, to bird feeders. The rats thrived by feeder theft, and on the spill due to our own carelessness and to the spattering dinner habits of the birds.

No doubt, too, the four-acre ecology we built up that way provided additional rat forage: eggs of the hundreds of birds we maintained, including birds that visited our large lily pond, herons that helped themselves from our thousands of tropical fishes.

The pair of foxes denned up in our long-unburned and unbulldozed property where the cover was tall because we refused to "improve" the area by fire. I was careful also to leave the fox palmettos untouched and even unexamined.

Our rats began to disappear. The foxes soon found that lying in our carport when we were away in the evenings was the best method of rat catching. Often, at that point, our car headlights, sweeping up our drive as we returned, would reveal the flash of a fox leaping from the carport or from nearby.

In time, however, the foxes realized that we and our car and its headlight glare were not perilous. They ceased racing frantically from such approach. We could eventually walk past them at night when they lay rat-awaiting on the lawn and they would not budge unless we came within ten or a dozen feet. Even so, they would merely trot off a little way—as if annoyed by the human disturbance of a rightful vigil.

One year, they had a pup. It grew up with the special information its parents had developed and handed on. Long before it was full-sized, it became even less disconcerted by human presence than the older two. It was almost what people call "tame," then—though no one ever tried to tame it. By that time we had so few rats we no longer saw any.

This ability to learn beyond instinctual knowing and to teach the particular learning (doubtless by example) was a tremendous forward leap in evolution.

But it entailed a new hazard, different with each fresh capability for that sort of adaptation. Consider that risk.

The wild creatures that have learned to live in the new environs of man's towns and cities and suburbs may in time forget the proper ways to live in their former, natural territory. Experiments suggest as much. And such is the possible fault in our three self-educated foxes.

We sold our acres a while ago. We were in Hawaii at the time, and no one told the buyers about the foxes—or about the birds, rats, tropical fishes, and our supplementary feeding that had set up a special ecology. Others moved into our house. Still others built more houses where our jungle had grown—doubtless bulldozing much of it for home sites, lawns, and landscaping less unorganized.

How did the three foxes react? I don't know. Perhaps the new people were like us and maintained the (quite expensive) food supply. Perhaps, though, like most civilized persons, they feared wild animals, or thought them vermin, fair game, potential disease carriers, rabies vectors, say, or liable to bite babies. So, perhaps, when they saw those man-trusting and handsome Florida gray foxes hanging around confidently at night, they shot them. Or, being humane in the common sense of that, perhaps they had the animals trapped alive and deported to the Everglades.

There is yet another possibility. The three foxes may have realized that the new tenants were another sort of human being, or the landscaping ruined their den seclusion. And perhaps in either such case they trekked off to a wild place and remembered the old traditions well enough to survive.

But since that fox family had come to trust not only my wife and me, but our family and our friends, I suspect they had learned as mother and father, or had been taught by them, as a young fox, that people and their vehicles weren't among the menaces their wild forebears had known. In which event, their new knowledge, so valuable to adaptation in our premises, probably led them to disaster. People in cars on driveways aren't fox wary.

Yet what those foxes had discovered and handed to their pup doubtless seemed as if a new truth about right-wrong. Certainly, if many generations of foxes had been able to live in the same way, their instinctual pattern would ultimately have come to impose that new, adaptive invention on all. The idea of man as not-a-fox-threat would then have become equivalent to a moral rule. A fox tradition. To follow it would seem right, to violate its truth, an error.

At that point in the fox line, wherever it might occur, the innate necessity of all animals, all living things, all of us, to "seem right to ourselves" would incorporate an invented, learned, and taught idea, but an idea that would be valuable in subsequent time only if its "use of the past" had been properly designed to meet future circumstances.

And, of course, it had not been for our foxes, most probably.

The sense of that in relation to human inventions, adaptations, traditions, and time-future, is, I hope, plain.

H. There is a still subtler aspect in the design of evolutionary ascent.

Tradition, the right-wrong system or morality of each species, is formed for the purpose of continuum alone. That is an observable and attested part of what men now know.

Nature is so "interested" in species continuum that it establishes for that aim an adamant ethos in each. But nature is even more interested in the evolution of species. So the most important individual is not the carbon copy but the usefully mutated member that has a rare but helpful alteration of form and, with it, of the old or traditional "morality." The difference will be slight, of course. It must be, or else its fellows would not accept it in the group.

Yet the implication of the circumstance is as lucid as stunning:

Tradition serves to maintain each species in order that the species may evolve.

It is, therefore, not the conventional members of a species but the individual that violates convention constructively, for which all the rest exist and reproduce by the old law. Yet the unconventional individual and a succession of its ever-less-conforming heirs are the members who matter most.

So long as that process of nature goes unnoticed among species (whose code relates solely to what appears the perfect means for changeless continuation) the value of the violator of tradition will not be known. Nature (or evolution) is doing the unobserved inventing by using past forms in present time to develop future-time creatures.

But once a form had evolved that could do the trick itself, the grand design changed. Man, so to speak, became more and more—and, finally, as-if altogether (in his opinion)—the inventor of his adaptations and also of the rules he dreamed up as appropriate to them. These he then taught to his descendants, both invented techniques and associate fantasies of right and wrong.

Like the new way of the three foxes, man's new findings and his invented new rules were fully and in every instance backed up and enforced by his animal faith in tradition. But he did not know that. The animal's need to be right became in man's conscious mind only a need to seem right. The old orientation was lost.

In other members of animal species, the evolved ability to learn and teach new moral codes to match changed situations was still perceived—and exploited, by men. It enabled men to alter animal environs and thus change their right-wrong moralities for man's purposes. That is the way he domesticated beasts and, with the act, made them dependent on him. In effect, he altered their physical territory and they slowly altered their territorial morality to match man-made boundaries, evolving new laws relevant to them. Species unable to accommodate in such ways could not be exploited.

Similarly, man domesticated himself. But he did not observe that the process made him as dependent as his tame animals on whatever rules he invented to give a seeming of order to his domestic arrangements. He repressed such perceptions to heighten his new belief that he was not animal, not, therefore, self-domesticated in ways requiring, still, new moral responsibility for each fresh "advantage," real or imagined. So he became lawless and thought the earth and all that lived on it was his, including, if he wished and was able to make the wish a fact, the territory of other men, nearby, and at last, anywhere.

Man by then envisaged himself as sole owner of the infinite and eternal span of time. So he set out to prove his grand delusion, that is, to conquer nature, or, as we tend a little worriedly to say, now, to control nature.

Most readers will imagine that man can, eventually, anyhow, at least control nature.

It is impossible, of course.

Elsewhere, I shall set down evidence of the perfect folly of that notion.

Here, let us merely note how man came to hold the imbecile idea, one that science reveals with each gain in knowledge it puts forth. For no scientific truth or sound concept implies that man can control nature. It is the applications of science—of knowledge gained from specific observations, experiments, and checking—that make people assume they can exercise control over nature. The immediate advantage of an application blinds us to its cost, always implicit in the principle thus half-used.

As men domesticated animals and plants, that blindness spread. Falcon to horse, weed to crop, all nature-use seemed evidence of a capacity for conquest. Stone ax to atom bomb, it all seemed clear proof.

People hardly noticed, till lately, that each new finding of science, or even of its primitive equivalent, usually was first tried out for its potential in weaponeering, and only after that, for even a present-time, constructive end. It still shocks paleoanthropologists to find that man probably made weapons before he made tools. Yet he still does. Gunpowder—in the West, anyway—propelled bullets long before it cleared away rock for roads. And the first nuclear reactors made bombs, not electric power.

Slaughter, then, seems to be man's primary imperative and one supported by some synthetic, yet presumedly adaptive belief; all other intentions come later and lower on his value scale. Meanwhile, his dependence on kill-power grows more and more difficult for him to discern. He does not see it or see what happens because of it. But the evidence is abundantly at hand.

He has domesticated the banana plant, for instance. Now, that plant has lost its natural means to reproduce. It relies entirely on man for continuum. Its seeds don't sprout. Man proliferates it from itself, its shoots. And man's domestic animals depend on man for their continuum also.

Every technological advantage, too, has a comparable cost. And, minimally, that of a new dependency. But men ignore their actually inescapable debt for the costly effects of what they gain, effects now myriad and universal.

Our principal evidence of our creativity, our greatest conquests of nature (or, say, our mightiest control) is in our capacity for destruction. What we think of as creation is based on ruination. To domesticate beasts, or to reform plants for food, we destroy their instincts (or genes) so they cannot even persist on their own. For energy, we use up fossil fuels. And uranium. The waters that hydroelectric plants use for any job we choose are spent energy of the sun. The minerals, the vegetation, and the animals—whether domestic or merely slain to make room for some human intention—represent loss. Even to cure disease, we slay germs. So as to live longer we destroy more. We refer to ourselves, not as vandals, however, but creators and consumers.

And always we count the immediate gain or even on some preposterous assumption of benefit without awareness that the knowledge we've exploited for the purpose is but half recognized and that the disregarded half states a commensurate, unmet liability.

What we thus believe in halves we teach as whole. And what we then teach keeps us half-witted. We are as the foxes with their new-invented morality that takes no thought of the cost elsewhere or in time to come, subject to sure collection.

Inference, you say? Not so. Cold truth.

Truth demonstrable within the known territory of science. Our summary advances with that.

I. Only in the last century have men contemplated themselves as even possibly instinctual, wherefore possibly mistaken about their own natures and all nature.

Freud, remember.

Then came a barrier, that half-century of imposed behaviorism. It was erased only recently as other than a limited concept.

Lorenz and the new students of animal behavior did that: the ethologists. What?

J. They discovered how behavior patterns in many species were imprinted at their beginning of life. Pioneer educators are finding analogues for that in man: They are finding the child is basically structured at age four to six; by age eight, its personality is firmly set, vectored, and oriented . . . or upset, misguided, and disoriented if that is the fact, as it is, with all our children.

These biological specialists next discovered that innumerable life forms have an instinctual pattern involving a territorial requirement of a scope species-described and absolute for each species. Whatever area is essential to the members of any such group is ritually defended but as if life itself required the rite. For them, it does. Yet material requirements alone do not define their range. Not food supply, not nesting room, nor water source, not mating space or mate room, not air enough to breathe or to fly in, or sufficient range to teach the young to hunt, or to provide the inhabitants with adequate room for exercise. No discernible body need of territorial creatures defines the extent of their minimal space needs.

Indeed, a territory can supply an abundance of what man thinks of as the necessities and even the correlatives of what seem a species' luxuries, but if the population within it becomes too great by the measure of some other, *immaterial* agent, that group will pay, often in terrible ways, by cannibalism, madness, fugue-to-mass-drowning, endocrine atrophy, and so on.

Territorial species require other than immediate or economic space for existence.

This so-called "territorial imperative" was seen, soon and easily, to be a function of instinct. The demanded space related to some para-material requirement of such species for their continuum.

I hope the reader has no questions about this new finding now. The facts are established. Proof is overwhelming and readily available.

Whoever has lived where mockingbirds live, also knows how that species stakes out its territory. How it drives off from the trees and food sources and certain other boundaries its own kind, if they invade that domain—and men and cats and dogs, too, dive-bombing all intruders till they flee, often in baffled arm-waving, hat-swinging dismay.

Bull seals first establish territories by combat. Harems come afterward. Many ungulates have a different duty of the same basic sort: The males fight for a specific courtspace until orders of possession are established, the best fighters in the central or highest courts and the others holding such inferior courts as they are able, stationed by battle decisions, or in what biologists originally called "pecking order" since they first noted it in chickens. Only when that territorial sequence of court rank is established do the females appear for mating. When they do, they compete for mates they desire according to the "value" of the little personal property each male has been able to take and hold. So the sex instinct, here, is clearly secondary to and a function of, the initial and profound imperative governing territory.

The advantages of that process for natural selection are evident. The males with the choicest real estate are the strongest and most durable and determined. The females with comparable attributes are those who get to such males. The group of each species is caused in that way to produce as its most numerous offspring those sired by the ablest males and birthed of the highest quality females. So the internal competition for property turns out to be a program for improving the breed, or, minimally, for maintaining the breed at its best possible level.

There are as many variations of such territorial behavior as there are species governed by the pattern. But all require a certain group range, a fact that will complete this summary.

K. Many leading biologists have concluded, on the basis of abundant evidence, that man is a territorial animal. Others await more evidence.

His history can easily be seen as proof. His cultures are clearly based on the characteristic drives.

And his perils can be stated as readily as the advantages man gains by his uses of territory.

We have reached *that* point of knowledge, that proven truth.

We have even gone a little farther.

For the ethologists have made it plain that all species (except our own) are governed by an exact morality and that such morality is fitted to each species and describes its good and its evil in terms of a single value: the continuum of its kind.

Where that natural law is used to study, however, the inferences, or, I could say, the logical deductions, are only beginning to be made.

Konrad Lorenz put one forward:

In all other territorial species, the aggressive instinct necessary for the defense of its dominion is subject to automatic limits. A group of monkeys will defend its realm against any outside group of its species, and even make a daily ceremony of threat, matched by counterthreat, involving the adjacent group. But this high show of aggression will never become deadly. It will remain a ritual and one that stimulates both groups without leading to lethal attack.

Men, as Lorenz has noted in his book *On Aggression*, seem to lack the mechanism that inhibits aggressions in the old way. Their territorial instinct sets them against each other in all fashions and the commonest one is murderous. Human groups are not ritually satisfied by scaring off their neighbors. They assault one another, as bands of head-hunters, as tribes, and as nations making war, for, as I've said, living space—Lebensraum—Hitler's big and maniac goal which so inflamed the Germans.

And men, alone, strive inside territories, for status, in want of a parallel and universal regard for the life of their competitors.

This human abdication of the territorial imperative is appalling. It is a half-use of a whole pattern. Men grab all the territory a group or an individual can seize, yet men recognize no law for balance, no rule that territory is to be defended only by ritual means. Thus men are unnatural, and as Lorenz grimly notes, their lawlessness is liable to lead to self-extermination unless men learn about instinct and what to do about its violation.

Man has no morality in the ancient, the necessary, the absolute, and the complete form.

3 / Some Inferences

Man must recover the morality of life to persist; for that morality describes the only way by which life could and can continue. He must find and serve his territorial drive and its inhibitive discipline, or bear the cost of his arrogance.

Other ethologists have noted some of those costs. Since man is a territorial creature, he is unquestionably governed by that codicil of the law that relates to overcrowding and to the result of that. But no one has yet been able to say, for man, what his biological crowding limit may be.

To argue with any of the formulations leading up to this point is, in my view, to reveal ignorance or decrepitude. The résumé (A through K) is of fact and logical deduction. Beyond, we but speculate.

At this level, some ethologists and many of their volunteer spokesmen tend to stress one aspect of the field and to ignore others. Another half-use of truth, that.

A common, contemporary response of this sort, to any demonstration of human instinct, is the following: a plea of innocence and of irresponsibility. If Freud is right, many say, then I cannot help my condition. If sex underlies all my drives toward (and away from) external phenomena—and since I grew up in a sexually repressed or antisexual society—I am a helpless victim of my instincts and my environment. Homosexual, neurotic, rapist, alcoholic, fetishist, drug addict, tripping hippie, moper, whatever, I am not to be held accountable.

The discovery of territorial instinct caused parallel responses. It *explains* man, some exult. It is why I, personally, want so much, in money, land, goods, services, national power, other people's resources, everything.

Sure.

It also explains why there must be a curb on just such reckless and irresponsible wants. Or else.

People who react that way—that is, most modern men—see in the territorial finding an excuse for their immoral ways, for their national immoralities, and for the immorality of all human history to this day. The revealed need to revise their impossible lusts, according to the new-found natural law, will not be allowed to enter their heads. Such people remain, by man's species-old trick of evasion, stuck in the moral scum where they have been and self-menaced as a species.

It seems logical, therefore, to examine more closely what

we have hitherto considered morality, or ethics, in the light of what has been shown the true nature of ethos.

And this is what I attempt.

Most of the above-listed biological facts and obvious inferences have been known to specialists for a considerable time. Many laymen have presented parts of them or contemplated them in separate bits. Among them, a few, including me, have tried to arrange the knowledge in meaningful patterns. And we have tried to show whatever over-all implications we then can discern.

I have long known that an innate morality is discernible in each species save ours.

I've long since written that the only basic ethical criterion of any worth must derive from species continuum, for man, as for all living beings.

I have also repeatedly set down my theory that when the pre-ape became man, the new species became able to use time as a dimension.

And I have published before now my theoretical picture of man's misappropriation of time when the ability to use it revealed to him that he would die.

Joseph Wood Krutch's insight about nature's need to "invent death" as a control of the evolutionary speed-up, which the invention of sex allowed, has been quoted by me in other work, and there, as here, used for further extrapolation.

I have also published my observation that, in order to hold power over masses of men, various religions have experimented with the manipulation of human instincts until they finally found those that could be most effectively captured and ordered about, by priests, according to priest-serving codes. Repressive measures proved more effective for human enslavement than permissive exploitation, as I noted. And I pointed out that the sequence of ritual repressions for that thralldom was set by the time factor implicit to each instinctual or animal function involved.

Man must evacuate bladder and bowel. Even the church cannot delay or restrict those two functions. It can but make them shameful and demand they be done in hiding.

Man must drink water and breathe air, too. The need is

immediate or nearly. Water cannot be withheld in God's name and so, church-rationed, that is, God-related. It thus can be used only as a holy symbol. Except to perfume the air with incense, the church does little about the management of breathing since that also is a constant function and not subject to ritual repression. Eating is less urgent, more time-freed. Feasts, fasts, and symbolic cannibalism, special foods for holy days, forbidden foods, and the like, therefore proliferate in religions.

Sex relations, however, are subject to considerable repression, or, at least, delay in time. And they are monstrously so used to sustain the holy grasp of the priesthood on their trapped believers. The rite of marriage is an example, a rite that, alone, permits church-blessed mating—though often hemmed by pious reservations, even rules for church-shriving after that sanctified act, which will otherwise remain vile. Childbirth requires church blessing of the newborn babes, in baptism. There are rites for adolescence, such as confirmation and bar mitzvah. And, equally adamant, are rites for that sex-required invention, death.

To reinforce its grasp on human sex drives by repression, some sects supply live symbols, nuns, priests, and monks sworn to chastity, and so held of a loftier piety than any married person, however faithful to the church rules for marital sex.

Roman Catholics and many Protestant fundamentalists are also chained in these prisons of piety by the belief that any chemical or mechanical effort to control conception is murder.

With such rules, many faiths try to outbreed each other. And in some, the command to breed, married by preference, but married or not, coupled with the living presence of holy asceticism in priests, monks, and nuns, is very odd in what it implies. For if asceticism is holier than married sex relationships, and if rational efforts to prevent unwanted conception or to interfere with unwanted pregnancy are murder, the superiority of chaste persons is not credible. Most ascetics wage a lifelong and usually losing struggle against masturbation, if not homosexuality; so it would seem that what is wicked and/or murder, when done with contraceptives or by abortion, is not so evil when fecundation is avoided by onanism, as such people call it, or by erotic acts confined to one's own sex.

All such seizure and rigging of instinct by contrived fear certainly reinforces religious belief and sustains the tyranny of its hierarchies. It still dominates our own land, and will, so long as we call it Christian; for Christianity has managed to suborn more of man's nature and integrity than any other religion. Church and state are not separate in our laws for sex.

All those insights have been clear to me for a long time and I have made some of them evident to many people.

But one related problem about the human condition remained a puzzle to me. I could not understand the intensity with which men were able to accept and defend any and every sort of belief about afterlife, in obedience to nasty rules plainly formed to keep them mired in holy ruts. No religion is rational and there is no evidence to sustain a single one. Yet men accept them and cling to them with a reasonless abandon that I, at least, found impossible to understand. And men adhere to secular ideas, to opinions, and to rigid bodies of belief with identical blind momentum. Even scientists.

You could have stoned my grandmother to death and she would not have repudiated her Covenanter conviction that a whale was home to Jonah for some days. Why?

How is it even possible to believe that the glorification of God is heightened by the filthification of man?

How can men imagine that the reasoning of Plato, the proclamations of Jesus, or what Kant thought of what St. Augustine ordained is more than interesting ideological relic? How, possibly, can the great majority of living people literally or tacitly believe and serve the concepts of men, real or legendary, when all they knew was the little men knew four thousand years ago, two thousand, five hundred, or a century ago?

It began to seem incredible to me at the age of six: The Bible wasn't sensible. At ten, these foolish beliefs seemed ridiculous. At fourteen, infuriating. At twenty-one, a horror. At thirty-five, a near-obsessive problem. Lao-tse said what,

soon, Buddha restated, and, half a millennium later, Jesus
tried to incorporate in his Essene creed, along with the
megalomanic idea evidently gained among Essenes that he
was their God-promised bringer-of-light. So it appears. And
if the Christians do not continue to conceal what the Dead
Scrolls report, or manage to destroy certain of them, I am
sure it will be found true.

Who are those hoary pundits, that they are given power
to restrict what we think, now, what we learn, even, or
how we use that? What writ can possibly be holy that was
derived in times when men did not know what they were
and had no idea what life was, by alleged revelation?

Love one another.

Do, as you would be done by.

"As you would be done by"; but done by for what end?

Ye shall know the truth and the truth will make you free.

Why did they not excerpt that last counsel and let it stand
for all time as the only necessary rule about knowing? The
one that at least suggests what should be clear: The more
man searches for and finds truth, truer truth, or images of
the real nearer its actual form (and function), the more opportunity men gain to be free. Why do men prefer old lies
and slavish fealty to them?

I do not believe many men have tried harder than I, more
honestly and with a greater amount of their available faith,
to meet, discover, encounter, sense, or somehow reach to
God. My failure is said by the godly to be proof of my in-
adequacy, my special skepticism, or owing to an experimental
attitude toward a process that forbids that approach, if not
to a premature abandonment of faith-as-method. To say such
things is to suggest what might be true of me but is surely true
of them.

There is a brink over which I cannot allow faith to plunge.
I cannot use faith predictively to commit my entire self.
What I know of that self, and know in the present-time way
I have described, is real and honest and I feel it must be
cherished all my life in a sufficient amount to allow its recovery, in full, anytime. I cannot say, unreservedly, "I be-
live," in order that I then shall believe. Plainly, were I so
committed myself, I would believe what I had chosen, in

that present for a future image. Obviously, if by predetermination, I made the image absolute and set my morals by the criteria I accorded it, I then would believe in the image as real, the morals, perfect. With what result?

No one would be left as *I* that then could be and be aware and self-aware. Even that "mustard seed" of commitment-in-advance could start the avalanche and make me "whole" as believer, nil as self. I could not learn more or other than what my pre-fab faith would permit. Truth beyond it, if any, would be lost to me. I would become irresponsible, save as responsibility was defined by that programmed religion or the God I'd bought. I would then seem perfectly right in my creed and my faith: Others who differed would seem wrong. My faith-inflated ego would be blissful, too, and what it blissfully did then could be as cruel and crazed as Christian mercy often is.

However, I soon saw I could commit that ultimate act for *any* sort of God or holy rigmarole with equal fealty and ex post facto certainty. My self would seem whole and righteous because it had been willfully abandoned, whether to Jehovah, Mary, Mary Baker Eddy, Zen, Jesus, Marx, Mao, or The Corporation.

I therefore felt, if there were God, then He made me as-is: self, imagination, reason, and values. If, to get in touch with that God, I had to abandon self, reason, knowledge, extensions of imagination, utterly and forever, that God was in fact a demon and malicious, the creator of me as an embodied dirty trick.

In my endeavors, I could not perform the psychological act that is the one essential, in some form, for God-knowing. I could be willing, passionately so, earnest, dedicated, honest, and full of hopeful prayer. But I could not will myself to accept God, first, so as to believe in God. That human capacity for believing what one has chosen to believe or been taught to believe, by "faith," seemed to me a voyage on a sea of self-delusion.

I have, in fact, taken that trip far enough to learn how it goes. On many a dismal night, years ago, I used to lie in bed, awake, looking at the ceiling of my room, which was off-white and faintly illuminated by streetlamps. To while the time away, in some manner that would block out grief, I tried to induce my open eyes to "see" that pale, blank ceiling as tinted. Soon I could do that. Then I willed my senses to escalate the tints to brilliance. That became possible. And ultimately, I was able through practice to paint that pallid plaster with stripes or polka dots or batiks, in colors I chose and in forms, sizes, intervals, swirls, and all other arrangements I desired.

For that edifying venture a schizoid use of "will" is necessary. One part of self is held back, in limbo, so the rest of self may be exploited for autohypnotic effects.

Thus, while I could create (or imagine and project) upon my ceiling, all manner of patterns in all shades and intensities of color until I seemed to be looking at phenomena as real as a stone statue, as vivid as Thai silk, I could, at any next moment, or even simultaneously, know the vision was illusion; illusion, however, so effective I have never been able to perform the experiment while perceiving at one time that the dazzling design I beheld was as-if "there" but that the same place was really near-white. I could not see both at once even though I could know that what I beheld as gaudy art was only my invention, a phantom imposed on what I knew was a pale and uniform area. I had, always, to abandon the colored projections if I wished to see the reality again.

In that manner, and many more of that sort, I've come to understand autohypnosis and the mechanism by which the will to believe, even when controlled, can fabricate whatever supportive illusion is required to give a seeming of success. We thus can have perceptions of whatever we first invent and then agree to experience.

So when I tried to discover God or whatever might be found as that for me, I knew I could not let myself be my own willed dupe. Yet that self-desertion is the very act of faith required of religious people. One must submit the will. One must surrender all personal entity including identity and imagination, itself. To believe, one must first believe that act is valid. God cannot communicate with a merely willing person. His absolutely willed existence is the prior demand for his discovery. And that requisite is one no man of insight and honor can accept and keep his dignity. It is one no aware man can perform and remain aware, in his most vital sense of the meaning of himself.

To use faith, I would have had in my autohypnotic games to yield up, also, the part of me I held in reserve, the part that could, on demand, always assure me that I was playing a game, however real seeming. Had I done that I'd have erased the knowledge that I was kidding myself, for no one else would be left to discern that. The ceiling would seem forever to be that color or those colors I projected and I no longer could even see it was off-white.

Any person with patience, self-control, decent imagination, and the time for it can repeat my experiment in that same form, or any other that suits his fancy. Once concluded satisfactorily, it gives a remarkable insight into the ease with which self-delusion can be achieved. Or it ought to give that insight. But those who believe by faith will not be able, perhaps, to make the test, or even willing. And if they make it successfullly, they will hardly apply their new information to other areas of conviction, seeing, then, what is delusion, what real, and how and why they came to fail to discriminate, willfully, through faith.

The phenomenon of self-hypnosis, or autosuggestion, isn't new-found. To test it takes a little nerve and a certain detachment, however. Hypnosis, of one person by another or of many by one, is a similar phenomenon which one can see anywhere and even in theaters. It is known, too, that the power of suggestion among masses of people is like a contagion at times when so-called emotional tensions are high. A multitude of individuals become The Mob, then.

We need to learn more about that because we often act, these days, as a mob rather than as a gathering of individuals.

Our feelings, as I've said, arise from our value system. On each of us values are engraved by genes, as heritage from evolutionary ancestors, and by family, environment, religious belief, given or gained by conversion, carved by all factors that establish each individual's necessary paired directives: his right-wrong, good-evil (and so, true-false) concepts. These program us, in a way similar to that of computers, with an instantly accessible mass of data we can process like lightning to determine, in any circumstance and moment, whether another person (or act or event) is one to love or one to fear.

And with a next flash, reprocessing that data, we can translate the message for behavior to suit our secondary value system, one we have previously set up that we project on others, arbitrarily. Love, then, can translate to greed and greed to whatever we think others will admire, or at least accept, thrift, say. And fear can turn into hate or righteous opposition, in that second processing.

The speed with which the brain constantly makes such prodigious calculations is sufficient proof of prior programming—of the lack of thought in the act. It is evaluation, alone. The values are then experienced as feelings, and they will only be as appropriate as the program was correct.

An obvious fact but little noticed.

Suppose we were not, fundamentally, evaluators? Suppose, then, on meeting a new person and in order to decide what we thought of him (nice or no, good or wicked, interesting or dull, right-thinking or mistaken in view, one, in short, to love a little, or fear) we had actually to think. To do consciously what we do automatically and often with no consciousness at all. We would then be forced to recall all the data gathered in our lives which would bear on our final judgment. The solid data and the prejudices, the proven values and the false, the real and the fancied—everything within us that would bear in any manner on our ultimate appraisal.

It wouldn't even be possible! Much of the relevant data would be unconscious, beyond reach—love-hate concepts we would not admit to ourselves since that would expose their fraudulent, deceitful, infantile, or otherwise discreditable nature. Still the mere application, consciously, of what we could recall, for an evaluation, would take hours, days, months, to collect and weigh sufficiently. But what we actually do takes a split second.

We do not, then, think. Not much and not often. We evaluate. It is my belief that we must first evaluate even to be able, then, to think, when we do think.

In any case, evaluation, automatic and swift, is our usual route to being and doing. We act and react according to the program of our value system and by our swift brain which first offers the computed feeling and then translates that by another computation into a feeling that relates to externals, things, people, and our intentions about them.

Without that capability, men couldn't even converse. It would take any pair a month or two for each offered sentence. We could not act by reasoning with sufficient speed to stay alive. No creature could.

Yet, to find out truly why we are drawn to this, or away from that, demands an inventory of the values of our stored images. To trace the etiology even of a single one may consequently take a trained psychiatrist hundreds of hours. Why does his patient hate cats? Dread heights? Find dressing in the garments of the other sex so appealing as to be a compulsion? Why? Go through the encyclopedia of his past!

The point of this is simple:

Our running and constant appraisals of everybody and everything are necessary. But the relative worth of our lives and life ways will be measured solely according to the reality of our collected opinions, conscious and repressed, about what is attractive, what repulsive, what we thus love and what we fear, what we then desire or detest, seek or seek to evade, and perhaps to destroy. Since our value system usually employs our local traditions for its principal criteria, and these rest on faith, not on self or on reason, it can be upset by an intense evaluation others make jointly—the mob, that is.

What creates the true believer (in Hoffert's phrase) is also what causes a man-unit in a mob to become the agent of values he, if alone, would repudiate. Conviction through an act of faith that is a promise to entertain no thought of any different sort, is, thus, parallel to the process that turns a good man into a demon, in a demonic mob. Both sorts of people are given into the charge of something we call "spiritual" in the "faithful," "animal," in the mob-joiner. We accord ourselves a spirit but deny it to other beasts, yet when men act savagely, we call that bestial. Why?

Chapter Seven

SEER AND SORCERER

1 / The Dreaming

THE HEART ASKS the question with agony; the head asks in near despair.

Why is mankind so evil?

Why is he full of sin?

Why am I?

Nowadays sullen answers resound:

God is dead.

Life is random and has no meaning. Morals are matters of expedience and present-time decision.

All is chance. Make it now or you've had it.

The answers are in, professor. All belief is mistaken; all ethics are false; there's only one solid rule: Keep your cool, cat.

"Every adult in America knows," a stranger wrote to me the other day, "that the whole show is crazy. And that they are, too. Only, nobody dares say so."

So I wonder, What about the show he calls crazy? And why does he think nobody dares bring that to general attention?

How many hundreds or even thousands of strangers have

written letters to me saying the same things? Often in almost identical words?

Civilization is mad.

Everybody knows it.

But nobody dares say so out loud.

I can agree with the first assertion. An individual would
be certifiable for displaying attitudes or performing acts
common to groups and even majorities. The very record
of man can be construed as proof of his serial lunacy.
Every belief, faith, tribal dogma, religion, and other ideology under which he has attempted to organize, prevail, and
flourish has monotonously failed within a few generations. He
was never a stable species and even when he tried to stabilize
as a group he wound up in a next landscape of ruins.

But I cannot quite agree that everybody or even every
adult American knows his society is demented.

Of course, many individuals and a great many groups can
see that others are crazed. But the sign of the true crackpot,
the genuine maniac, is his unshakable conviction that his
conspicuous aberrations are sound. The adult Americans I
have had the honor, duty, right, and the misery to observe
seem to me, in the main, confident that our way of life, our
ideals, our political means, and our social intentions are rational and the best of anybody's.

You can fear you are going off the deep end and even
be right about that. You can then become schizoid or paranoid or both, but at that point you will not know. You may
also recover and then realize you were insane. But in the
time of being crazed you will only be able to notice that
state in others among whom it may be relatively or actually
true or among whom sanity will seem to you as madness.

So if we are crazy, we don't know it.

What surprises me most in my correspondents is their third
avowal. "Nobody," they say, "dares tell the truth" about
American lunacies or, for that matter, about any other aspect
of American behavior that sorely needs exposure as evil,
stupid, hypocritical, and psychotic.

It surprises me because I've spent much of my life publishing just such manifestoes. That, indeed, is why these folks
write me. And I am surprised at their feeling that we no

longer have enough freedom of speech to permit criticism, cavil, not to say, anathema, wrath, and the outraged exposé.

There is, of course, a growing sense that the public isn't told all the truth by anybody in government or business or the professions. And in a world where part of knowledge has been made secret, including our American world, there's a basis for doubt. But in general you can publish the truth, still, even when it offends great corporations, haughty professionals, or anybody else. You can, of course, if you're willing to have detectives tail you and research your background in hopes of finding something that can be used to blackmail you into silence or something to publish so as to occasion mass doubt of your true bill.

You can speak up if you don't mind losing your job. Or if those who are in power resent your verities but "cannot destroy your assets"—as an indignant corporation found of me once, while seeking to shut me up.

But, in a lifelong struggle to find out such truth as might be available and to use it for a diagnosis of man's ills, I have managed to learn a good deal of what's known and what's reliably theorized. And I've said what I then thought without being jailed, tailed, or having my assets destroyed. To be sure, people have tried to bribe me into silence, and once a pair of hired hoods threatened to murder me if I kept on using local papers for airing facts not welcome to their employers.

But such side effects are of minor importance where truth is concerned and a person determines to state it. The honest man has a counterpunch no others possess; but he does need to learn how to use it with skill equal to the treacherous cunning of his adversaries. Just knowing and proclaiming an undesirable truth at any cost is not enough unless one's object is martyrdom. To survive one needs lessons and experience in sociopolitical karate.

Given that, the honest man can speak with an advantage the others lack. For they will always be off-balance owing to their dishonesty.

Those who write to me and tell me our country is mad fail to see how hopeful that very notion is. If they are right, they still imply that sanity is possible or conceivable. How, otherwise, could they bewail national insanity?

Furthermore, two hundred million Americans, even though all crazy, cannot be afflicted with identical manias. The lunatic who thinks he is Napoleon may accept the word of the lady who claims to be Joan of Arc. But another idiot, sure nothing exists at all, will doubt both the other two.

Diagnosis of a delusion is possible, then, even for people deluded in other ways. And group therapy often aids in relieving mental ills thus disclosed. There are specialists who help the demented to see their warp and to recover, also.

As a man aware that his own conduct was disordered I spent two years in analytical effort with a Jungian and two more with a Freudian. Overlooking any benefits to me, perhaps a questionable matter, the six-days-a-week, two-hour sessions with those experts did give me some of the advantage noted above: insight into the nuttiness of others. That may even have been my main reason for the lavish outlay of money and time so much psychotherapy required.

In any event, the information gained led to a series of books of many sorts, beginning with the one mentioned in the forematter. I have been and remain far more cognizant of your aberrations than mine, so to speak. I was unable to learn enough of what is known by man about his environment and himself to satisfy my lifelong desire for insight into what is called "the problem of knowledge," the "measure" or "temper of man," and also, the "human condition."

Bits and pieces of the matter came clearer and I published them. But I went right on looking—not, I feel, owing to neurotic compulsion, or even to that notion that knowledge is valuable "for its own sake." Knowledge was and is valuable to me because it can widen human understanding and because it can be used, sometimes, for worthy ends.

What seems obscure to most knowledge-seekers and knowledgeable folks never was, to me. The motive for gaining knowledge, any sort, every sort, all through life rises in the fact that one is a man. A human being. That makes the accretion and contemplation of knowledge mandatory. Our species has heaped up knowledge and is working at that effort on an accelerated scale. The act is evidence that an appetite for such feasts is innate and normal. Our brain is designed to find and feed on knowledge.

So I feel that a human being ought to want to learn as much as possible about as much as is known merely to justify his membership in the league. Children, as I've said, start out that way. But soon their education, their religion, the culture, and probably their parents put a stop to that transcendent drive. Most of us are taught early not to learn and to try not to want to learn. And many leading educators, sociologists and scientists keep stating man now knows so much that he is probably near his learning limit.

This attitude appeared repeatedly in a recent issue of *Daedalus* devoted to predictions and guesses about our "condition" in A.D. 2000. Yet some of the colleagues of those pessimistic and pedantic people could have told them that man currently makes use of about a fifth of his cerebral capacity, another example of non-communication between the Ivory Towers. But I was not oriented in childhood toward belief in the impossibility of continuous learning or its "own sake" value. The assumption was, for me, that being people means being as minimally ignorant and stupid as possible.

The result is the slightly absurd anomaly that bears my name. However, my goal of trying to understand why everybody seemed to be leading irrational lives, including me, did not become imaginable until the ethologists had provided all who cared to read with the information on territorial animals and the observation that man is one.

Then, rather rapidly, the fragmented insights I'd gained and the knowledge, such as it is, coalesced to lead to the theory I have written this book to state.

Indeed, the experience of the initial vista was so vivid and "other" that, had I been mystically, politically, or organizationally oriented I could and would have tried to transmute my exciting idea into a me-first operation. I could have reacted as Saul did on that Damascus road when at least something he thought was a revelation hit him. I could have started a business enterprise to profit from the dissemination of the concept. I could have founded a new church, a new religion, a dynasty.

Luckily, I'd already determined the speciousness of or-

ganized belief and found that even a solid idea, used to gather
disciples who would presumably spread it as a gospel, in-
variably became dogma. My theory, so employed, would also
cause an organized and bastardized surge of creed. So I
could see it had value only as a challenge and an opportunity
for each and every individual willing to examine it. True
gain of insight is exclusively a do-it-yourself operation.

I have already indicated my discovery—the perception that
man, when he used his imagination to enter the territory of
time, thereby became a man, and couldn't stand it.

Wherever that happened and whenever—possibly in the
Olduvai Gorge region two million or more years ago—
the animal exploited the capacity to duck its cost. His imagining of an afterlife to cover up his realization of death
was only one early dodge. He really did need to get a
better hold over nature, then. But as he contrived to do so,
a little, he assumed, forgivably in that epoch, his successes
proved his supernatural status and supranatural eminence.
With that inner orientation he soon began to behave as if
his imagined realms were real and territorial, requiring a defense as irrational as the delusion.

And as men wandered apart and altered their techniques
to suit new environs, they changed their mythical territories
accordingly.

We have clung to that inner cheatfulness to this day.
The "kingdom of heaven" is believed by millions to be as
solid a piece of real estate as any cattle ranch. And our
uses of reason in science produce imagined realms that are
also seen as much proven terrain as the fundamentalist's
heaven. Where clergymen disagree with priests about their
domains or physicists with physicists about theirs and either
sort with the other, border fighting erupts. The scientists even
identify their assorted territorial claims, with unconscious
verity, as "fields."

But the blunder in the whole affair occurred when the
first man mistook some imaginary kingdom or field for terra
firma and his own. After him, nobody ever noticed what had
gone haywire.

Since all products of time-use are artifacts of human imagination, their defense required just that obtuseness. And since

all such immaterial constructs were used, from the invented first one onward, to give the inventor and his followers added support of the basic error of seeing man-as-more-than-nature, the territorial imperative was applied as reinforcer. But that otherwise universal mandate and moral law cannot possibly sustain what is but imagined, be it the Egyptian faith that set out pyramids or an invented but rational logic leading to some more nearly correct hypothesis in the field of chemistry.

The imaginary dominions do not exist, whether proclaimed by faith or entered by scientific logic. Man, to this day, has therefore used an imperative related to the real for the defense of the unreal—as a territorial animal with an ego-centered and self-aggrandizing motive for the fabrication, maintenance, and defense of what he but dreamed up. He finds himself obliged to go to any limit possible, however, to support his fantasy or to extend its borders. An effort of mere ritual would seem, to such a being, tacit admission of error in the concept he imagines as his true and necessary turf. Self-deceit requires total force, legal or not.

Three billion years of past behavior will be exploited in a new, totally displaced fashion to feign all such phony goals.

All the needs of animals will remain for the player, and must be met. But now the right-wrong systems for meeting them honestly will be revised according to the crook's dream-world and his dreams of himself. What he holds as his heaven and its furniture of gods or God will require equally specious elaborations of and violence to what had been moral. Since he cannot prove a dreamed domain exists, man must dream on, certify its falseness. As his territory, that is easy to do. His territorial imperative is corrupted for the office and the act is called "faith."

Similarly, as man uses his imagination with more skill to invent logical systems and finally to define his scientific method, he will see that imaginative feat as a different proof of his original self-canonization. Each step he makes toward understanding nature will be applied, if possible, to escape or defeat what he regards as the foe, nature. Agriculture, animal husbandry, water power, steam, the artifacts of present technology, will be imagined as evidence of his superiority and used, in turn, to reinforce his image as God's top product—or as godlike. The fact that no belief and no technology, no faith-founded religion, or any other man-inflating concept of purpose has led to human success is clear. The reason, however, is within man's imaginative grasp, at last.

2 / Self-Enchantment

Our ability to cast spells holds us spellbound by those we cast.

Heirs of a long process in which the living parts knew what to do and what not, certain of their moral authenticity, we have felt it essential to be exactly as certain about our many ideologies and attendant "moralities." When some special use of imagination produced an image truer than the local "truth," but at variance with its central fiction or with the attached right-wrong notions, we have taken steps, usually, not to salvage the truer truth, but our myth. A scientist whose logic produces a heresy can keep it quiet. Properly, he assumes it, by that act. Or he can use it to his personal and material gain, letting a few in on the way the theory goes, but permitting hardware spin-off for profit. This is the holy condition of science, today, ruled by what Lapp calls "The New Priesthood."

To demand that people who make use of gadgets learn how they "work" would be to require them to learn (and evaluate) nearly all the theories of science. That would upset their spiritual beliefs. Not to require it, however, is to hold a sacred view of science as a territory above and so in contempt of man.

It is difficult to imagine that we do not think, reason, abstract, or do any of the acts the schizzy terms that psychologists, philosophers, scientists, and plain people employ to describe their mental processes. The data for such an unprecedented idea are too recent. Human faith, and the mightiest human intellectual feats, have never before been open to such vision, owing to the illusory way we have hitherto imagined ourselves and our awareness, as conscious, sure in belief, logical of reason.

All man does in his "mind" or "psyche" (or with his brain and nervous-wiring and his body) that animals are not able to do, or can do only slightly, is a single act: He imagines. Imagination, as people involved in the study of man fail to perceive, is the underlying source of the other processes of mind to which we give so many and such absurdly nit-picking and hair-splitting names.

To see what I mean by that, I offer an example of what "goes on" in an animal X—and of where something more goes on, in man. Consider, then, a mammal, good-sized, faced for the first time by another, unknown creature of cryptic (and so, perhaps dangerous) sort. A panther, or tiger, say, with no inherited, learned, or prior personal knowledge of what now appears before it: a man.

The situation sets up the familiar alternative-choice problem: fight or flee.

The panther or tiger has sense perceptions only slightly different from our own though some are sharper. Still, its picture (imagined) of the real world more or less corresponds to man's. Light and shadow, perspective, relative size, distances, colors, numbers of objects around it, are sensed in a way we comprehend. So are smells, if any, and most things smell. Such sounds, too, within auditory range: rustle of leaves, crunching halt of man, distant bawl of ungulate, chitter of near birds. The animal is "aware" of all those, or could become aware on notice of need.

It is similarly aware, or able to be, of itself—as body and so as furred and hairy, as warm or cold, as breathing, as toothed, as clawed, as very powerful in its environs and pretty safe from predation. As, perhaps, having a mate and cubs, somewhere near, as hungry or not, or thirsty; and aware of such data in relation to many other creatures, when they are present, as well as its kind, as panther, tiger in sufficient degree to recognize other panthers, tigers, and the rules for own species responses.

But now its awareness rises one level. It perceives its first man, and about this creature it has no such "knowledge." Here is an animal, obviously, but one with crimson head-hair, a red fur down to the place where blue, slick skin begins; and below that, black feet. Standing like a bear on two legs. With a complex aroma so unfamiliar as to be incomprehensible—unless, perhaps, in part, as a sweaty scent of fear.

But what to do? What not? Flee and lose face for no cause? Fight, and risk being killed? The panther will flee almost always. Not, though, the tiger perhaps. And our panther may have cubs behind and a lamed mate and a sense that their defense is more important, perhaps, than other risk. Not of death, but of defeat—since the panther cannot foresee death. Stress rises, and awareness of stress, another lift of level in awareness.

Without any conscious effort, automatically and in a split second of time, the panther runs its baffling image of man through a cerebral computer for analysis and analogue. All the heritage of its ancestral beings is stored there in shorthand form and also the enormous library of panther facts. Its own experience is coded there, too. If the other animal were familiar, that sorting would suffice when checked against the panther's present situation, and its current mood, its individual nature, cubs to defend, matters of territory, and the rest. It would then know what to do, or not, from its innate moral order.

That knowledge would not be palpable to it as such. All the computer will finally furnish is a cue in the form of a *feeling*, that is, a sensed result of an evaluation, for what could and would instantly be translated into the appropriate act—a leap toward, or away from, the other being. Or even the ignoring of it, a passing on, alongside, or a skirting of it.

But this panther has to decide without any complete way of evaluating the data and then experiencing the correct feeling for action. Or for non-action. This state involves a still higher level of awareness, a sense of stress that obliges the creature to be aware of itself as under pressure and as forced to *imagine* what to do—using time and past experience to the degree they may help for that end. Whatever the panther, or the tiger, then does is the result of the feeling it gets by imagining itself in a new way, so as to imagine something about the unknown reality it faces for evaluation, all alone, to get an individual feeling. It will conjure up a feeling that will lead to its act, appropriate or no.

People have that identical capacity but in an unlimited

degree or one nearly unlimited. And people make every determination save a few special sorts in exactly the same swift manner of panthers or tigers. For all either animal did took an instant.

The human computer can be programmed in as many ways as can be imagined including insane ways. But what the human being does to "think" is merely to react to a feeling that is the aware end product of reference to a stored value system, sensory, learned, and personally encoded. If it were not so, what people say to each other in a five-minute phone conversation would take a year or two. Our statements, questions, answers, opinions, exchanges of verbal symbols of every sort—all these—arise nearly instantaneously but after computerlike evaluation. They represent translation to feelings, not to thoughts. To mere sensations that are the "print-out" of automated process. These are retranslated as verbal symbols in our phone talk.

In face-to-face talk they are also translated into the vocal inflections (that the phone carries, too), but the spectrum of kinesic "talk" is now visible. Often without the exhibitor's awareness. Hands, brow, eye rims, a hundred or perhaps many thousand bodily movements, give clues of the speaker's evaluations, which are often opposite to or different from his verbal statements. So we are preposterous when we assert we are rational and fair, just and equable, lucid and reasoning. We but imagine that.

We imagine it and act out the imaginary "reality" exactly as does the animal, panther or beetle, to their limits. Nothing or near-nothing in our aware activities is reasoned. All is imaginary. And nothing is true, in consequence. All is merely an evaluation of images we ascribe to ourselves and then project on others, the world of matter, realms of "belief," theory, and even admitted images. We do not have access to *any* dependable, fundamental data.

We do not know what the universe is or why it exists. So we cannot know "who" we are and merely cling to imaginary notions about that. Our perceptions, sensory or fictitious, are not the accurate, dependable concepts we assume. We cannot hear most of the vibrations that seem to us the whole of sound. Our ability to sense the electromagnetic wave spectrum is minute. We sense more only with the aid of apparatus. Our sense of smell is probably one thousandth of that of some insects, a billionth of the smell range.

What most of us, most of the time, and all of us some of the time, conceive of as "self" and as "another," or as "communication," and as "intelligence," "reality," suitable "judgments" and so on is but a fragmentary image of limited evaluation rendered as a feeling. Thought, reason, logic, the entire rest of the human aware acts, and those unaware, too, are artifacts, themselves end products of images.

Even "original thought," a supposedly purely intellectual act, is the result of a feeling. Before the genius makes the step forward that abets human progress, evaluation will have led to a feeling that leads to his new image, poem, sonata, or scientific theory. And to the scientist who now demurs, who insists, perhaps, that there is "more" to art, creative thought, and the discovery of "new concepts or categories" than that, it might be asked, at least, with a certain potential of elucidation: Why did he choose to become a mathematician, biologist, chemist?

If the answer does not finally emerge as a statement of a feeling that scientist had for his choice, he hasn't given the true answer.

For unless a career, or an errand downtown, is the response to a feeling, the career or errand do not take place. The innate right-wrong programming of the individual is involved to every end, and it gives all the directions there are for living things. In that basic and unarguable way it can be stated that all "thought" and all other allegedly discrete or detached "intellectual" processes are but *rationalizations* of feelings. Rationalizations made unconsciously of evaluations the ancient moral machine printed out. The results can be good or bad, gain or loss, mental achievement or madness. The source is one; the process, single; the whole affair, to the point of action, imagined.

From what I've read, seen, and heard of the images of educators, psychologists, anthropologists, and others engaged in the study of awareness, however, I think they would list imagination as about the fifth most important capability of human intelligence. Still, it takes both selfless and informed imagination to see imagination as the sole source and form of our aware being, belief, knowledge, and all else that goes on in our heads. To see, also, how men assume most of that their images as territory and, in that enormous self-deception, how they seize and exploit the basic force of life to support fantasy requires more imagination than most men have, or rather, allow themselves to use. A moral health is needed for the achievement. But very few men, even now, have access to a sufficiently honest value system for imagining what they are, or do, think they are, feel, believe, or assume about the world and themselves. Man is the medium, his act, the message—both but image in source and manifestation.

Perhaps it would be of use, here, to consider specifically how we attribute reality to what is imaginary, and what that leads us to fabricate as objects for our imagined ends. To some, the following example will have been understood. But for many it may be a little new and so, a little helpful. And I cannot offer much more of such aid, here. The reason is this:

Once it is seen (or, correctly imagined) that even our sensory and other animal awarenesses are but dreams on which dreamed territory is founded and spuriously held—the record of all man has, is, does, did, and intends will take on so many new and more nearly proper shapes, that everything will be an example of that new means of understanding.

Once that image of our actual condition is adopted, all morals will need revision, all ideas and artifacts, review.

Let us imagine, however, a man looking from a window of his home at a typical, suburban scene.

Does *he* realize that most of what he sees is derived from a moral fantasy so incorrect and ill-conceived as to be a threat to his very species? Does he even recognize another truth, that the "who" looking on is his own invention, not real, and in its main part anti-real? Is he even able to consider that what he thinks of it is a set of feelings, rationalized into his notion of sense?

Does he also note that his reactions to the scene are not real, either? Not real, but a product of beliefs, ideas, and values that were, themselves, invented by other men? Or by himself? Hardly!

What he beholds is therefore not even felt by any other person exactly as he feels it. But they employ parallel processes.

The houses, streets, and vehicles are, of course, presumed to furnish the best currently possible means to his own and his neighbors' needs, comforts, luxuries, and aesthetic or other desires.

But many of these objects have their form and function because the owner was induced to imagine he needed or wanted them, not because that was the actual case. Many, also, were fabricated to enhance his and his neighbors' sense of status on a purely imaginary value scale, dreamed up for the end of making him believe he had a need, or the want, till he bought the thing claimed to fulfill synthetic desire.

And all these artifacts are imagined valuable by him in short term ways, alone.

Only recently, and only a little, has this looker-out even been able to be aware that what he has thitherto imagined as wholly good in this scene isn't. The exhaust of passing cars, the fecal trail of jet planes overhead, the silent surge of his own and his neighbors' sewers, the waste that the city garbage trucks collect, the smoke from a visible back-yard incinerator, the DDT that a man across the way is spraying on his shrubs, and endless other items connected with the scene are not pure boons but partly malign. What should have entered the imagining, here so incompletely exploited, now somewhat shows the suburban achievement is not sound.

But even a more than ordinarily imaginative beholder will hardly increase his use of imagination enough to contemplate his view in a broad relation to its net cost for future men, through waste and pollution and irretrievable devastations of the earth's resources.

Likely, the traditional American values of the man in the window—and false logics he has accepted—will prevent him from any true evaluation of what he considers reality. The Great Society will emerge, in his dream, as more and more people are born, to consume more and more goods and employ more and more services. The absolute cost and self-limiting fact of such a fantasy will not much register with him, if at all. He will reason, as did a young woman, who recently said to me when I spoke of these matters, "They'll think of something."

"They" will "think," then, of ways to reduce the pollution and repair the ruin of man's terrestrial environment. Of substitutes for whatever is being and will be annihilated or exhausted of the materials man derives from living species and inert matter. Ways, she meant, that would allow the crescendo of human consumption by that ever-accelerated proliferation of commodities and services. And of people.

The young lady, when I asked, could not "think of something," herself. She plainly felt my question both unwarranted and mean. Yet she was a college graduate, and as I was told by the lady who introduced us, "very brilliant." Her brilliance was the near-universal American sort, flashy and so, small-gauge, a fixed point of present-time dazzle, scanning nothing else. Its irresponsible focus is as minute as nearly universal and will write the signature of our doom if it persists much longer in that meager degree. What she imagined as logical and true, what she assumed from our tradition, was as mistaken as faith in human sacrifice for the appeasement of the God Bubb.

She could never look across a suburban street and perceive that what her eye beheld was a scene not-real, not logical, not true, as purpose, but only a clutter of imagined artifacts created without consideration for future-time. Solid enough in seeming and as things, but the spawn of dangerous dreams in fact. And she'd not ever discern how false her feelings were.

How insubstantial are all our values!

Return, for illustration, to the home-owner looking at his suburban scene. The house across the street was built, let's say, by a Mr. Williams. He and his lovely wife, two charming sons, and two delightful daughters lived there till recently. Then Mr. Williams sold the house to Mr. Johnson. Who has a lovely wife, charming boys, girls, etc. Both men are high-school superintendents. Mr. Johnson, the new resident-owner, is more learned than Mr. Williams, more talented, handsomer, and better paid. Mrs. Johnson is far lovelier than Mrs. Williams. In every such measurable way, the new neighbors are

either like the former people or superior to them. There is
one difference, but it is minute, a matter of their relative
amounts of dermal melanin. The Johnsons are Negroes, and
the first Negroes to buy and occupy a house in this suburb.

Now, how do the values of the man at his window change?

Again, suppose we are not looking from that window but
showing an album of photographs, taken there, to a bright
boy fifty years from now.

How will his imagination evaluate the same scene?

Will he exclaim, as the album leaves turn, "All that
room, for just one family! Look! The people getting into
that car—going to the city, you said—forgot to take along
their breathing gear. They'll have to come home. Or smother!
And those men in that other car, the ones you told me were
leaving for New York—a thousand miles away? Have they
got throughway permits? And assigned times for entering
the throughway? You mean anybody could go anywhere on
any road, without a permit, or a starting time? Imagine!

"And—all the kinds of trees and bushes and vines and
flowers growing completely outdoors! My, it must have been
confusion when so many things could grow that they practically made a jungle in anybody's yard! And—let me see—
two, three, four kids. In that *one* family! They sure must
have gotten a high gene rating on the federal tests to be
allowed so many! I wish my father and mother had passed
that high. Then maybe I could have a brother. Or a sister.
Still. People in those olden days had worse troubles than
now. Like—cancer. All those diseases. Hardly anybody lived
a hundred years, either. And now, most everybody can, and
millions already are a hundred."

Will that be the sort of reaction of a youngster, in half
a century, to our small scene?

Will such a boy go on, this way, "All that what-you-call-
it? Yard! It's about a thousand times the square meters we
get in our flat. And people cooked at home, too! Whatever
they wanted to eat! Even, outdoors, on that—that—barbecue?
I'd like, just once, not to be handed the standard meal from
the air chute. And I'd like—once, anyway—to be able to
start walking in any old direction as far as I pleased, and
no permit, and come, even, to the end of the city, and then

go on in that noplace, any direction, where there might even not be people, or crops and machines, and I might even perhaps come to wild trees, finally!"

That?

Or would such a boy say, of the same pictures:

"My! That was really ancient times! Look at the smoke! Look how close together people were! How they could even see into each other's houses! And the raw meat they half cooked on that fire-thing. The lousy prepared food they ate! And the waste! Think of mining and raising all that junk, just to build crummy hovels like those! Ugly, uncomfortable— and, you said?—torn down in twenty years? Out of style, already? How crazy could people have been? Why make anything not to last? Look at the clothes, too! And warm day I'd say! Boys and girls, all in those sex costumes. And, didn't I read, not allowed even to undress together? Were they nuts? Didn't the mother and father even like sex? The kids too?

"And look at the colors on those shacks! One makes the next one ugly. The vegetation—all tricked out to seem machinery-made. There's one of those—in this upper corner—jets. With all that four-track smoke! And the sky! Missing, I thought. Clear, you say. Clear—my foot! And look at the way that car is being steered—and going fast, for the olden days. How old is the driver? Sixteen? And that rotten at it? No wonder everybody slaughtered everybody else with cars like that and such lousy operational technique! What's a louse, incidentally? And, you say, this sort of house-and-lot mess went on and on, for hundreds of square miles, around the old city centers, where people used to die in smog? Like that? Oh, yes, with shopping centers at intervals. Sure. Where you bought all that stuff you didn't need or had to replace because it was made to come apart soon! Imagine! And that was what you called a TV set? With the Indians fighting white men on its front? Was that a—what's it? The program? Oh! A Western!"

A minute for meditation, then:

"I looked at a couple of those old Westerns in school. Part of history orientation. They said even educated men by the millions, watched those Westerns, hour by hour, a their lives. With almost identical plots and characters. You know what? Our teacher asked us to write down why we thought grown people would even bother to sit through more than one of them. I got 'A' for my answer on that quiz. Know what I said? I said they liked to look at practically that same show, forever, because of two things. In Westerns, they could still imagine a place where value choices were easy. Good and bad guys, only. Good girls and wicked, but, even so, pretty, right? Sneaky, that! And the mountains, desert, plains, too. I called that the main reason, besides the idea that simple values and violent fights settled status. Pecking orders, I said. The shows always were about places where there was immense room, which people didn't have then. Watching Westerns probably kept them from going mad by being overcrowded, even though they finally did, before the Change."

A moment's further thought. "One more thing I could have said on that test. I mean, would they have watched Westerns to keep up a dream, anyhow, of natural and ample space if the films or tapes or whatever had been made in the West as it was at the time they watched the TV. I mean, all messed up with litter, beer cans, dead cars, thrown-away refrigerators, or those—air-things—conditioners, and garbage, and trash? With trailers for camping parked in every canyon, or on those rivers? And foamy filth on the water, too! Outboards roaring everywhere! The noise! Fences! Billboards all over. Some mine, or mill, smoking, right at the Pass where you headed off the bad guys. The sky dirty, like it really was. I mean, I bet Westerns made in the real West, as it was then, wouldn't have had anybody looking! I could have used more to prove my idea that intelligent men watched Westerns to seem to escape their crowded and filthy living places. Like these in the album."

Which sort of reaction a boy would give, or which of any such specific reactions one might have, fifty years hence, to our vista from the window in the suburb, I cannot say. Those I've dreamed up may not be near the mark.

But I think their orders of magnitude of difference are more or less right. What our average suburban householder thinks real and valuable about his scene will seem that much other, as reality and in value, fifty years hence. And perhaps it will seem near unbelievable, then, either as a picture of human bliss in some past golden age, or as a reality men put up with, as best they could, in a then-dark-age, called late twentieth century.

In any case, most of what appears in the photographs of it will be gone in fifty years. What replaces it may be wild woods taking over ruins with no man left to see that. Or it may be different and lovely and occupied by human beings who live and act, believe and feel, behave and think, in ways they find very real, very loving, and very true, that we would, nearly to the last American, call abominable, vile, communist, perhaps, and immoral, surely, though those terms would not fit the facts. Reality, even that palpable, is not real at all. And when it is contemplated in relation to man's (and life's) true ethos, and then in regard to form-as-function, it changes, and is seen as imagination more than as substance. If our moral values are added, the change is even more subjective but still more vivid. Obscenity (say), like beauty, is in the eye of the beholder. So is a suburb.

I have taken some of your time to juggle that illustration. I hope it has served at least a little to enable you to use your imagination, if you have any left, to discern that man can improve his image of truth or reality only if he sees that both objective fact and subjective value are images and, mostly, needless fakes.

Nothing is real, in our sense of the word, these days. Nothing.

If the man at the window is a Baptist fundamentalist and his neighbor across the way a devout Catholic, even that will change the imagined reality of the beholder toward all he sees that his neighbor owns. And even if he is a non-believer, tolerant, a humanist with the best ideals thereby attainable, he still will not see that setting truly. It will remain man's work, for human ends presumed both known and attainable either now, or soon. To this humanist, life will seem sacred, but the only "sacred" thing, human continuum, will not be his criterion.

Such a man will look out at the moderately affluent scene and wonder how he and his fellow Americans can "bring the

twentieth century" to . . . Hottentots, or Amazonian tribes-
men, or even to the benighted Roman bigot and unfortunate
across the street.

Even humanism, then, is not a sufficient use of imagination
to find what truth we can.

For man is not all. Nor anything, without the other beings that support him. What he is, **at** his present best, is
nothing to regard as wondrous; and to deem that notion a
golden export and wondrous gift is asinine. Not any human life is sacred. All are sacrificed, will it or no, after
good or evil lives. Humanity is not precious, saving only
as it is intent upon becoming—and becoming what, it cannot guess, since all it can know there is how to enable men
to evolve themselves into better kinds of men, and perhaps,
into beings no longer men, but greater.

There is a way to imagine, always more realistically and
truly, how to proceed toward that unknowable goal, by one
pair of orders: love for man's continuum, fear of what
threatens that.

Chapter
Eight

SCIENCE
AS PIETY

1 / The Gospel According to Reason

AS LONG AS scientists, themselves, have been unaware of
the possible seizure of any region that imagination establishes, as if territorial, they have been liable, at least, to
the surrender of their reason to a corrupted instinct. It
has been, and still is, in consequence, possible for a scientist
to become attached to his concepts with the same senseless "faith" that dogmatists exhibit toward their hideously
unreasoned domains. My discussion of the authoritarian
stupidity and paranoid zeal of the behaviorists was an awesome example of such rigid fealties amongst scientists.

I can recall vividly others. The hot denial by mathe-
maticians and physicists of Einstein's first news. Believers
clung to the prior, Newtonian "universe" with the passion
of Christian fundamentalists. Today, classical and molecular biologists are at war.

Since doubt is, nonetheless, a constant requisite for truly
scientific process, the most adamant groups of entrenched
scientist-believers will, sooner or later, be obliged to yield.
But their frequent reluctance to accept a new enlightenment
requiring change in their ideas can be explained, I am sure,

158

only in the way I have done. They have been converted by faith to the imaginary borders of a time-territory: and then they've been trapped in it by an instinctual process that evolved billions of years earlier—for the establishment, maintenance, and defense of what had been, till man appeared, three-dimensional and real.

From the first, modern science and its growing "territories" conflicted with those of the godly. However, the two regions were able somewhat to coexist owing to the fact that science, taking reason and objectivity as its method, did not believe it could or should enter the area of morals. And for a long time, it did not much attempt to do so. Thus religion served for a few further centuries to seem to most persons (scientists included) as a different domain and one not open to scientific investigation. The instinctual necessity of some right-wrong system was met by religion, though in diverse fashions, but scientists constantly asserted that particular area of moral inconsistency was not their business.

It seemed possible, even in A.D. 1900, to be a good chemist and a good Presbyterian, too. The instinctual animal could use his imagination to invent the logical systems needed to observe, for example, the cause-and-effect relationships in molecules and compounds, while still finding his essential right-wrong pattern in a creed based on a Trinity of Gods. The irrational dogma of a denomination satisfied the unseen, but absolute, demand of the human animal; the rational pursuit of chemistry could then go forward in supposedly separate dimensions.

From the first, however, scientific findings shattered religious ideas, regarded till the crash as undeniably true and so-supported by the blind-faith technique. In time, and by our time, all the specific dogmas of all the faithful were proven false by science. For evidence, one needs but to read some works of contemporary theologians in which the authors make efforts to accept the truths of science and at the same time to reconceive of God. The honest reader will realize the theologians have nothing left of tenable religious territory save words, and their use for surmises without plausibility of any sort, or even sense. The effort is like a rhetorical explanation of why a drowning man snatched for a straw he merely imagined in his wet environ.

During the brief centuries in which the scientific method proved so fruitful of new knowledge and ever-truer truths, a great conflict for the supposed two realms was waged. It still goes on. The religious believers have generally done, and do, whatever lies in their power to deny what science proves, or to hide it so as to hold their ever-emptier territory as certified by "higher truth." To that end they still maintain a grasp of education and law.

As territorial coexistence grew less and less possible, some sturdy scientists (and increasing numbers of persons who accepted various scientific facts contrary to religious dogmas) were martyred. Laws serving pious fantasy still lead to the occasional punishment of such persons. And scientists were held inferior beings, ridiculed and ill paid, also. Until after World War II, in the United States and other Christian lands the total support provided for scientific research was a pittance compared to the annual treasure poured out to sustain and promulgate religious faiths and their compulsive antics.

Not surprisingly, scientists found their best protection from harassment in their claim to objectivity. Their territorial defense was made by withdrawal from the greater realm of man's beliefs. And so, quite unconsciously, scientists called that a virtue and negation defined their limits. Each division and subdivision of scientific territory, furthermore, required a new language, since, in each, new, wherefore unnamed, phenomena required fresh symbols.

So science came to occupy its ivory tower where churchmen rarely asked admission and even tended to let the workers be, so long as they stayed put. Because each major realm of science broke into plots where those new languages had to be invented the ivory tower has become (if a contemporary, official index is correct) about one thousand towers, and these, with their different idioglossaries, a thousand Towers of Babel. The occupants can no longer talk to one another. And the lay public was encouraged to develop its present conviction that it cannot comprehend even one tongue spoken in one tower, let alone the thousand languages and dialects.

The tower people, with few exceptions, also shared with religious believers one other majestic delusion, old as man and powerful as man's piety: the idea that men both could and should conquer nature. Or, in the mealy-mouth rewording of nowadays, "control nature."

That notion led to man's first reappraisal of himself as superior. His new entry into the territory of time with his new imagination had truly made him the all-killer, the limitless exploiter of tree and plant, and lake-crosser, river-swimmer, fire-builder, and so on. Then, as his religions evolved for his attempt to defeat the shocking cost of time-territorial access, the foreknowledge of death, beliefs in his heavens and hells soon made earthly realities seem inferior. These are, still, seen as merely "temporal" things, acts and experiences, upon which the godly look with smug disdain. The blunder was as absolute as the invention of afterlife and part of it: not to die required of man that he also assume he was supernatural, not the one who does die, the beast.

The Holy Bible authenticates that wicked notion of man as the lord of the earth—of earth as that lesser domain than God's, or the Devil's, both deemed infinite and eternal. Jesus Christ was not aware of any scientific fact worth mentioning, either, and to him, also (according to such hearsay records as we have), the earth was apparently nothing but a temporary place where human right-wrong related to the everlasting hereafter. To Jesus, all things except human beings, all beasts and plants and rocks and seas, were fit only for exploitation as man chose, so long as his choices were weighed against good and evil as defined by the path to "many mansions."

Science, until lately (and even now, save in discrete, small, and occasional fragments of the field), accepted that pre-Christian assumption of nature as malleable to man's will. Man need but to understand in order to manage. With all sorts of invented, but sound and demonstrable, logics and processes, it examined the temporal realm, while it left the alleged regions of eternity and infinity to the priesthood. Science thus came to define itself as altogether reasonable. And it believed that, by the continuation of the use of its method, one I have elsewhere called "applied honesty," it would not only uncover the secrets of nature —and even, perhaps and finally, all of them—but that science ought ultimately to enable man to take complete charge of his environment and mold it to his exclusive ends and wishes.

Since that had been the seemingly correct intent of our species from its origin, and since the discoveries of science swiftly led to numberless means of revising nature to man's ends, it seemed perfectly sensible to believe in science as the best means toward man's endless effort to manage nature for man's sake—a species-long endeavor that had seemed to man exactly like war and, in any victory, identical to conquest.

Today, scientists still tend to believe that they act (in their disciplines, at any rate) as reasonable beings. Reason has triumphed over all other mind-uses, in science, they think. And they widely share the common assumption of civilized laymen that nature has already been greatly conquered and can ultimately be suborned entirely. The assertion is incessantly made, or implied, in scientific journals, popular magazines, newspaper editorials, and in all other media. It is rarely disputed anywhere.

This illusion has a corollary that is as deeply imbedded in the general mind:

Where it becomes evident that technology, which is not science but the special applications of scientific ideas, has upset some feature of nature, or wrecked its balance, man assumes he has but to extend scientific research, or to apply more carefully what's already known, to eliminate or redress the mistake, in order to proceed unscathed, or salvaged, on more efforts at control or conquest.

So implicit is this attitude that very few laymen and not a great many scientists are properly concerned about consequences of on-going efforts to manage nature, or, more accurately, to exploit the whole of nature and science for short-term ends.

Imagination has failed here, also.

A man sufficiently sophisticated to realize that the earth's resources, all potential materials, are finite, will perhaps know that this is a "have not" nation, in respect to what is either not available within the boundaries of the United States, or not producible here. Such a man may also be aware that he and his fellow citizens are rapidly exhausting the available supplies of on-hand materials. But he will probably not feel apprehensive. Science, he calmly explains, like my bright lass, will find substitutes. And what we don't have can always be imported.

The actual damage being done by man's attempts to exploit nature has lately become a matter of some concern in relation to a few of the most conspicuous examples. The contaminated waters, polluted air, diminishing fresh-water supplies, and the perils of pesticides are the principal subjects of such anxiety as is felt. But virtually every person who views even those increasingly palpable matters feels quite sure that somebody, soon, will take steps (of a technological kind) to ameliorate the trouble. Most scientists, indeed, would agree that these situations merely require applications of their basic function: reason.

That their reason is dominated by laws of instinct, very few even imagine.

True scientists, the so-called pure sort, the theorists, finders, pioneers, discoverers, the men and women engaged in the search for knowledge, for what they call its own sake, are not aware of how territorial they have made the enterprise, and its artifacts of imagination, too. They do not dream that they are acting as animals, not as men, near-absolutely, in one major fashion: They have not seen how exactly they stake out and fanatically defend their special territory as if it were holy as heaven.

Let us make an imaginary visit to their megalopolis, to study that phenomenon.

It is a supercity of metaphysical ivory towers. Skyscrapers, now. With a Borough of Biology and a Physics Plaza, a Chemistry Quarter, and a Midtown Mathematics Mall. In these various districts, the size and the height of the towers differ as well as their locations, some being more prominent than others and many much newer than a few.

The pace and even the dress of numerous occupants differ and some of the people no longer do any actual research, but act as executives, while many others spend only part of their time in the city, the rest being devoted to teaching, which those so engaged usually do with reluctance and only, if it can be managed, for the edification of graduate students.

Many engineers and other technicians work in the sacred city, but only as lowly employees engaged to turn out apparatus and gear for the purely scientific experiments conducted here. Laymen who visit the place will be shocked, usually, to realize that not one of hundreds of thousands of scientists working in this vast urban complex is trying to make or do anything primarily meant to be of use, that is, "practical." And a layman might soon become annoyed to find that these people look down on applied scientists, who are busy elsewhere, in all cities, on efforts to use the knowledge found here for some "practical" end. There is a reason for that disdain, but lay visitors seldom appreciate it.

The question "Who pays for it all?" would be natural, of course.

The answer is rather peculiar.

Of these brilliant people in Research City, many are paid by colleges and universities where, as a rule, they also teach part time. A multitude of them are paid by the federal government. They are able to pioneer owing to grants made by the National Science Foundation, the Office of Navy Research, and a hundred other research-sponsoring bodies in the central government. Tens of thousands are paid by industry directly, or through corporation-owned institutes. Other hordes are sustained by grants from private foundations, such as Rockefeller and Ford, as well as hundreds of smaller and less well-known bodies of that sort.

Some of the most renowned men (and the relatively few similar women) are entirely free to choose the area in which they will work and to follow their own course of investigation as they please, without any limit or outside direction. Small numbers of these mighty minds are allowed merely to think and talk, in the hope that by reflection and reason and imagination and interchanges, they may solve some enigma intellectually, or perhaps find a new hypothesis to explore, or new means of exploration, and the like. Most of the investigators, however, are somewhat constrained in their work, either by organizational command or owing to the fact that to obtain funds for any work they will have to design research projects they know will appeal to the money-granting boards and federal officials they approach.

As a result, perhaps only one in twenty or thirty of these people is engaged in purely "pure" science, that is, in a quest for knowledge upon which he is able to pursue his own course without guidance, yet with every advantage of time and resources he might wish to call upon for his unstated ends. Pure science, then, is, in the main, a delusion, even here!

Each skyscraper has the same mighty motto carved above its entrance:

KNOWLEDGE FOR ITS OWN SAKE

Under that, each has its general and special designation. The several hundred towers in the Borough of Biology, for instance, bear that word, below the slogan of all science, and beneath "Biology," one may read:

Energy transfer: photosynthesis

Energy transfer: bioluminescence

Invertebrate paleontology

Genetics: Deoxyribonucleic acid

Genetics: Ribonucleic acid

Ecology

Morphology

And so on. But those seven named structures will hardly give any idea of the complexity of work even in this one Borough of Biology.

The Physics Plaza lies close to the Midtown Mathematics Mall. And its buildings are more neatly grouped than those of the Borough of Biology since its subdivisions have been, in most instances, recently formed. Astrophysics, for example, is pretty much gathered in a clutch of rather new skyscrapers of more or less the same architecture; and the

building housing Radio Astronomy won't be very distant
from one still under construction, called Quasi Stellar
Objects.

That gives us something of a picture of the territory of
pure science. It seems very real, just as religion seems real
when one looks at churches and cathedrals and temples. But
all that happened, happens, and will happen in this megalopolis is, in fact, immaterial. It arose first in an individual
mind. What arose was then checked experimentally. If it
was thus proven sound, it was disseminated. It then became a part of the past-time, or remembered (and, here,
recorded) information, upon which all workers then oriented current endeavors toward some future goal of, hopefully, an increment of the same sort of knowledge.

In spite of the reality of the great city, then, and the
tangible, sometimes immense and fabulous equipment employed, the only product is concept, something that arose
in human imagination and is extended by that through invented systems of logic and by means of dreamed-up procedures, all arbitrary, and all limited absolutely to what
men can currently imagine about whatever men can perceive directly or with instruments or by inferences.

But what the people in this Holy City have imagined is
a very great deal!

The search for knowledge for its own sake is, of course,
mythical. Knowledge hasn't any "own sake," as I've noted:
what is, is; and doesn't need to know about itself. The
search for knowledge in this city, then, is a search conducted for man's sake. But not, mind you, in the sense
most men imagine as "their sake." The effort here is conducted without ethical or moral or social aim. It ideally
represents the extension of curiosity through its logical and
imaginative use, in any and every direction that men can
go, with their minds and their invented equipment. The
ideal's faulted.

Where a given man or team here seeks added knowledge
may depend on one man's wondering, or upon a corporation's area of interest. It may rise from some purpose of a
branch of the government. Or it may relate to the mere pas-

sion to get some feature of nature, such as insects or stars, typed, classified, named, and counted.

So the knowledge that arises is of a random sort and the advance of it in any special direction, though dramatic, is often the by-product of some program and neither expected nor welcome.

The next and greatest peculiarity about it all is this: The increases of knowledge are published, when confirmed or even when mere theory and still open to criticism, in journals that use one of the thousand appropriate languages. And that's pretty much that, insofar as these discoverers are concerned. Each of their triumphs is a new and more accurately imagined image of a reality of some sort, which is then put on the record for any interested colleagues to read. Perhaps it is also reported by the press and TV— if it's dramatic from the lay viewpoint—though such reports are often inaccurate and misleading.

The only further public effort made by the citizens of this city (with growing unwillingness) is to teach, to a few classes of students who have usually been chosen in their special field, what they need to know in order to enter it and carry forward the work there.

And with that observation, we reach the main point of this part of this chapter.

Scientists cannot be held responsible for what they will discover, of course. Nobody knows what that may be till they find it.

But these pure scientists feel no responsibility for what is done with their discoveries by anybody. They are, plainly, gathering knowledge for man's sake; using his imaginative curiosity, which keeps wondering What? Why? Where? How? When? In what way? With what result? And then—? But they never define or consider that "man's sake" relates to them.

All the answers they've gotten and all the paths toward added answers they follow are, then, special territory or its approaches, in the dimension of time, where only the human imagination can journey any distance, or in any degree, on any vector. Yet, since this is the territory of pure science, it is, like all cerebral image, ruled by instincts that relate to territoriality in every facet of man's being.

Among territorial animals, patterns of instinct have specific intentions, we will remember. A group must defend the boundaries of its established real estate. Aggressors of the same species must be driven away. In all such animals but men, that act is ritualized and instinct is limited so that defense of one's domain against neighbors of one's kind is never a matter of war-to-the-death but one of stylized conflict that stops short of killing.

Individuals within each dominion are also involved in aggression, against each other, to set up and maintain a pecking order, and to establish leadership for breeding purposes, as well as to assure that adequate territory the species demands for each member.

Men never behaved in this manner.

They, alone, regarded all physical territory and all possessions therein as booty, and suitable for taking or holding, by homicide, as in war, owing to their fealty to some fantasied idea of subjective "territory." And men have also apparently disregarded the law that demands of territorial beings a minimal space for each. Space competition within a territory is, for man, also a grim and deadly affair, when measured by its results.

Toward his imaginative territory, that is, what he believes, thinks, feels, and knows, man has displayed an identically unnatural behavior. Many of the great religions, for example, are promulgated as if by the policies of ruthless colonialism. Here, the territorial-holders, evangelical Christians, for example, presume the only real and true "territory" is their Christian sort, and in consequence, their horrible aggressions in the name of their Jesus and God are executed with the same bloody "righteousness" to be seen in the troops of a civilized nation as they assault a primitive people, to grab their land for its gold ores, petroleum resources, or whatever happens to be the tangible aim of such abnormal greed.

Communism can be seen exquisitely as an idea served, territorially, in this same, solely human, and utterly lunatic way. Its thesis is that its system will furnish the promised bounties and joys when all the people of the earth have become Communist, and become that as a result of the Communist use of any and all means to that end, however amoral.

When we look at pure science and its human exponents from this viewpoint, however, we see that the idea-territory involved is not subject to exactly the same insane expression through unconscious and perverted instinct.

The scientific researcher is aggressive in his work, to be sure, and often in a degree matched by few other sorts of men. Each thrust to gain more knowledge, a truer image of reality, requires great intellectual courage and sometimes incredible physical bravery, too: aggressive behavior, indeed! Internal "aggression" is common among such people, also. They are continually in conflict with one another in their specific fields over matters of experimental interpretation, new hypotheses, and the like.

But their aggression does not often spill over their established boundaries to become an evangelical act in the outer world. When it does, in fact, as with behaviorism, it is often owing to the process I have described: a discard, by scientists, of their true function, as men using reason imaginatively, turning them into men who have taken up an idea with the irrational and passionate drive of religious fanatics.

In many ways, the conventional use made of their ideological territory serves scientists well. It tends to prevent attack from the ignorant, dogmatic outside world. It permits them that seclusion essential for objectivity in their working hours. It expedites their achievement in each cell of their whole, wherein a special language has evolved, of necessity, and where those who speak it feel no need to teach it to others, and so, many spend their full time in productive effort, or, only a little, in explaining to students.

But one can find a cosmic flaw in this affair. For it is sensible to guard territory in order that work there may go forward at its best pace, but it is another thing to regard the fruits of such work, the knowledge, the treasures increasingly multiplied in the territory by the work, as if none of the workers had any responsibility for their fate. At that point, the territorial instinct acts among most scientists in a manner opposite to its action among people whose territory-of-imagination is not described by reason, but by faith, or by some other irrational belief. Most people, that is.

The latter are bent on taking all possible men into their "fold," as Christians call that real estate. And by vigorous or even amoral means. They will not have it, even in America, in millions of cases, that a non-believer is an equal citizen to one who says he believes in God. They suspect an atheist of "Communism," while they scream like raped women when a constitutionally minded, free citizen manages to get some gobbet of their dogma out of secular schooling, or the Bible off the bench of justice.

Scientists are not aggressive in any complimentary manner. On the contrary, their animal reaction to such assault evokes the other and opposite partner of that instinct: flight, evasion, and retreat into their fortress. This takes visible form as irresponsibility. They are never, save as individuals and then rarely and feebly, given to any defensive foray against border-challenge. And knowledge, the precious images within their borders, is simply set there, and then abandoned.

Anybody (in, at least, a free society and so, our own, till lately) can seize any part of any such prize and use it for whatever end anybody wishes, within the law—which, however, is of prescientific design. If a great chemical corporation snatched such information in order to manufacture pesticides that endangered the world ecology, the chemists who had learned how to chlorinate phosphorous compounds (that is, found the now-swiped treasure) couldn't care less. None of their affair.

What's done beyond their territory—which they term a "field," with an instinctual aptness they aren't aware of —is not relevant to their "belief." Even when some application of a valuable finding in one field is known to be dangerous, foolish, or wasteful in another, its inhabitants do not deem it mandatory to call attention to that peril. Decent, perhaps, but not obligatory.

The irresponsibility of these people is even greater and

more shocking than the kind just indicated. Most have no sense of any requirement whatever to acquaint mankind with their terrain, its contents, or contents being sought.

Thus pure science can be seen as a region in which the inhabitants act as if they were not men at all, that is, not any part of the species, not human, not really anything related to other men. Non-people, when in their territory. Or out of it. How is that possible?

How can that be, when all they do and find and know is the product of man's imaginative uses of reason? When they are, as workers, the most reasoning and reasonable of all men? How do they manage to go on in such an unhuman manner?

Some tentative answers can be given, I think.

Scientists are not responsible for what they will find, which fact I've tried to make clear earlier. But that situation does not automatically relate to what is found. That becomes real and usable, therefore, care-demanding. Their use of logical imagining is, however, local. Outside the laboratory they are, as a group, only somewhat more rational than other people. And also, as reason-users, they cannot be expected to employ their territory of knowledge in the same way unprovable dogma is so widely used, by people whose territory is faith-founded, or religious. Good scientists will not be compulsive preachers of that sort.

Nevertheless, scientists could use their knowledge in a different though correlative manner.

They could, if they saw the necessity, insist on what might be called "equal time," to state their case, as do religious and other irrational exponents of images. They could, were they aware of the territorial condition of all mankind, and of their own, too, demand that every untrue, irrational, or misleading utterance of the dogmatists made in violation of known truth be subject to debunking and/or correction, in the same media, with the same prominence. They could engage, in sum, in a constant and ubiquitous public debate with the voices of non-truth, of superstition, and of all unscientific ignoramuses.

That effort would greatly retard their present way of working, of course. But it would be the required act of any normal, territorial animal.

Scientists could also insist that education be conducted according to truths established in their domains. They could require all teachers to learn their basic methods, their uses of imagination with logic and reason, and to have a sufficient grasp of what they know and propose to seek, to be able to instruct all children in such means, the main results, and the prospects.

American educators, however, do not even know, save in a few instances, what science is. They, like most of the public, think of science as technology. And that damning, near-universal delusion is owing to such an absence of responsibility in the scientists as I have defined.

They should and could also make themselves responsible for the applications of their knowledge. They do not. They should and could have made themselves responsible for that freedom of thought and speech which is the only, but the absolutely essential, liberty that permits men honestly to call themselves free. They did not.

Such suggestions will seem outrageous to most Americans. And to most scientists, as well. For the former, freedom means their right to occupy any mind-spirit-territory they choose or are set in. For the latter, freedom means, among other things, freedom from any duty related to their field, insofar as it concerns their species.

Their aborted condition becomes, finally, comprehensible, just as the otherwise utterly incomprehensible state of man in his religious territoriality is now understandable. Once we saw ourselves as outside nature, superior, and the intended conquerors of nature (let alone, when we saw ourselves as possessed of infinite and eternal territory beyond our graves). We lost contact with nature, that is, with reality, including the life force and its clear, absolute and dominant morality that is followed to the one end of species continuum.

Species continuum is not the ruling value of religion. It is not relevant in patriotism, either. And scientists, as men, have set it absolutely aside as motive or duty. When we see that, the grisly vista of today becomes vivid:

"Faith," faith in holy writ, in revealed truth and all other mythical rubbish, is an iron lid clamped over the believer's faith-restricted territory, defining his allowed plot and confining him to it.

Yet man's faiths can be comprehended with a certain compassion. Our predecessors led their lives by faith in the perfect morality of each kind. Man's reliance on what might be called an inner sense of faith-as-real is natural—and purely animal, of course, on that account. With the first living cell-creature, a need to trust its urges was innate. And the need but intensified as life became complex in form. Faith is as near "real" as that; and it betrayed living beings only as man corrupted its essence to sustain his delusions concerning himself and nature.

Reason, as the scientists have used it, has merely created a different but equally terrible trap.

Of course, in recent decades, many scientists have become perturbed over various calamitous applications of their new-found knowledge, and over public ignorance.

But few of them, indeed, have recognized even symbolically the true cause of this, their rather recent access of worry. I can remember only one instance of an adequate perception. After he had led his physicist-colleagues in the atomic-bomb manufacture (an application by previously pure scientists of a pristine artifact in their realm of concept—an engineering feat, then) Robert Oppenheimer said sadly that, somehow, ". . . science has known sin."

It took an application of a truth for a thing of gigantic size and menace to draw that little sigh of perceived truth from one scientist.

But the central question about this observation on the evaded duty of science will still seem this:

Why should pure investigators be obligated to take part in appraising all the applications of their findings that others make? Why should they be bound by duty to refute ignorant and erroneous public utterance by clergymen, quacks, and all those making similarly false claims? Why should they require that education incorporate the teaching of their method and main findings and current goals?

2 / Free Is for Fools?

This is a free country, not a dictatorship. True?

A man has a right to believe whatever he chooses. Correct?

Well, first, no.

Freedom is limited as an absolute to the freedom to think, believe, and speak as anyone wishes. But that area of freedom must be unbounded or no freedom will exist.

Even that minimal freedom is dead in America.

Part of abstract knowledge became secret when the American people failed to realize that the principle of liberty, itself, would collapse if they did not, after World War II, demand an open and non-secret world, especially vis-à-vis our antagonists, the Soviets, as the inescapable requisite for continued liberty of mere mind, in America.

So far as I am aware, only Robert Oppenheimer (again!) and I are on the record as having discerned and advocated that requisite for continued liberty: To have remained free, we should have demanded an open U.S.S.R. by ultimatum—and war if that had to be. The idea wasn't even comprehended. So the principle of liberty perished, violated by default.

And I hardly need to note that nobody save those "cleared" for military reasons now knows what he does not know, because that's secret. And I need scarcely point out, either, how secrecy has spread like a dirty river emptying into a clear lake, everywhere, and with it, inevitably, a national disease of suspicion, distrust, and hysterical (wherefore mistaken) hates. All predictable; and all predicted by me, publicly, at the critical moment, before America flunked her last chance to stay free.

Freedom, then, even to scientists, who should have best understood its essence, freedom to know, went undefended. With one exception, the very scientists who were frightened and angered by the impending abdication of freedom in their special field did not manage to say so out loud.

People, they assumed, have a "right" to believe what they wish. And to act as self-governed in that condition.

Here is one more way to discern the crux of our present calamity.

We do have a right to believe as we choose: our so-called religious and intellectual freedom. To be sure, in every region of the nation, that right is subject to abrogation according to the barbaric tenets of local prejudices, faiths, dogmatic beliefs, suspicions, and hates, in sum, local fears, all classically "un-American."

However, for as long as we were to consider ourselves a self-governed people, that general "right of freedom of belief" had an invisible but potent corollary.

Let me repeat it, in this connotation:

People can govern themselves only when they are sufficiently informed to make, in their majority, appropriate decisions.

With scientific knowledge self-immolated in its separate territory, general knowledge has become general ignorance; and the gap between what a few men know (but many exploit without, usually, adequate understanding) that most men don't know at all, and cannot be made to understand (owing to lack of suitable education) is already a Grand Canyon. A breach that heaves apart farther every hour. We are not a properly informed people, and we are becoming less and less informed, every hour. We have long been too ignorant for self-government; and the idea that we are still self-ordered is mythical.

Not any president, representative, senator, governor, or other elected official has the knowledge essential to govern any broad aspect of civilized enterprise. There are not ten scientists among the topmost of the elected officials in Washington. Who'd vote for an astrophysicist? What biochemist would even run for Congress? Every president since Hiroshima who has ad libbed on nuclear subjects has exposed his ignorance by some preposterous utterance. Even Kennedy, by far the most intelligent and best educated, once made a serious mistake that I wrote him to explain. I have his letter of admission and thanks, along with the public evidence of his self-correction. If our presidents cannot talk with knowledge even about modern weapons, they are plainly that much more ignorant in less urgent-seeming areas of science.

We are governed, then, by experts, appointed by our officials. We don't know who they are. Or how capable they are. Or even how honest. But our elected representatives have to rely on them for decisions. On specialists, frequently, who are paid by big industries and private enterprises to take their aims as a presumedly scientific course for the nation and world.

Eisenhower, as a last (and therefore bearable) official risk, warned America that the Department of Defense and big industry were gravely endangering the sensible and safe conduct of the state by their use of power. Who even knew what he meant, in that too tardy tocsin?

Yet it contained a truth we should have understood.

The departing president gave us the gist of his eight years of experience and knowledge.

Our civilization is technological and technology's biggest customers, defense and heavy industry, are taking an increasing charge of national destiny for their own ends.

It is the pure scientists who, among themselves, have the information necessary for proper decisions, by any majority or other ruling group. Their information may not suffice; but it is all men own that might. They shrug.

How could they insist it become known by all able to learn it, for the recovery of self-rule?

How could they suggest making the effort, since free men have the right to believe what they please, whether true or as batty as . . . astrology and the Gospel according to LSD?

Supposing these men saw their obligation as human beings to humanity and undertook to fulfill it?

Would the great majority of self-proclaimed Christians permit them to counter their doctrines in all media with their holy force? Would they face informed men in debates accorded the newspaper, magazine, radio, and TV time and prominence that religious (and all other scientifically disproven) utterance now virtually monopolizes?

No, I am sure.

What pressure, then, could scientists bring to bear, if they became moral men?

They could cease to work. And since we are here dreaming of scientists suddenly informed by the new morality, we might as well assume that the applied scientists and all other sorts of men whose professions and trades and skills derive from scientific knowledge would quit with the research people. Doctors, for example. All engineers. All technicians.

Such a strike seems ludicrous, I know.

It won't happen, I suppose.

Yet, if knowledge is power, should not the men who have the knowledge and those who most apply it have the power? The power, at least, as I've here implied, to see to it that their knowledge becomes public, and the property of an informed public, which then, and only then, could regain an ability to govern itself?

What is politics, now?

The science, I am told, of the possible.

If one accepts that, one must assume that same science also is aware of the impossible.

However, politicians are unaware of either.

Unaware, at least, until evidence of impossible conditions reaches them, not from scientists, but owing to a clamor of enough people to make of a given impossibility an issue—and one where the votes will be found.

Politics is not even leadership by the use of knowledge and reason in any scientific sense. Hardly an art, either, being creative only when that becomes mass-compelled. It is the strategy of occluded followership.

And in our funny world.

Our upside-down America, the greatest nation in all human history, that leads the rest and has a mystical sense it is ordained to do so.

Leads where and how? What's its definition of means?

The economy of abundance. That's correct. That's the twentieth century.

But think how strange our slogan is! What did "economy" mean, originally? And how is "abundance" achieved?

What does that banner really say?

The thrift of waste.

Those peculiar and changing prophets, economists, aren't checked up for their past records of right or wrong prediction. It takes a depression to discredit any one of their theses—that, or some other national calamity.

Yet when the ruling minds of America wish to study the Big Picture, when the high federal officials, the state leaders, the burgraves of business and industry, want a projection for the ensuing fiscal year, or more rarely, of the next ten years, who's called?

The wizards who think in that non-think way.

Nobody seems aware that the right men for the job are the ecologists. The men who count what's used and measure it against what's left. The men who know the laws I've already implied:

Production is destruction.

Consumption is reduction.

Affluence today impoverishes tomorrow.

Spending is expending.

The more men use the less there is for men to use.

Ecologists also know another and different truth.

Mankind breathes green plants and eats them.

As this was written, a remarkably graphic study of that appeared as the feature in an issue of *Time* magazine which in general carries the flag of affluence and free enterprise. *Time* made it very clear that America and all other industrial nations must swiftly and dramatically end their rapid and reckless ruin of the national air. Green plants, *Time* explained, are no longer able to clean and restore the earth's atmosphere fast enough.

But one curious thought occurred to me as I read that excellent and courageous effort of public enlightenment. *Time* pointed out with proper horror that though the air reaching the U.S.A. is cleaned in coming across the Pacific, should China become industrialized, the arriving atmosphere might well be polluted before our contamination was added. True, no doubt. But since the article also noted the grave state of

European air pollution, I wondered if their air, crossing the narrower Atlantic after being made filthy here, is already presenting Europe with just such pretoxicity as China's industrialization would bring to us?

I do not know. The information would surely have made, if true, a neat and logical addendum to that report. *Times*'s projection was *Time*-centered, as usual.

Elegant half-think.

Business, as we conduct it, calls the mere attempt to think ecologically interference. And as we become overwhelmingly an urban people, we lose touch with the mere evidence of ecological reality, the green world we depend on and will forever, and the spectacle of its devastation for our interval of progress.

To understand mankind is part of a chain of life that, broken in too many places, or generally retarded to some certain degree, will cause the end of progress and the destitution of humanity, one probably needs a direct experience of the links in the chain. One needs to see at least something of the green world and learn a little of its interdependencies, as well as those of the microscopic world on which the green one relies.

To whiz through the countryside in a car on some great highway and perceive how much of America is still verdant is not to know what was in the same place before man came to it, that is now of reduced strength as a link in the great chain. And to snarl around a lake or river or bay, noticing the second-growth woods and the meadows on the shore, is not to realize that this greenery, also, is inferior as agent of human sustenance to the same but prehuman scene. It is not to appreciate, either, that the petrochemical swill of the snarling boats has changed the aquatic life-links for the worse also.

Even such information leads, usually, to rationalizing.

Loren Eiseley told, in one of his lustrous essays, of a college student who asked, in effect, Why can't we just kill everything that is of no use, or troublesome, and leave alive only what we want and need and use?

Eiseley said he couldn't even answer the youth. I suppose because the answer would require complete re-education and probably rebirth, for that end.

Ecology can, and will, answer such people if they learn it. And its answer will be dreadful.

3 / A Scientist's Sermon

There have always been a few scientists who, from time to time, leaned out of their towers to attempt the act of participation in man's affairs. Rachel Carson was one. She broke the territorial rules in that endeavor and was roundly scolded from the tall towers.

Another example intrigued me as I edited this work. In the technical, but not exactly disciplined, pages of *Playboy* magazine for January 1967, Sir Julian Huxley offered his thoughts on "The Crisis in Man's Destiny." And a more articulate scientist could not be found for the job.

In the piece Huxley points out early on that the greatest shock to mankind science has so far occasioned was its proof that men are part of nature, and within it, bound to it and by it—not, as men had always thitherto assumed, supranatural.

What Huxley means by the reminder is that man must adapt to nature since man cannot hope to alter the order of reality by managerial, technical, rational, religious, or other means. However, multitudes who assume they are knowledgeable, including multitudes of scientists, have not reached that high a state of shocked awareness. And most men survived by simply ignoring the import of such news altogether.

For example, in a somewhat earlier issue of *Saturday Review*, there appeared an article entitled "What Modern Science Offers the Church," by Emmanuel G. Mesthene, executive director of the Harvard University Program on Technology and Society. In it, the author held that man could, should and would conquer and control nature by technology. The fellow wrote as if that assumption were not only universal and valid but not open any longer even to question.

Just what that might offer the church, even if true, I was not able to discern. But I could see that the author's point of view was opposite to that which Huxley presumed basic among scientists, at least. And I could guess that the director's attitude relates to the program directly, one financed by a long-term grant from the International Business Machines Corporation, a firm obsessed with the idea that technology is the means to all human good.

Sir Julian Huxley had a better idea. His essay lists many of the familiar but grievous blunders of present-day technology and many aspects of civilized behavior that represent threats to our species. He includes the swiftly stepped-up ruination of our living environment, the rapid exhaustion of resources, the pollution of air and water, the population explosion, and the geophysical certainty that unless we soon change our industrial techniques entirely we shall make the planet uninhabitable. He also mentioned the uncontrolled aggressive and nationalistic postures of an animal equipped with H-bombs.

Another of his observations especially beguiled me since it is as sinister as it is strangely obscure to the layman. Our expectation of boundless atomic power from present-style reactors is not warranted. The process involves dealing with highly radioactive reactor components by their hazardous, long-term sequestering. That produces an ever-bigger storage problem, one likely to concern men for centuries and one that will grow while power reactors multiply until it creates a cost factor unacceptable to our debited heirs and assigns. Since the fossil fuels are already earmarked for short-term squandering and since fission is clearly not an unlimited yet practical power source, we must hope that fusion will lend itself to power generation in the relatively near future.

The engineer-physicists in that field are fairly confident it will. Should they fail, however, our hopes even for an ever-greater supply of electrical power will be shattered. In that case we shall be thrown back, at last, on such energy as we can take directly from the sun and from water sun-lifted to turn turbines, along, doubtless, with devices to collect tidal power. These will be costly and their power-yield relatively low. At the moment, then, even man's hopes of an expanding industrial society rest on the possible but unsure exploitation of thermonuclear energy.

Huxley's index of crisis-realities is, however, merely a multiple alarm in the ivory towers, not a program or plan for action. He sees and foresees these certain physical perils, along with some others innate but undefined, within man, yet his suggestions for remedy are near nil.

Humanity must change these ways, and swiftly, or the collision courses cited by Sir Julian will lead to just that, crash, and repeated crashes. One agrees.

But we cannot begin to do anything, the author admits, till we find out what to do. Find out from ethology, he suggests, or Zen, or psychedelic revelation. Broad-minded, that man! Or is he? Psychology offers no hopeful answer, he indicates—which seems rather odd in view of the various fields he puts forward.

Once we get the proper value system for action, though, we mere lay human beings must make the correct changes and in a generation or two, evidently, if Sir Julian's schedule for imminent desperations is sound. Those changes would involve a revolution in a brief period of a magnitude approximately equal to that represented by all the changes men have managed from the Old Stone Age to the present.

By what means are we to find the light and pursue it in a manner that would alter all our goals and shut down or rebuild our factories? Suppose Zen fails us, and LSD?

In Huxley's words, we must do it, "somehow or other."

If that is not a clear illustration of the territorial jail of science, no jail exists. Huxley is in such control of local reason that he is almost nitwitted about unreason even in the territory of scientific minds.

Pure science?

Pure piety!

"You must," sayeth the man in the ivory tower, "for if ye do not, ye shall suffer hell on earth in punishment for your sins!"

So says the preacher in his pulpit. So calls the muezzin from his minaret. The Pope on the balcony. Obey God, Allah, Huxley.

Who the hell's in charge here, and responsible? Who's

ethical? The moral superiority of all beings but men has been plain since primates started to do what they still call thinking. To say an end is mandatory and means thereto must be found somehow is to ignore the central point of all such effort, and here, what Huxley isn't.

Chapter
Nine

THE NATURE
OF THE BEAST

1 / This I Tentatively Believe

EVEN TO TRY to see all mankind as one is hard for many.
To see their future generations as the meaning of those alive
is harder still. Humanism in its many forms does not en-
compass such classical biology. And the discovery that mankind is but a recent event in evolution did not break down
many standing images of what man had thought he was. The
power of invention is great and its inner realms are held by
a force too formidable for most inhabitants to resist, and for
most, a force unseen, and so, unknowable.

Getting over the great shock caused by Darwin was not
much of a problem to orthodox religionists, the fundamental
believers. They followed a long precedent, one of great weight
and effectiveness, where contrary reality had been met before.

They ignored the checkmate. They moved their now-im-
mobilized king, anyhow, taking the piece that had mated
them and calling it a pawn, beneath their higher knowing,
or a castle that their glorious faith could seize, but never
a truth that had put them out of honest business. Orthodoxy
imagines its game is fair even played that way. If a defeat

of dogma is absolute, all that's needed is a change in the rules.

The mechanics of that trickery involve what men call Mystery, and Mysticism and Mystique.

Whoever resorts to mysticism seems to me his own dupe and I cannot bring myself to truckle to that non-ideology.

There are unknowns. There will doubtless be unknowns for the time of man and into time beyond, when man himself may have taken charge of his evolution and become other. In a billion years or two, our descendants might know all. Or might not. The effort to add to and use what's known is the only important enterprise.

Mysticism is no way to do that, but its negation. There is, says its practitioner, a great Mystery here. A Paradox (perhaps). A state beyond human conception. Something transcendent. Just being aware of it as Mystery is a goose-pimpling thrill, and a privilege. Next, the Mystery-maker tends to take charge of his Enigma. To explain it in non-terms and to make rules for its acceptance by non-comprehension.

Odd place, this world, we men, the universe, he asserts. Mystery, here. Have to show you the magic for dealing with it. Set a day aside in each seven and close down all the business activities of people, even though their day is another, or they have no magic day. Then, set aside Lent, Easter, Christmas, Ash Wednesday, Good Friday. Better stick to those attached rites, too, owing to their mystical meaning and significance. Failure to go through the motions is worse than mirror-breaking, ladder-crossing, or salt-spilling. Better eat the symbolic body and drink the blood, too. Operational aspects of the mystery.

So are Buddhist firecrackers, Gothic gargoyles, temple bells of the Ind, the Hebrew holy days, the architecture of cultures and their acts that reflect the inner images of their mystery. We can show you the Way, they all say, and hold séances, get out tarot cards, peer in glass balls, consult horoscopes, toss pennies, because there is something going on that they don't understand or want to understand. They but want to be the people with the inside track on their "fact" of the mystical reality and the proper hocus-pocus for dealing with it.

The catch is as funny as it is ghastly. Simply because he's the animal with imagination which, rightly used, can find out about mysterious-seeming things, man has a hunger to be knowledgeable. But since he has misconceived himself as a non-animal, he seems justified in assuming he knows, even when he says what he knows is mystery. He has so big a self-image he cannot let truth penetrate, though that would be more real than his conjuring.

There are, then, no mysteries in the canonical sense. There is no mystique in the sense that word is used. There is knowledge, truth, and the way to make better images of those. That way is to regard what perplexes as a problem, not a magical dilemma. To be a mystic is to be a certified illusionist. All a man should do when confronted with the riddles of these many Merlins is to answer, "I do not know." Unless, of course, he does know, as he may, since many mysteries have long ago been erased that now perplex dolts, only.

I, then, am not mystified by the synthetic quandaries others find so fruitful of primordial tremor and glorious (self-induced) trance. I am ignorant, nothing more. What you may say is unknowable is not beyond knowing. The Great Mystery, to me, is merely your moral error to my current ignorance. And I can live contentedly in my sense of ignorance without trying to incorporate it as something I can make money with by magic passes. To have to pretend one knows everything, or has The Answer, is sad, if arrogant—and both when that Answer is "Mystery."

You can't fool me, says the mystic. And you can't: He has already fooled himself past a point of no return—of return to sense. Our modern world is alive with these automated Merlins, in costumes of the medieval era, windrows of self-pixilated people who claim to know what to do on the grounds that what they know is not knowable. Their insubstantial ghosts must stand; no truth is allowed to show them the dream is their own, not real, and that their incantations therefore mean nothing. They are but setting-up exercises for self-made spooks.

The truth has become, by necromancy, impossible; the confession of reality, their words: I know because I don't know.

Yet no image can be brought nearer reality, no territory held in the head can be extended, till the present figure is doubted, some border acknowledged arbitrary. And that demands the first step of admitting ignorance, not proclaiming mystical certainty.

Darwin didn't shock many people much or for long. The invincible proof of evolution, of man's place in the chain of life, did not lead at once to enlightened responses by the modern primate. An animal, bizarre and perverted, he is; a predator, but one that acts as if no restraint of his predecessors bound him. A being whose prey is anything and everything, animate or inert, real or imaginary, that he can sell. One who destroys all life forms in his path toward his intended prey, or its transport for sale, or his travel. A carnivore that stalks with a flame-thrower to clear the route to meat and the route for dragging it back. A vegetarian that kills all other herbivores because this one brooks no competition—and then kills the predators of the competitors, as nuisances, or for sport, or in "mercy." And a terravore, a tyrannosaurus of earth, mining it to sell, consume, eat in that way. The infinite wastrel.

That vision did not leap from the pages of Darwin. What came to many, instead, was a convenient, new disillusion. Since man was evolved from lower orders, men reasoned, he no longer need be even a little ashamed of his universal aggression. That, he had decided (to seem other), was the nature of all animals. What was true of his image of himself, and terrible, which he had falsely bestowed on other beasts, he now took back, a little, and with a lessened sense of guilt he behaved in his old way, which had never been that of any beast.

He widely yielded up his big Mystery, God.

What remained for him as image, thereafter? Materialism, only, he decided. To get, to have, and that, now. So he made himself a pure scientist and a non-man as was demanded by that notion of purity: irresponsible as man and to man for what he found. Or, by the hundreds of millions, his fainter mystique and stronger lease on lust made him a technological being, armed for every predation by machines and attacking the universal prey with redoubled self-assurance and a strength multiplied a millionfold and more by engines. All substance was his meat, and ecology was still a myth to him, as was his long-hid instinct. He could eat mountains, Mesabis of iron, or a continental wilderness, and nothing like him had existed—or long could, which no one realized for a time.

Disillusionment seems painful to most men because they live by illusions in their heads that they spell out in acts. Yet, to any man who searches for truth, his most welcome and desired experience is disillusionment. For when he achieves it, he knows that he has erased one error, and set up a better image, or a way to one, as his question, in the place of a folly.

But that most glorious experience is not ardently sought. Illusion itself, as the basis of man's usual image, means that to be undeceived in any one way, however small, threatens the sum of all delusions.

Men who became disillusioned about their divine otherness in nature, owing to Darwin's truth, bade farewell to God and eternal life in countless cases. Others moved the checkmated king into a limbo where they lip-served deity as a hedged bet. Still more men put their dimmer deity to work by new rules, in the service of progress and industry and of nations and races. In effect, they decided that what is good now for American industry, or for Britain, is good for God.

The men who had already taken apartments in the ivory tower city of science and those who increasingly rushed there also tried to concede some space to the inhabitants of the Kingdoms of Hereafter. Religion has a value, they said, looking down their noses; it gives men an ethos, a moral code. And well said, that, by those chaps who had eschewed morality to attain the new purity! Their old animal felt, though never saw, the necessity of a right-wrong system; and most scientists, in their version of the default, waved foolishly to the proponents of moral systems founded in fierce, ridiculous wishes.

Both sides gave some ground, shifted the rules, exchanged means of cheating.

The so-called conflict of religion and science thus appears to be lessening.

But that is not so.

There is no conflict. There is no possibility of conflict. The two territories are discrete, utterly different, and the inhabitants cannot communicate.

Why?

Because the two separate domains are imaginary. Neither is real. What is said inside either is not true talk; hence all cross-talk becomes twice nothing.

They come near to stating that fact, at times.

Faithful people speak of the "grounds of being," now.

Scientists, of "logical grounds."

Grounds. Territories. Where the uttermost boundaries never approach near enough to be discerned.

The people in the two realms will never be able to speak to one another unless they see how and why their two dominions are inventions and not correct. If and when they manage that—the greatest quantum jump so far demanded of the human psyche—they will be able to talk together. But at that point both territories will have been abandoned for the new one, that of man in and of nature.

The possibility of such an advance in human awareness has not existed till lately. For I do not consider the endless and semi-seeing intuitions of philosophers, poets, and other men of sufficient value to cite here as true discernment. The essential for that is not intuition but a solid, theoretical and experimental means to prove our true condition, our nature and that of Nature, so as to enable us to define a value system of the sort Sir Julian Huxley said we must contrive to do "somehow or other" to save ourselves from ourselves.

I have attempted to lead the reader to such a system.

Here, once again, is the idea:

Man's morality can have that name only if it is based on the eternal morality seen in other life forms, the morality that nature has decreed as absolute. Man must, to become moral, define good as that way of life which is dedicated altogether to human posterity. Whatever men do that diminishes the prospect of men unborn is evil, that way.

It's simple.

But men have never attempted to use any such criterion for morality.

Those who believe by faith have taken time-future of their species into their own possession, and robbed posterity of the energy and effort and birthright they stole to get to their artificial heavens, to evade their nightmare hells or, at least, to believe in God.

Their morality then became self-serving and in no way related to nature and its law.

They persist, as I said, because such a territorial seizure of time-future does lead to right-wrong systems, false, yet false or no, in a deep and unseen way, necessary for the animal instinct that rules man.

Modern religion tries to avoid even that proper task of the moral imperative. Tries to imagine an intellectual God without Satan or even, sometimes, without any place for the soul to go in a dreamed-up afterlife of mystical remix-in-God.

But such rarefied theology is still demonology, aware or no.

All deism is satanism.

For the minimal notion of God connotes a notion of meaning in existence. And meaning is conceivable only when it defines purpose, however vaguely descried. Where purpose is presumed, right and wrong arise as inevitable components. So, every idea of God is bound to produce its Devil, if only in the unconscious mind of the God-inventor.

If reason be the imagined and sole means to truth, sin appears as but illogic. Man's unreason and his demonic behavior must, then, to be set outside the tabernacle of reason-using men.

It becomes necessary to press imaginations into a new dimension to transcend both systems.

And when we do, those who still occupy one or the other are going to be appalled. For the kingdoms dreamed up by faith will vanish, along with the realms of reason as inviolable and free of moral requisite.

Man will then appear as he is, evolved, a single species, an experiment, an animal, instinct-ruled.

But a new kind:

A magical species.

One in which nature allowed its own imaginativeness to emerge. One wherein that gift has functioned only to the evolutionary reach of imagination is at last possible. An animal, in sum, that need no longer pervert his imagination for the historic and prehistoric ends. Man the magician can finally cease to be a sorcerer who believes his tricks are not that, but genuine; his faith, proof of miracle; his reason, of his moral nihilism.

To do those things he has used Black Magic for hiding himself from his trickery or hiding the trick from the clever prestidigitator.

White Magic, the use of imaginative reason to find his way back to nature and reality, is now at least conceivable as a true way to make images.

But if we employ it, what then?

Suppose we agree there is no afterlife and no god we can invent? That nature cannot be conquered?

Suppose we agree that instinct governs us as it does all life and our one morality must be based on future generations and their needs and potentials as we can assess and serve those in self-sacrifice?

Then we will be animals again, but true animals, not our libel of beasts as the savage ones.

Resurrected animals, we can become. Our values based on the eternal course and aim of instinct. Animals at last aware of the price demanded by nature for any and every violation of that one criterion of true good and real evil; not reasonable then, by any scientific limit.

Animals.

But image-makers, imaginative, and so, able if we will to imagine the realities of all being that we did not try to adduce, even when we were finally shocked by finding our animal place in nature.

Animals, now, who will know they are mortal. Know their only eternity is a hope that rests in the future of mankind. Animals who, however, if they imagined that much, that truly, could accept the implicit morality and begin to use their then-infinite magic as it is meant to be used, according to natural law, not man's bastard perversions of that.

But the hope of such imminent vision and reformation is slight.

So my answer to the question, What do you think of the world *now?* must at last be manifest: *not much.*

We have failed the experimental test of evolution, which we embody but abuse.

We but exploited our magic for present illusions of grandeur, a gift that was meant to enable us to become within nature what we have only pretended to be: the heirs of evolution who can take charge of that great work by taking control of man's own evolution for moral cause and by moral means. Having failed, we are become the terrible antagonists of nature. Our wickedness is as long as our span and as total as men have been able to make their acts through their self-inflating corruption of their monopoly of a new capacity, magic. The measureless power was snatched for self-enchantment and now that spell is near infinite, near universal, and doomful for that mean seizure and its two imagined territories designed by faith or by depersonalized "reason."

2 / The View from a Non-Pompous Head

To me, then, how the world seems is mad.

It has always seemed so, to me, as to many.

For though I have compassion for the efforts the believers by faith put forth in order to follow their multiple moralities, I believe their endeavors are futile.

And though I understand the main truths found by magic applications of wondrously invented logics in science, I am revolted by the failure of these equal wizards to measure or even be concerned with what lies outside their chosen, arbitrary, and monastic province, and likely, their tomb and ours.

Nobody, in sum, is acting in what must be a moral way for all doing, however imaginative.

Nobody is basing his life on his view of the needs of

human posterity. At best, effort in that direction is secondary or of a yet lower order, and there pursued with our provincial fantasies in corrupted dichotomies. No one keeps score. Score?

God does no miracles.

God does not violate natural law.

Nature cannot cheat, wherefore, cannot be cheated.

All reason is but man's, moral or no.

Our American goal is founded on the belief that we can conquer or at least control nature by reason, or owing to God's revelations, whichever, or both.

Yet a moment's honest reflection should show the idiocy of all such premises. Man cannot even hope to rule Nature. *Think!*

A cool sun not yet sighted by our astronomers may be about to loom into view and then seen on a collision course with the earth. Control or conquer that?

Anti-matter, some scattered rubble of it, may be on the way here. A scintillant night-array may commence in the sky as it encounters bits of our reversed-sign style of matter and in each meeting flashes pin-bright news of an annihilation. But suppose the mirror-image rubble is too massive to expire on the way here? Or to be erased by all the rockets we can hurl at it? Enough clotted debris to cause the earth to vanish. Possible, it seems, any time. What to do? Nature, only, but how will man save himself?

The sun need but enter a relatively unstable phase to wipe the earth bare of life, boiling away the seas, and the rocks, too. A mere jostle of its delicate balance, a bigger sunspot than any yet recorded, might occur, may have occurred before. What fire brigade have the nature-conquerors ready for such a trivial but lethal flare?

The earth is still hot and changing form. Let volcanoes again open and belch forth a not-inconceivable amount of gases (of a large number of possible compositions) and we will be unable to breathe the air, then. Even minor emission might add to our poisons a deadly surfeit.

One of the unknown but multitudinous hunks of errant matter in space might smash the moon upon us. Or bring a splatter of the sun's fierce-heated fluid into our vicinity, a little gobbet, a wisp, but enough to spell finis for man.

The ice age can return, and will, for all we know. It would alter man's circumstances for thousands of years if it did. But we could probably do nothing to prevent that, or even to halt its eradication of our major belts of civilization.

Some possible rearrangement of the massive and hot core of earth, some shift of its ambient currents, might tilt our globe and turn the temperate zones to polar positions. Our small planet seems to have been swiveled in such a way before, for whatever cause. And even a small tilt, if sudden, would bring all man's works down upon him.

A new bacterium or virus might arise owing to such gene-change as is constant in all life forms. It could be a sort that would reduce our species, in a season or two, to a hundredth of its present numbers. Or to zero. Science might not find a way to prevent that, in time, since it cannot prevent many known plagues, or even cancer, as of now.

Again. There was a star that exploded almost a thousand years ago; its gas and fragments, now called the Crab Nebula, are rushing across space toward us at a terrible speed. They will evidently reach us in a time but generation distant. And if they do, the collision, or its radiant energies, may eradicate all who exist in that near hour.

Other on-rushing and lethal spatterings of matter may bring other ends. What we discern as light, heat, and radio waves may not be all there is to find, oncoming, doomful, and even very close.

A nearby nova, like many stars we see explode into terrible brilliance at safe distances, may be projecting its radiation toward our solar system right now. That annihilating energy may arrive tomorrow, when we might then see the giant sunburst of a few years ago, for a moment and as a great, unbearable light, before we and our nation become red-hot, or white-hot, and the earth turned on to be scorched to death in that swing of the meridians. We cannot know what is that is a light-minute away or a radio-day from here.

Insects might suddenly evolve in kinds, and in decillions, and all resistant to every toxin we have or could quickly invent, and they might locust up the green world to a degree at which there was not enough plant life left extant—or perhaps merely not left green enough—to maintain the balance of oxygen and carbon dioxide we must have to exist.

Glassy tektites spattered widely, and in many ancient periods, suggest that big bodies have hit the earth before now. And that the blows reversed the magnetic poles. And, further, that in the demagnetized interval the sun's most terrible rays reached our planet's surface. With the apparent result that in all life forms great and swift evolutionary changes took place. Such an event could occur tomorrow and some who are doing research in this odd area think it is about due. If they are correct in these surmises, our genes may presently be exposed to rearrangement by radiation we cannot prevent and, as seems to have happened before, the shape of life will change. But how, exactly, could men fend against that?

Many readers will regard such sample calamities as unrelated to the definition of nature conquering. In their minds that term does not refer to what they see as "acts of God." Their opinion of man's great victories concerns acts of men—our lengthened life expectancy, other medical marvels, increased crop yields, pest control, our light-swift communications, and expedited travel. The technological cornucopia, in sum, certifies our mastery of the primeval.

But each such triumph was, in effect, gained over what till then had been an "act of God," a natural menace or impediment or misery in the uncivilized environ that technology banished, rendered manageable, or diminished as horror, handicap, peril, and hardship. The possible and uncontrollable circumstances I listed ought to show any sane reader the fallacy of our general trust in technology as able to control nature.

My sampling of what may seem like science-fiction lacks a specimen of yet another sort, one that is not fiction, but a dire certainty if we do not soon take proper charge of the causes. This is the long list of collision courses on which we knowingly race, Huxley's samples, that are of our own making and not even subject to rationalization as acts of God.

Many people believe the news of these homemade perils came yesterday. But the information was always available. Available in deserts of earth man fabricated to get the trees for charcoal to smelt iron, or to make ships, to burn and to build with. The datum is visible in tropical forests where prehistoric men burned out a space to plant with edible crops, and then abandoned quickly to burn out another, since the tropical duff, if stripped of trees, soon erodes into the rivers and so to the sea bottom. And that way of farming is continued.

In our century, learned men have repeatedly tried to tell you of this calamity wrought by the conquistadors of nature: William Vogt, for one, in his *Road to Survival* and Fairfield Osborn in *Our Plundered Planet*. Even I was publishing facts about the dearth and dirtiness of American water twenty years ago. Ecologists have tried to get your attention, and we few who listened have tried to interpret their truths in terms you could comprehend.

Only now, and a little, do you worry. But you manage to change the rules there, too, for easement of anxiety. The fact that people know of the perils, voters in myriads, congressmen in some instances, industrialists, supposedly, is taken to mean that remedial action will follow. That remedies are being designed, financed, put in effect, required by new laws, and so, good as done, or sure to be done.

What dreams men make, to pretend their clouds are so effortlessly dissipated! What reader, with such a dream, has even speculated on the sacrifices of comfort, convenience, affluence, and private goals that will be required of him for any true effort to end the present mangling of the earth environ, let alone to recover its lost quality in any way?

Present planning and acting does not embrace one hundredth of the order of magnitude of technological changes we must make, and make in this century, for assured survival only. Pure science, in fact, does not yet have sufficient data for all parts of this necessary effort to save ourselves from ourselves. Much more must be learned by hard, particular research in hundreds of areas where, at present, the smallest amount of investigation is being done because the smallest fraction of research funds goes into it—the gigantic area of biology. Biology not even including medicine.

Every week, if not every day, some new finding is made of some man-made harm, local and easily remedied, or general and not susceptible to simple or even known remedy. The people who, as infants, lived downwind from the Nevada bomb-testing grounds suddenly show an X-times-normal incidence of thyroid cancer owing, apparently, to radio-iodine they absorbed before open-air testing was stopped. Yesterday, there was a fifty-people collapse (and high death incidence) in one place in Canada and another in the U.S.A., owing to the use of cobalt to fix the foam in the beer those groups drank. The cause was soon found, in a sense: cobalt; but not why the small amount which made them deathly ill, or dead, had that effect only on those particular beer-drinkers.

Every day, every week, then, we find our present and presumably successful attack on nature has backfired in a new manner, while prior and known backfire is plain wherever men live in our nation.

To see such toll and such unknown but imminent toll as the cost of progress is to put a too-high price on alleged getting ahead. A price that will become beyond payment if we do not alter our values soon. But our thinking, there, is still of the conventional and mistaken sort: more technology will halt the dangerous side-effects of present technology.

In some cases, it may. In many, no. At best, technological additions to stop or decrease current and intolerable hazards from technological processes will raise costs of the products of those processes. At worst, such industrial endeavor will follow a Gresham's Law, multiplying machines and devices and processes to damp-down lethal side-effects of the going gear, thereby creating new hazards of kinds and violences not predictable till the multiplying gadgets are put in operation for enough years to reveal their nastiness.

Here, it is not out of place to note that our fundamental economic thesis concerning mass production is apparently in error. At first, it seemed that the techniques that have made us the relatively most affluent society in history would be ever more effective in that way. Mass production, we held, would cut costs, broaden markets, thereby raise income at all social levels, and so, lead to the Ever More Abundant Everyman. Economic and sociological statistics supported that idea, for a while.

But the truth is different. Even when we make adjustments for the decreased value of the dollar, it does not explain the rising cost of things. Better quality is given as one reason for that. Higher wages. But none of the textbooks quite shows why one could buy a new car in 1925 for a fifth of what one now costs. Or why mass-processed foods cost ten times the old amount yet often lack even a pretense of the old quality.

So there must be hidden or rarely published causes for that immense increase of the cost of the GNP to the consumer. I suggest that economists look into these following possible reasons for ever-rising prices, when, by their theology, mass production should have had the opposite result:

The population explosion, and, in the U.S.A., its doubling of potential demanders for every product;

The growing scarcity of raw materials and minerals used in production;

The result as added cost of reducing remaining, less-rich ores, and of the longer haul of such materials from still-rich sources that become more distant as nearer lodes are worked out, nearer forests are denuded, and fields are farmed out or obliterated for other uses;

The ever-greater need to import ever-larger quantities of raw materials and minerals needed in the ever-varied ingredients of the GNP but not available or producible in the U.S.A.;

And, perhaps, an ever-rising rate of profit-taking.

To project the GNP for any next generation, doubled in numbers, again, on a curve of rising expectations and rising affluence, an economist would need a great deal of vital information that not one of them seems to consider important —information probably few would understand or know to be relevant, or to exist, even.

The data of ecologists would have to enter such a graph. Data from a hundred other biological disciplines, a hundred chemical fields, and as many special branches of other physical and natural sciences. I am sure economists fail to use such data in their projections because they do not even ask sensible questions in such areas, or any questions.

Yet our nation relies on economists, along with their equally unscientific colleagues, the social and political "scientists," for every major projection in which American industrial planning is based.

But at least one economist, John Kenneth Galbraith, in his book, *The New Industrial State*, has faulted our society and technology in another way. It is a wonder that spectacular flaw had not been descried sooner.

To manufacture the goods that stand for our affluence, he points out, industry must plan ahead. What we will be offered in five years, in ten, must first go on the drawing boards and next, be made as mock-up and model for testing. After that, the machines to turn out these products must be designed, built, tested, and fabricated in sufficient numbers. With that, Galbraith notes, what was economics is no more. For the cost of such planning and preparation cannot be sustained by a competitive society; and the risk involved cannot permit the buyer to prevail. What we will be offered as the GNP in three years, five, or even ten, will necessarily be what industry has estimated, by surveys, polls, and shrewd psychological inquiry, *what we can be made to think we want* in our future.

So the need of industry to plan ahead has, by its very nature, shelved the old economy and turned most of us into managed consumers, pretested to discern what advertising and publicity can cause us to think we want, and to buy, that industry has decided it can sell us in years ahead. The laws of marketing have been rescinded by that. We are buyers in a rigged market which our wants and needs no longer determine but are as much fabricated as the GNP.

And since the earth's crust cannot long sustain even the current rate of industrial productivity, the question will increasingly become: Who gets how much of what?

We are, even at this moment, deciding that millions in India, millions in Latin America and elsewhere won't get enough to eat to be well, or even to live.

But the underlying cause of such horror hasn't been faced here even in respect to this one matter of famine. We have not reached the decision that Americans must limit their own people-production if they are even to hope for effective limitation anywhere else. That necessity of example is not being contemplated, partly owing to the fact that the right to breed is still regarded as implicit in American liberty and the notion that breeding is a religious mandate—one held by fifty to a hundred million American citizens of or near breeding age.

If, however, we do realize we cannot hypocritically urge and abet birth control elsewhere unless we practice it here, illusions about liberty or God to the contrary notwithstanding, we will then be faced by the next, ancillary, yet sure question: Who, when reproduction is limited, will be allowed to reproduce?

A rational and just system of population control will require an imposed quota system. And quota will connote assignment. For a limited reproduction will have to relate to all, and when that is seen, it will be clear that no nation can sanely let all its citizens reproduce the same limited number of offspring per married pair and per unwed couple.

Genetic regulations will be seen essential at that point.

These currently seem not merely contrary to multitudes of religious beliefs, but unfree, unjust, and individually unacceptable. In some minds, moreover, including those of some scientists, genetic criteria are held not subject to scientific definition.

There, again, one sees how any rational effort of self-management of man can be assaulted by informed-seeming but territorially bound specialists. How irrational their claims become can then be descried, and the exposition provides another illustration of the deluded ideas even trained men hold, where managing reality or nature in their own is involved.

The main arguments against trying to sustain our gene pool by breeding laws are two.

First, that superiority of a breed cannot be achieved in any over-all sense. To breed one improved attribute is to lose some other, equivalent value: the dog bred for keener smell becomes slower, or less acute visually, and so on.

That may be true, although a long and careful study

of many hundreds of people who exhibited superior intelligence in their youth and who have been followed into middle age reveals that they are bigger, stronger, better looking, less subject to mental illness, physically more healthful, longer-lived, more stable, better paid, contract better marriages, and have children of a similar, all-around superiority, compared to the equally studied control group of average-intelligence people.

However, the argument of genetic loss for a bred-advantage is irrelevant. Genetic management of man need not aim at producing special people, super-thinkers, super-athletes or super-anything. It would aim to produce, merely, a population of more normal persons, or of increasingly less abnormal, subnormal, and defective persons. That would not require the limitation of mating to superior males and females. But it would forbid the current and massive mating of genetic defectives. For, even to breed plain dogs on a basis of mere dog-viability, mere wholeness of form and of intact function, puppy runts and culls must be disposed of or at least rendered sterile.

The minute we, or any nation, effectively undertake population control, it will be seen that limited breeding must include means to inhibit the present, unchecked reproduction and rearing-to-breeding-age of human runts and culls.

Yet there is, currently, a self-styled scientific argument ever against that need—obvious though it is to any animal raiser or even to any observant gardener.

Persons with defective genes, it is known, may have some compensation for their liability. Groups of people who inherit a strain of sickle-cell anemia, for example, have a greater resistance to malaria than those without the gene-blemish. There may be other proven instances of such advantages as that demonstrable (if inexplicable and unpredictable) asset accompanying a defective gene, or several such flawed genes.

Here, however, the salient truth is, again, evaded by the opponents of gene-pool control. To get the extra resistance to malaria that somehow accompanies the sickle-cell anemia defect, the causal gene must exist as a recessive entity in the individual's gene structure. That is, a son must inherit the dangerous-advantageous gene from one parent only, not from both. And from a family line, in keeping. Defective genes are usually recessive. But if a given embryo has received in ovum and from sperm, a pair of like recessive genes, then, the defect they cause will afflict the individual at a statistically unacceptable rate and it will be handed on if he or she lives to have offspring.

In the matter of sickle-cell anemia, the inheritor of two such genes will exhibit the disease and die of it. He will hand it on if he lives to reproduce—hand it on as recessive, perhaps, depending on the sexual partner. But nobody wants to be born with the sickle-cell anemia death sentence. Nobody wants to be born with any of the known hundreds of genetic defects that cause that many human horrors and deaths, already known and those as yet unfound. Even if such faulty heritage can be surgically remedied, or improved, and inherited ills can be medically controlled, those now commonplace procedures do not affect the passing on of genetic woe.

Thus even if it should prove true that many, or all, defective genes provide some peculiar advantage to those who are born with them, so long as they are recessive in such individuals, the application of that fact in a birth-limiting population would be necessary and would involve an enormous and exacting control of mating. For in that case, any male and female desiring a child would have to be gene-screened in a degree not now even possible to make sure that neither would-be partner had the same flawed but advantageous *recessive* gene, so as to ensure their offspring would be free of the horror of the blight therein contained and so doomed to their own and future biological disaster, whatever the advantage would have been.

Both so-called scientific claims used to oppose any thought of genetic screening prior to permission to have children turn out on scrutiny to be more proof that genetic compatibility will be an absolute necessity at whatever degree is feasible, after birth limits are set.

Thus, again, we can see how a sensible effort to limit population will give rise to the need to manage—as much, and as far as man can, by law and by tests and enforcement according to their results—the simple matter of which of us may mate with which, and which may not with some, and which may not at all.

Few contemporary people are able even to think of man in such terms. Our present and vast technical ability to salvage all sorts of genetic culls is regarded as one more splendid evidence of victory over nature. It is, actually, evidence of our increasing defeat by nature, since we use it not to keep our genes as normal as possible, but to permit a rising incidence of genetic decay.

If some of the geneticists make such illogical and mistaken inferences as I've noted from their data, how can we expect laymen to interpret them?

Laymen, who have not yet even acknowledged the fact that a nation can do nothing decent about overbreeding abroad until it has shown the way at home. Laymen who have not yet dreamed of the fact that man must choose mates by reason or else be pruned as a heedless swarm, by genetic laws we already know but do not plan to apply even to maintain average men?

No voluntary gene control system will work, since the last breeders to volunteer self-limitation will be the least able to grasp the need and learn the means, owing to their intellectual disablement by religious dogma, to an already low level of inherited intelligence, to impoverished despair, to all three, or to any pair.

Genetic control is essential not for breeding super-people, but to halt the present genetic decline in every national population.

These truths add up as a current and unforgivable contempt for the very bodily and mental rights of our own posterity.

The whole matter again connotes that technology seen as means to nature-conquest is a false view. All it does as we apply it in breeding and the salvage of culls, and to industry, is to create a condition of human eutrophy. Our artificial species overproduction and our goods productivity push us toward a condition so lush it will ruin its environ and then, itself, rot the agent, mankind, in a surrounding of putrescence, its own, and that of the other life forms it will have destroyed by merely becoming too many for their survival, also.

The truth is stark and gem-clear.

How do we react?

Are we ready to reduce our own numbers simply to go on having what we possess, or will be made to?

What does management say here? The bosses of technology? The demand-makers?

3 / Industry's Mirror: Image of an Image

It is difficult for a knowledgeable man, these days, to look at any mass medium without revulsion.

For that which interests most of us, our fountainhead of affluence, industry, has taken charge of these media, as Galbraith revealed. The sponsor determines what we see on TV, mainly, and so, indirectly, what we don't see. Often, however, the sponsor's interest actually determines what's censored; for he pays the bills of TV and radio.

The same covert control is exercised over mass circulation magazines and newspapers. Advertisers hold innumerable swords at editorial throats; without advertisers there would be no mass magazines and no jobs for editors, either. Newspapers used to be, at least in some cases, independent. Their editorial policies were often at variance with or contrary to the planned purpose, prejudices, and pretenses of their advertisers. Now, however, newspaper publishing has itself become big business and that primarily.

Some faint charade is made by the press to appear free, still. Some is made by some magazines, also. But a man whose professional life involves the communications media knows how near-to-completely business-as-end has taken them over. Even book publishers, the last redoubts of free expression, are becoming big industries too, and trying to publish what sells, in the main.

Neither free enterprise nor the profit motive, as theory, is the object of this criticism. But profit as the sole motive for any business is not a sufficient aim. Mass media operated for gain above all other purposes are contemptible. News then is but show business and truth becomes only that part which attracts more customers, listeners, or viewers. Where industry has the power to censor mass media and to use them as an advertising underground, let alone to own them, all hope for a properly informed electorate vanishes. And what is called managed news is no news or lies, often.

But it is claimed that TV has made a greater number of Americans better acquainted with more truth than they were in pre-TV days. Nothing could be less correct. More people doubtless have a slanted half-glimpse of more events, ideas, so-called scientific marvels, the faces and voices of prominent people and so on, then they had before. But fewer than ever have any background for appraising these unrelated, unevaluated, and random bits. Time was when a Vanderbilt caused public outrage by allegedly exclaiming, "The public be damned!" Today, damnation is universal and the public either does not know it or, if it knows, takes damnation for granted.

Industry now presents an "image" and nobody says it's only that. Nobody laughs. Real knowledge is so rare, indeed, that not many persons can spot fraud in the fakery though it appears in four-color advertisements. For example, the lumber interests are using pretty pictures and rapturous texts to report that, where they cut forests, they are replanting trees, by helicopter—indeed, growing more timber than they fell. Doing more good than harm is the inference. Nothing is said about what else they destroy that cannot be replaced by them, or by anybody.

America can raise all its needed lumber, maybe. But what happens in cut-over regions while the seedlings take root and start growing into trees worth logging?

Rains fall in the long, barren years. Winds blow. In summer the dust flies. Winter comes. Ice solidifies in depths of duff, rich humus, subsoil, and the cracks of rock. Ice chops up all these and the freshets of spring then carry the riches away. No true forest remains to hold the fertile base. In such man-fashioned barrens, the ecology is wrecked. Ten thousand life forms, or a hundred thousand, lose their habitat and move on or perish. The potential of the replanted forest land to sustain new trees, mere groves of one kind or a few kinds, is thus a net loss of incalculable degree.

What is lost, nobody can fully reckon. Only a part of that national deficit can be guessed. The forest soil rides muddy torrents to the sea. Urban areas down-river experience floods unknown when the virgin trees and the environ they built held back the seasonal rains and loosed it gradually in drier times. The cut trees spent millenniums to make soil. Those that are seeded will be allowed to reach board size only. Redwoods, these lumberers tell us, for example, grow quickly; they reach commercial size in sixty years or less. But commercial size is not ecology-restoring size.

The work done by ancient forests to create man's environment and keep it livable cannot be done by trees planted as crops. Man suffers a universal loss and irreparable damage when he turns a forest into stumps and mere seedlings. His air is not any longer processed in the same volume by the new groves. His rainfall is diminished by the many-times-lessened transpiration of small trees and by the ruin of the old water-storage system. The organisms that were turning the vast annual debris of the original forest to soil and plant nutrients are reduced, or gone utterly with the erosion of their sustenance.

And if we look at this same reality from my concept of morals we can perceive yet another feature of the shame.

I tried once to explain it in an article but not with much success.

Everywhere in nature there are ecosystems and ecological niches, regions both immense and tiny, in which exist interdependent multitudes of life forms and many peculiar to that place in that they can exist nowhere else. These worlds within worlds evolved over thousands or even millions of years by adaptation of their life forms to that one kind of region, great or tiny, and to each other, there, as territorial owners.

Some ecosystems are county sized, even as large as a state or several states. Many are very small: a few square miles. And many are smaller still, such as some in Hawaii where one species of a plant thrives in a spot the size of an executive desk but cannot live in any other place. These little and unique niches also abound inside greater ecological dominions; and a man with a bulldozer can annihilate a dozen of them in a day.

What matter?

Each niche by definition contains species found nowhere else on earth. But such a fact impresses no average man today.

That man, godly, or merely pragmatic and a nature conqueror in his view, believes life that cannot be exploited for profit is worthless.

Call him an omni-predator.

A holocide.

The creature who has so contorted instinct and reason that he now has but one limitlessly aggressive criterion for all the rest of his planet's life.

Every animal he cannot domesticate or trap for fur or use to make money somehow, man calls wild. It is vermin. Banish it!

And every plant he cannot eat, or get some industrial juice out of, or sell as seed, nut, root, or leaf to smoke, and so on, man calls a wild flower, if it's not too near his premises, and, if it's near, a weed. Kill it.

Many animals have damaged some feature of their environ by necessary acts that were only incidentally the cause of deprivation to other life forms. But when any such lethal act renders their environ too poor to support them, they have moved on or perished.

But no animal, till we evolved, has had the imagination and a concomitant moral perversion to kill all species, or any, merely because they were in that animal's way, or because they annoyed it, or because it feared other animals as an urban-dweller, or, may cosmos forgive us, for fun.

My point about our daily despoliation of hundreds of irreplaceable niches was, simply, that when one is gone, whatever future value to all men it might have had is now forever lost as humanity's potential wealth.

I tried to illustrate. If, I said, lumbering interests had wiped out the cinchona tree before men had found its bark contained quinine, and used that to treat malaria, we might still be ridden with that mass executioner of men.

And if the baking industry, in its constant war against bread-ruining molds, had managed to exterminate just one species before Sir Alexander Fleming happened to notice its exudate killed bacteria, we might still be without antibiotics.

A thousand examples could be added here to show how some single species of plant or a particular animal organism led scientists to the way to present mankind with one of our majestic boons, and one that could have come in no other manner.

But when that (far-more-abundantly illustrated) statement was printed, another authority, a pharmacist, refuted it in a later issue of the same publication. He explained that the medicines, wonder drugs, and other chemical marvels I had noted as found owing to the study of a single species were not even used as first seen in nature. They had been replaced by synthetic, and often better varieties, of the original material, he said.

I suppose his statement made me seem an idiot to the usual reader. It was true. But what the pharmacist overlooked was the fact that the synthetic substitutes would never have been dreamed of if the natural precursor had not existed and its use been learned then.

What I'd intended to show about ecological niches and their unique inhabitants, from virus to redwood trees, was only this: each time we eradicate one we wipe out a potential for future mankind of a magnitude we do not know but one we can reckon, accurately enough for caution, from what single species have already taught us.

We will never know what value might have existed in what we have exterminated—only that, in such niches as a whole, fabulous marvels will surely be found if they remain intact for future study. The idea is, evidently, not only unacceptable to industry and business but not even comprehensible to the average educated American.

So we forge ahead with real estate developments, highway and reservoir construction, flood control that turns rivers into chutes and leaves their banks a barren shingle, lumbering, farming, animal husbandry and everything else we do to reshape the natural environs, without the slightest regard for what we destroy, which no man can ever replace, but all men would surely benefit from had the niches been preserved.

We could know, and should, how our crude ruin of the treasures of ecology robs our posterity of irreplaceable wealth. We don't want to know, however. We try, like that pharmacist, to disbelieve the truth, and go ahead with acts of annihilation. One square yard of habitat under one stand of trees might be worth billions of dollars, fifty years from now. Cut the trees and the value will not exist; those who lack it will never know their loss—save as rueful generality about all we took from them in our stupid folly and greedy contempt.

In my state, Florida, thousands of those niches have been bulldozed, dynamited, scraped up, and abolished by machines. In your state, too. Why? To make a few paltry thousands of profit, any sleazy parking-lot impresario or trailer-camp promoter can steal possible billions from all men yet to be, and myriads do it, daily, everywhere.

So when the lumbermen boast that they are replacing what eternity created, with seeded stump-lands, they are deceiving man, and perhaps themselves, too, if they can be so close to life yet so ignorant as to commit thefts too great to estimate. But how false is their "image."

Another illustration of corporate image-making comes from the final line of a speech delivered to close a conference of petroleum moguls and their hired scientists on pollution. It was quoted in a national newsmagazine. After days of considering petrochemical duty or need, in respect to its violent ruin of the earth, the man summarized the attitude of his oil-oligarch colleagues thus:

"Industry must not be stifled in our quest to improve the environment."

That jewel of industrial utterance is remarkable for its perfection, as diamond in seeming and paste in fact.

One's first reaction, providing one is sane, is laughter. If industry mustn't be stifled in any way by efforts to deal with pollution, then who will be stifled? People, obviously. You and I and everybody else who hasn't the private fortune of the top oil people that enables them to buy country acres for home sites.

But one should also note the subtler hypocrisy in the sentence. The conclave was held to consider what to do about the catastrophic condition of American air and water, here stated as "our quest."

A phrase suggesting the speaker and his associates had really made such an effort in spite of the rest of the sentence. But had made it as if the desperate situation called only for a quest, a seeking, with no finding demanded, or necessarily to be expected.

And even in that feeble-minded frame of reference, the quest was said to be aimed simply to improve the environment, dodging, with that phrase, then, the last shred of sane purpose. For we are not trying to improve our environment, but to recover it or at least to alter it so as to keep it viable. This need involves no quest but a compulsory achievement by whatever violence of industrial "stifling" may be mandatory.

I doubt, though not with any supporting evidence save the internal sort, that the president or board chairman who wound up that conference with those words was their author. I suspect the sentence was constructed after hard labor by writers talented at image-making, with, perhaps, the help of motivational psychologists and other experts in mass deception.

Yet how many who read the sentence in that powerful magazine stopped to note that it was a complete disavowal of what it pretended to proclaim? How many of the magazine editors noticed? And if some saw, why didn't they point out that those few words represented a naked rejection of any intent to end pollution in the great petroleum industry?

The weasel words of industry, of lumbering, of oil, and of nearly every great corporation are samples of the images most Americans regard as rightful and their media of mass communication worship.

If every advertised quote and broadcast image and claim were measured by the value scale I've used here (and every one should be, of course), very few would much increase sales and many would result in a public assault upon the product and corporation guilty of image-making, a false act by the very term.

You may or may not have perceived, however, that such shrewd and informed appraisal is nearly impossible. For how does one find the truth so patently hidden by these barefaced images?

Those publishers of books, large companies and small, who do refuse to consider profit their first aim are penalized. Bigness pays and big dividends to stockholders pay, too. Magazines with editorial policies devoted to a true and balanced account of all matters of interest don't get the advertising money or the circulation of the mass-circulation journals. Industry prefers to advertise in media that support industry with great enthusiasm and little or no adverse criticism, however urgently needed.

Many other "interests" in America have also used their power to jam the wheels of freedom for mass media. I once conducted an experiment to detect the nature of editorial taboos in American newspapers by writing a syndicated column. It appeared in some thirty leading newspapers. But since I wrote my columns without let, fear of, or regard for anything but facts and my opinions, I lost papers as fast as my syndicate salesman could find new clients for my usually indignant essays. The multitudes of cancellations made it very evident that the press, as a general rule, is not willing to print an attack, however justified, or reproof, however factual, if it relates to business or to religion, or if it is a critique of contemporary sex morals, sex ideas, and our medieval sex laws.

To name a religious body, the Catholic church, and, perhaps especially, that of Christian Science, in any disparaging way isn't allowed, as a rule. Religious organizations have powerful members who are ready to pull their advertising from such an offending paper, or other medium, in punishment for an exercise of liberty that reveals, as I tried to, how they hamper the liberties of all by insisting we conform to their rites, their special ideas of "natural law," their sick fantasies of what is "moral" in sexual behavior, or even the "right" to reject for themselves and their helpless offspring medical therapy known to be correct and, in the case of some special true believers, withheld in God's name at terrible cost to adults, and children, also.

When we say America has a free press, we do not say that the major media use their freedom in its full and necessary extent. The image of our media turns out, on such scrutiny, to be cowardly and unfree in a very great though not inclusive degree. To make the most profit, the media, in their mass-circulation or mass-viewed forms, either foster industry's synthetic image, or remain silent about the rot, mess, lies, human debasement, and the best of the unfavorable truth hid behind the idol. They go along, too, with the support, at least by silence, of pious interference with liberty.

But when one puts forward that accusation, one is usually told that not only do Americans have the right to believe in whatever religion they wish, or have wished on them in childhood, but that it is cruel, wanton, or at least meddlesome of a man even to want to disturb a coded faith that gives so many so much comfort.

Such answers beg my question. As a free American, I readily grant the right of my fellow citizens to all the comfort they can find in any belief, religious, magical, or faith in flying saucers. But I feel they also have a duty to be informed enough to vote and to act in ways the current knowledge of truth demands, for self-government. I am opposed to all ballot by superstition. And when believers act to hamper my freedom, or that of anyone else, I claim the duty, as a mandate of our constitution, to try to reveal the dirty deed that such ruthless minorities foist on majorities in the name of freedom of belief—which has nothing to do with public acts. When dogmatic believers make their comforting fantasy my limit to speak, or act, or yours, by their public and imposed will, then I say their comfort has made them unAmerican and their acts must be stopped in liberty's name.

The image of industry is, of course, pro-technological. Impositions of religious image by law, or blackmail of media, are different in motive but similar in effect since they tend to espouse scientific ignorance in support of some ancient or antiscientific notion. Technology as the exploitation of science to provide goods is acceptable there; but insight into pure science is often deemed hostile to creed, and rightly, for it is frequently the nemesis of creed.

The net result, as those two great forces act to form a false image of known reality, is appalling. Moreover, as most of us are living in urban, suburban, or slurban areas, on a tiny fraction of the nation's area, we are out of touch with nature. Young Americans, most city-born and reared, and soon to be the majority, will, therefore, in general, have no concept of the reality on which all of us forever depend. They will not even have any way to imagine it, or think of it rationally. Their urban, technological world will seem reality, and a fence against nature, their unknown. They will not ask right questions.

Where do their clothes come from? (Shops and mills.)

Whence their food? (Stores and supermarkets.)

Does coal, gas, oil, or the splitting of atoms provide the current when they switch on their air conditioner and start the blender whizzing? Or is it Niagara Falls they're using? Or, perhaps, water stocked in some reservoir that is silting up rapidly behind a giant dam the Army Engineers built at an unimaginable cost to taxpayers, to man to be, and to the ecology now drowned?

They don't know.

Where does their trash go when it drops from their hands into the apartment house chute?

When they wash their faces, and flush their toilets, how does that detergent-polluted or fecal surge finally return to the source of all water?

How many trees went down and how much land was left naked, to make their plywood boat and its metal fixtures?

What goes into a windowpane and where is it obtained?

What are the natural components of the packaging in supermarkets?

Of what is a cement block made? A rubber tire? A synthetic rubber tire? Where is the origin of these?

What's a carton?

Where do we get aluminum?

What's in stainless steel?

They don't know, these city-blinded technophiles. Don't

even wonder. They assume others manage all that, and the supplies are infinite. Our very economy rests on the assumption that, in effect, our goods-sources are as infinite as our image of God.

The assumption is so false that one wonders how any human beings can make it outside insane asylums.

When I walk about or drive through or fly over your world, however, I do not see progress so much as I see an endless cemetery. Every skyscraper, highway, suburb, car, truck, and man-made thing is, to me, a corpse and corpse-maker. What progress the scene appears to exhibit was managed by a retrogression in nature and an irrecoverable loss of man's wealth.

And in this partial view I have looked only at objects, and your way of seeing them that is in error.

4 / Crowds in Collision

One universal aspect of the territorial imperative is the result of local overcrowding by such a species in any one area, a matter mentioned earlier.

Overcrowding is, of itself, dangerous.

Each individual of a territorial kind requires a certain area for survival; and its minimum is not defined by physical need. As I have speculated, that irreversible imperative perhaps relates to the need of many species for survival, even at the cost of local self-extinction of the too-crowded sort.

Whatever the reason, the fact has been proven.

Man, being a territorial creature, must also have such a minimal per capita room-equipment.

That thought seems, on its surface, not very tenable.

In civilized history men have repeatedly been crammed into cities and city-states for centuries on end.

Asia and the Orient have teemed with people for millenniums.

And in our country, accelerated crowding-up is the dominant way of life. Nine-tenths of us live in a fifth of the national space, and that ratio rises yearly.

Aren't we all right?

There's some scattered doubt about that question now.

It seems plain that crowding increases crime. And raises the level of nervous disease.

Last year, a picked group of medical men and women held a conference on that matter, a crowding-effect they termed "mental pollution."

But (again) from my viewpoint of man as part of nature, I suggest that other and different evidence might at least usefully be examined, by those competent to do so, in the light of possible relationships to territorial over-crowding by us.

Such extrapolation can give rise to rather horrendous ideas. And they should be checked if only because they are so shocking.

For instance:

The cost, in death and crippling, of the American auto-mobile is so great and grisly as not to be acceptable by any rational person. To kill half a hundred thousand of our-selves annually, and permanently maim a million or so—just to use cars and trucks—is to do something no human being who cherishes human life as we pretend we do could possibly allow for any presumed gain or end save victory in genuinely defensive war.

But the car is already a bigger killer than our wars have been.

Why we sustain such massacre is therefore a most im-portant and obvious question—yet one rarely even asked in that frame of reference.

To hold our mayhem-murder factor to sensible levels would wreck the economy, which may be one reason for our lack of interest in the query. We would have to make cars crashworthy, a fact Nader used to rock the automotive industry. But we would also have to screen all persons who propose to drive cars for capability, emotional stability, drug use, reflexes, law knowledge, understanding of road rules, age competence, vision, hearing, bodily integrity, and many other human factors.

For it is perfectly evident that of all persons now operat-ing motor vehicles, at least half do not or cannot drive well enough to be allowed to. Any even moderately sane screening of all drivers would oblige that half either to take an elaborate training they have not had or, for half of them and at least a quarter of all present operators, to give up driving for good.

That, of course, would ruin the automotive industry, the oil industry, and others relevant, since the abrupt drop of twenty-five percent of vehicle-users and/or buyers would not be supportable under the current economic system.

So, in one manner, we support our bloody traffic to keep the economy of the land going at its present pace.

Removing drivers who shouldn't be allowed behind the wheel would cause instant depression.

Still, is not depression better than an infinite graveyard and a million-per-year increase of mangled, crippled, wheelchair casualties?

So, why do we fear the unbearable?

I suggest that our lethal love affair with the automobile is the result of territorial overcrowding.

The automotive havoc is greatest in and around cities where, also, the crowding is greatest.

A car gives the man who drives it and those who are its passengers a new sense of territorial potential. With it, a man need not feel jammed inside his populous flat, up against his suburban neighbor, or touching others on the thickly peopled streets and in offices and stores.

I suspect the curve showing our movement from thinly populated regions to congested or urban areas would parallel a curve showing the rise of automobile production.

And if that is more or less correct, my thesis may be, too. The passion for a private vehicle has made mass transportation falter and collapse, where most needed to relieve downtown and feeder-highway congestion. Is that owing to the instinctual drive of a territorial animal, man, who cannot tolerate his ever-tighter packing in small areas without some means of instinctual redress? A bus or a train won't do for that since they are crowded, like his city.

But in a car, his own, with whatever actual inconvenience and inefficiency, he can seem to have a space he may need to exist at all, as he commutes on however overburdened a road to his work, and as he or she shops, makes social visits, plays games, and the rest.

Only some invisible instinct, of that order of magnitude of power, I feel sure, can explain our otherwise incomprehensible toleration of the death-mangling cost of cars.

However, even if my surmise be someday authenticated, that explanation of an irrational act will still seem, itself, irrational. For the cost of cars in money, material waste, mayhem, and death, then seen as payment for crowd-escape, will still relate to illusion. The more cars we use, the less effective they are, even as space-providers assumed the result of ineluctable, instinctual demands.

And our price for that deluded end lowers other values.

For example, I still hear my fellow Americans proclaim how "cheap" life is, in Asia, or in Latin America, or some other distant and people-swarmed region.

They have no right to the assertion.

Life is cheaper on the American highways and streets than anywhere in the world, save similar places where people pay the same ghoulish toll for cars: other technological societies, nature-vanquishing nations, city-living and car-using to our degree.

Of course, in all things, abundance decreases esteem.

That is as true of general life-evaluation, in cities, as it is on auto-crowded roads.

Because we have doubled our numbers in my lifetime, we have, in some not-yet-defined way, halved our sense of the worth of people.

If we become, as we expect to, twice as many in the next thirty years, we shall hold human life as of only a quarter the worth it had when I was a child.

And I would think the curve showing the rise of car-killing and car-mutilation followed that hypothetical graph of decline in man's value of living.

It may be that all history supports in a strange way the idea that man cannot tolerate overcrowding any more than other territorial animals are able to do so.

History has never been contemplated from that ethological viewpoint but perhaps it ought to be.

One immediate datum is clear. No civilization has managed to persist for more than about thirty human generations. Man, more adaptable than other animals, may have a longer time span for crowding-accommodation. With his imagination, his unique ability to use time as a territorial dimension of an imagined sort, perhaps he can use that to postpone the consequences of overcrowding, for a while.

But isn't it conceivable that, whenever a civilization reached such an overcrowded condition that the imagination of its inhabitants failed to sustain even an illusion of tolerability, his society collapsed for that biological cause?

His city-state was too crowded. He had armies compressed in legions of a density unbearable for any long term. He reached a compaction beyond which he could not capture other regions by conquest. Maybe he was no longer able to find a drive for grabbing space; perhaps could invent no added palliatives and illusory remedies for his state. He began, then, to be "decadent."

To consume, in his present, the wealth and the technological artifacts he had, up to then, been busy amassing and increasing while he was extending his realm. The religious belief, by which he had come to assemble, and under which he had established his empire or republic (as is the case in all civilized beginnings and rises) now ceased to give him additional illusions. The old and productive images had reached their limits as agents of progress. He began to disobey, rather than improve or "modernize," the right-wrong code, whatever it was. He then was oriented neither toward some route to eternal life after death, nor to his prior aim of conquering nature, here, by the conquest of other peoples, civilized or barbarous, for more space. Either way, he commenced to live in a materialist now.

And that was the end.

Toynbee's great design of the burgeoning, rise, zenith, and fall of all past civilizations is not, of course, accepted by all historians. Herbert Muller argued with it, as have many others. But there was a visible cycle in the story, a psychological implication of Toynbee's thesis. A yang-yin concept (that Jung, for example, might have given great and lucid definition) is historically undeniable, however explained.

Ethology may now, perhaps, offer a description of history that is accurate.

All past civilizations failed. All reached conditions of crowding that, for the technology and the understanding of people, at the time, may have caused such collapse as is routinely observed in groups of territorial species suffering from comparable circumstance.

Technology, of course, enables (or would seem to enable) men to increase both their density and the time span of toleration for increment. But there has never been a way to advance technology and the congestion it demands over an unending period. It seems that may still be true and the collapse point may be near in spite of the immense advance of technological processes.

Technology perhaps became a direct factor in the ruin of crowded cultures, too. We hear, for example, that Rome may have faltered because its leaders and rulers, its upper classes, used leaden vessels and lead pipes. Their found bones show signs of lead poisoning. Technology thus may have slain Rome's brain trust. Slaves and lesser citizens lacked lead-pipe plumbing and used pottery plates and pitchers.

We Americans will show, and far more generally, various grievous substances in our bones too—all, the fruit of technological progress, for weaponeering or industry.

It seems to me that somebody besides selected members of the American Medical Association ought to begin studying the phenomenon of overcrowding, as "mental pollution" and as bone poison, too, in relation to discovered ethological laws that reveal the certain fate of other creatures, like men in overswarmed territories.

Scholars who contemplated the cyclical rise and fall of man's cultures from an ethological viewpoint might find still another relevant datum about overcrowding by an obverse method. Our species has endured over long periods where it has not been urban and compacted. Where cities have not risen, or did not attract the populace that remained stable. Where armies were not massed, or slaves taken in throngs to congested capitals.

In China and India, city cultures rose and fell as countless hordes conquered and destroyed them, rebuilt, flourished, and decayed. But in those immense lands, *villages persisted for thousands of years, unchanged.*

To fly from Calcutta to Benares is to behold their size and arrangement, which have not altered for millenniums. A half dozen clusters of huts are spread around a somewhat larger village and connected to it only by footpath or track for beasts of burden. Each such cluster is bordered by like sets of neighboring villages, all connected with slightly more prominent trails. And that pattern stretches for hundreds of miles. India has half a million of these villages and though armies were levied from them, and slaves taken in them, the changing city rulers did not alter the village patterns, the perfect design, perhaps, for survival through biomathematical distribution.

The conquerors and rulers wanted the cities, forts, seaports, and big centers of people; there, the dynasties rose and withered, the invaders came and ruined cities only to build metropolises on the rubble. In time's proper scale, they, too, soon vanished beneath ruins.

Those abiding villages have a design that suggests a management of human density, arrived at by prehistoric trial and error surely, but maintained in ecological stability, by natural processes, infant death, famine, disease, the Malthusian control that prevented an increase of thin-spread peoples to a point of general collapse by killing off the excess. But in city-states, immigrants or slaves frustrated such control.

In many regions, North America for one, and for another, Australia, a meager population existed at an evidently stable level for fifteen or twenty thousand years. When Columbus reached our shores there were no more than two million Indians in the land, from the Rio Grande to Hudson Bay. There had been such a number, or even one smaller, in that region, for ten or twenty times the period that any city society has managed to endure without collapse.

But south of there, in Central America and Peru, fantastic congregations of peoples built tremendous cities (or, perhaps, not cities in our sense but religious and governing centers)

—Incas, and pre-Incan societies, Mayans, Aztecs, or Toltecs and the rest. All vanished. Amongst Mayans, collapse seems to have been as sudden as that of massive suicide in an overcrowded society of lemmings.

There is, in sum, a great deal of as-yet unexamined evidence to suggest that men are territorial animals, because they obey territorial law, including the law that forbids territorial overcrowding. Opponents of ethological theory, whether their motive is to defend religion or reject any theory of human instinct, may here find another cliff of fact they cannot scale.

Certainly, nothing that historians, anthropologists or archaeologists have suggested so far seems to explain such events and circumstances as I've outlined. But the ethological findings that demonstrate instinct and its compulsory effect in territorial species do, indeed, offer a force strong enough, innate enough, and invisible enough (till now!) to clarify innumerable puzzles about man's past, and, of course, to furnish in addition a terrible suggestion about our present.

The speculations (and, perhaps, logical inferences) to be drawn from ethology in reference to man are numberless and will appear as better imaginations than mine use the new science.

Here is another. Men are now just starting to explore space. Our own concentration of skills, industry, money, and productive capacity on the effort may represent an unconscious passion of civilized and overcrowded people, on a too-populous planet, to seek unoccupied territory, or even to set up and maintain an illusion that such territory may be found beyond our earth. Certainly, there is no rational understanding of man's haste to reach the moon—even as, admittedly, the first step essential to traveling beyond it to other planets. Far more valuable and vastly more essential research could be done with what we have poured into that aim. But terrible needs are neglected or not perceived, and even denied, as we concentrate on our space-lunge, in a possibly occult but perhaps instinctual drive that is stronger than reason.

At this moment, too, another space probability occupies

the minds of many people. Astronomers and astro-physicists currently tend to believe that, in our galaxy and others, there are hundreds of millions or even of billions of suns, like our own and with planets like those of our star. Theories of the formulation of galaxies, suns, and planets tend strongly to support that idea. In time, lunar or orbiting observatories may prove (or possibly disprove) the hypothesis.

But if the theory becomes fact we shall then have to assume that, in probable billions of other places in the universe, life arose, as it did here, and has evolved, in the same or some similar way.

If we carry that concept a little farther, we may logically ask if the evolutionary process would be likely to parallel our own. Did nature, in these countless similar places, invent sex after inventing replication by cell division? It seems a likely event, early in any evolution for the acceleration of that process. Territoriality, as another useful phenomenon, seems likely: it greatly increases the efficiency of any species, in ways I need not recapitulate.

If, then, conscious beings have often evolved that were two-sexed, territorial, and, finally, intelligent enough to own nature's inventive power through an ability to use time by imagery, would they not also have reacted as men must have, inventing an afterlife to imagine an escape from death, and defending that imaginary territory with the terrible might of half of instinct exploited to hide its opposite half? Would they not, also, rather swiftly develop a complex technology that enabled them—that, indeed, appeared to drive them—into crowded cities? And then, however unlike us in physical form they might be, would they not, perhaps, repeat our history, for the same causes?

If we suppose so, on the grounds that earth's way may be a logical evolutionary procedure for other life forms, we can wonder about results elsewhere.

Do all intelligent beings (supposing ours is how what we call intelligence often evolves) undertake in the parallel seeming of sanity, but in actual delusion, to evade death? To conquer nature?

I have suggested that the evolutionary "reason" that re-

quires overcrowded groups of a territorial species to falter has the aim of saving the territory for the many other
non-conflicting species that live in the same place (because
the salvage of many species is more important to nature
than that of any one). Suppose that idea is sound and that
law holds everywhere?

In such a case, beings on the other planets may have
reached a condition similar to our own. One in which they,
a single species, will have embarked on the attempt (impossible for "lower" life forms) to take command of all other
orders in their worlds. They also will then act as lords of life
and of nature, destroying innumerable species for immediate
ends. And, that being against the fundamental ordinance
of nature, will they not be forced by their instincts to collapse as an intolerable breed, a dam in the path of evolution,
a species that, like all, was experimental, but one which,
like many, failed—owing, in this instance, to vanity and
the illusion of some utterly incorrect status above or outside
nature?

Will they, then, have arranged means for that, without
knowing why, or knowing at all till too late? Developed
and then used their H-bombs, or some equivalents?

Will any such beings, in effect, ever have managed to
use their imagination correctly enough to discover their
kind as part of nature and dependent on nature, thereby
managing to readjust to that simple truth, so as both to
prosper and to endure?

Perhaps.

But perhaps not.

Perhaps the gift of imagination is self-defeating.

Perhaps the error that new ego makes with its new imagination will be identical and not ever rectified.

Perhaps that is why the universe may keep blowing up,
expanding, and recombining as one titan ingot, only to
explode again and scatter in more billions of years. Perhaps
nobody evolves who can understand nature soon enough
and thoroughly enough to get on with the business of
stabilizing the inanimate catastrophes that evolve life for
that end.

Whatever minds may call God, which they are not, and

could be, then die and are resurrected by evolution to try again and fail. And so on. Their self-intoxication never self-seen sufficiently for grand purpose.

And if we assume the evolution of intelligence proceeds according to the steps observed here, another and less cosmic speculation becomes logical.

Multitudes of people, these days, insist on believing that creatures from elsewhere are visiting earth. And of those fanciful persons, most seem to imagine the visits are of a kindly sort—surveys by higher souls who intend to show mankind his errors and bring security and peace to our species, ending present perils and all anxieties.

But if territoriality is a universal pattern in the development of instinctual uses, such ideas may be very mistaken. If that be so, any being visiting earth would surely come from an overcrowded planet, because of that, and in search of additional habitat. That possibility, taken with the technical superiority demonstrated by an ability to get here, bodes no good for man.

They'd want the place. And want us out. And have the means to arrange that, in all likelihood. Else, why come at all?

But, as I've suggested on a different logical basis, it may be "they" will never come and have never touched down here, just as, I feel sure, they are not doing so, these days. Their non-arrival may be owing to a different effect of instinct: perhaps, before they attained a technology sufficiently advanced to leap the tremendous distances in space, their kind had destroyed itself, in order to give the other, lower species the opportunity that nature demands, according to its very understandable law that I have tried to relate to man, the fool that sees his images as territorial and righteous.

Whether such private efforts of imagination are warranted by such presumed results is not the question. What is relevant to me is only that they seem to me to show the ways we ought immediately to try to use for imagining reality or, as most would say, for thinking.

We ought to try to look at life and man and nature in other categories, as Ouspenski suggested. Especially in the other categories that ethology has disclosed. For, surely, men have not been successful where they tried to "think" most urgently and with the most ingenuity, in civilizations. And, surely, modern man does not seem either stable or safe. He is not even committed to his own continuum as mankind.

Many ghastly but common acts of people in cities reveal a lack of normal humanity and are attributed to the crowd itself, to Reisman's "lonely crowd." These appear in our disorientation and anxiety, our loss of empathy and sympathy, in what young people like to call "anomie," in the gruesome refusal of city people to become "involved" at moments when their participation is required for self-respect and in the hostility of such crowds as spend idiot hours screaming to some would-be suicide teetering on a skyscraper ledge, "Jump! Jump! Jump!"

These are symptoms of a recognized sickness, that "mental pollution," which worries doctors and sociologists, who attribute it to crowding, in a way. But it might be more clearly diagnosed, I think, as an inescapable effect of overcrowding; the early symptoms of a too-confined group, Americans, and the onset of an act that will make us pay the penalty of all overcompacted territorial beings. Rats turn cannibal. Lemmings flee to death by drowning. Deer suffer endocrine atrophy. The human evidence of the response may begin as this madness; and we are surely crazier than we realize—losing sanity, perhaps, as means to our necessary disintegration by the age-old law.

My reader may even find some symptoms within himself, small evidences of the disease, or of futile efforts to stave it off. Evidence of the lemming kind.

To the car, we now attach the boat-trailer and the house-trailer, adding technological gear to our effort to move away from crowds. Yet, when we enter uncrowded regions our fear of nature, which is as old as our breed, and our reliance on mechanical aids for safety, cause nearly all of us to see the initial urge, unconscious but violent, as its frustration.

We "escape" to a place where we can plug our portable houses into electric outlets, water pipes and even sewers, amidst a thicket of other trailer-people, joined for reassurance. One glimpse of a wild animal may send us flying back to the city, as a contributor reported doing in the *Reader's Digest* not long ago. That nemesis a porcupine. But his family panicked. Yet the editors seemed to sympathize with their absurd flight since they printed the sick little account.

The boats towed on our highways in such growing and impeding numbers are one more aspect of my idea that motors give us an illusion of range. People who have found the highways inadequate are now moving onto water. Rivers, lakes, and seas aren't built up and have no roads but only, sometimes, channels. This taking-to-boats by millions, however, ends up as a new compaction. For not many of our urban citizens plan to launch their vessels in an uninhabited region and proceed to areas where no crowd will be found.

So nearly all our navigable waters are relatively as jampacked as our highways. And, of course, we are paying a parallel price for the new illusion. Few boatmen know enough to push away from the shore safely so, in their loud, stinking debauch of once-unpeopled waterways they drown and burn up or get their heads cleaved by propellers as they fall overboard.

Another possible evidence of man's overcrowded state is worth more detailed note, though its hideous and wide-spreading reality has not, so far as I am aware, led any other diagnostician to see its cause in territorial instinct. This is the rioting of Negroes (and some whites) that has turned our American summers into hell.

If man must in some fashion obey the mandates and taboos of other territorial creatures and if his present passion for the city subjects him to those rules, those urban dwellers who are most crowded and least able to obtain even illusory relief would obviously be first to exhibit the ancient and self-destructive tenet of the great law.

Those would be people in slums and slumdwellers with the least chance or hope of getting even false means of imagining they have space enough. Negroes. Among them the imperative of overcrowded animals would be operative soonest and be most dramatic in its forms. I hardly need to say that the increasing number of riots in our cities occurs among just those sad citizens.

Psychologically crammed together, and physically, too, by segregation, with fewer jobs available and a lower wage scale, wherefore closer to pre-human levels of existence and feeling —through no fault of their own, inhabiting the least desirable tenements and shacks in the greatest density, Negroes would, if my thesis is correct, demonstrate the law that requires space enough for every individual within a group territory. A city, and cities.

If, then, I am right, all the present effort to ameliorate rioting is vain. It is not based on reality. The diminution of poverty, the opening up of better housing areas, improved schools, and, for that matter, the furious and (I believe) deluded efforts of Congress and local officials to meet threats of black power by violence will fail. What these luckless and maltreated folks need is room, primarily. But, being captives of white cultural ideas, they do not know that and merely seek the slightly greater space and the somewhat more abundant deceptions that Whitey has. But Whitey's room is constantly diminishing as more people leave the farms and hamlets for cities and as more of us, black and white, emerge from the womb in our lunatic excess of reproduction.

However, if our leaders were aware that the Negro riots in our cities are expressions of an age-old pattern and its drive, they would not act appropriately. For their ideal is the city and megalopolis is every man's Mecca. So it might be posited that Whitey will someday riot, too. Indeed, white people have already joined in the havoc.

And one should notice that when the burning leads to looting, what the participants attempt to snatch are usually escape gadgets that delude Whitey: TV color sets and liquor, the lone legal American means to cop-out, along with miscellaneous housewares presumed to accord status to their owners. Cars aren't so widely stolen, though. Maybe even Negroes know that the automobile doesn't really provide a man or a family with the space that is man's essential. So, in riots, cars are burned—another and different but suggestive hint about how overcrowded territorial animals may respond to what cannot be borne.

We are trying to rescue, restore, and refurbish our cities. We have not considered that cities may be untenable by men, for long. And suburbs do not much diminish our presumed infraction of a natural law. I do not know and no man has yet determined the minimal room for man at any and all stages of life. Viewed as the predator man certainly is, however, I'd think one family in each fifty square miles might be too many. The ivory-billed woodpecker required about a fifth of that range—and man is bigger, as big, indeed, as his machines enlarge him as a holoparasite. So the identical houses in our development and even the acre-zoned lots of suburban snobs may not remotely do as a means of survival. And, too, the individual need will vary. There will be cultural variations, too, no doubt.

I've said that the more numerous we are, the less we cherish our kind. I now add that the closer we are compacted, the shorter will be our history.

Yet, every day, news comes of the effort of some corporation, or of an Army engineering project, an urban reclamation plan, a swamp drainage program, that will destroy, reduce or degrade the ecological values of vast areas forever. Such "land improvement" is done directly or indirectly to abet urbanization. The loss is unreckoned, unknown, for engineers are only engineers. Who needs the countryside? Well, farmers. But seven percent of our labor force raises a crop surplus. The jobs are in town. The excitement, too—though it is becoming a kind sensible men do not desire. Meanwhile, an opposite stimulus leads many of our young people to tune in, turn on, and drop out in protest to all this. But generally they make their indignant acts of rejection in cities—in city slums.

Chapter
Ten

THE MOTIONLESS
ESCAPISTS

1 / Instant Everything

MAN SLOWLY REDUCED the time and labor he expended to obtain life's necessities. When he was able, that allowed him to supply some luxuries for his rulers, priests, and heroes. The process, technical advance, was uneven and did not occur everywhere. Over and over, technical skills were developed only to be lost as the inventive culture, or civilization, collapsed.

In this last third of the twentieth century, human beings in myriads still pull their own wooden plows. And no people, till a mere two hundred years ago, had managed to harness for "industrial" power other sources than those in natural being. Their ships were moved by the wind. The wind worked their pumps, the water, their mills. Domesticated animals added their muscle-power and furnished overland transport. Men built dams and aqueducts to store energy for water-driven wheels. But fire was used for cookery, warmth, and smelting; not for propulsion, or to move machinery. Save in powder for weapons.

Then Watt invented a steam engine, using a discovery that

had long been buried in the records and never put to practical purpose, in any case.

It is only a matter of some six generations, that span of our age of power.

Its first phase was the era of the steam engine, the period of thermodynamics.

Living men knew men who saw the second era begin, that of electrodynamics.

Its subdivision, electronics, is younger than this writer.

And the Atomic Age burgeoned as this century neared its midpoint.

Mankind has passed through three orders of magnitude of accession to energy sources in the reach of time measured by that of a great-grandfather of a great-grandfather. And in about that same period most of his knowledge of medicine, chemistry, biology, the planet, the universe, evolution, and other, equally spectacular sorts has come to him.

From the first man who added to his muscle by adapting or inventing a thing not-man, till the American Revolution, some two million or maybe more years passed by. And in all that time, man contrived little to add to the power of leverage of a spear-thrower, or of a bow, the energy he could capture from beasts, and the winds and running water. In that time, too, his biological condition was regulated almost as it had been before he became man.

For even when his technology enabled him to build pyramids, or the roads of Rome, or the cathedral at Chartres, man perished, as infant or as youth and young person, from myriad natural causes he neither understood nor dreamed he might understand. And, to those Malthusian pruning factors, he added war.

When we worriedly wonder if early man's brain grew as he needed more of it for toolmaking, or whether, as now seems all but sure, his intellectual ascent was owing to his need of more brain to make better weapons, the worry is superfluous. Surely man needed weapons first. In his dawn environs he was a relatively weak creature and prey for other species. Even foraging for his own food was mighty risky. Indeed, his initial rise, owing to his weapons-making, seems to me to show his good sense, and not that man started life as a killer, in the present meaning of that word as synonymous with vicious.

If early man was a cannibal, that is no proof, either, that man is innately and uniquely hostile toward his kind. For, clearly, our ancient grandsires were near enough to their prehuman progenitors to act according to the universal law that makes the welfare of the species as the chips-down criterion of morals. If he ate his relatives, or ate out-tribe people, it was originally owing, no doubt, to the fact that somebody had to eat something for anybody to survive.

All such efforts to exhibit our present nature as intrinsically violent, murderous, savage, brutal, inhumane, and so on reveal skimped thinking or unwarranted excuse—however useful to the consciences of many anthropologists and others who need to rationalize their own "modern" feelings.

The too-often overlooked point here is that, until only a page or two back in man's long story, the need to conquer nature was seen in terms largely sound and very vivid. Here, then, is a being with a million-year tradition, who, suddenly, became a technician and found he could work his will on nature in ten thousand new, seemingly advantageous ways. It had till then been his lifelong enemy: source of dreadful, deadly acts of providence he could not anticipate, explain, or escape.

We cannot, therefore, be altogether amazed, or wholly disgusted, at mankind for hoisting his archaic conviction, like a flag, above every one of the countless technical means he developed after finding the principles involved.

For the first hundred years of our recent and geometrically accelerating achievements, men did not even know they were evolved from lower orders and so, equally of and in and dependent on nature. Darwin threw the first bright light into that black immensity of prior unknowledge. And biologists have only now enabled us to see the wondrous furniture men had amassed there as magical and nothing more.

For a mere quarter of a century, scientists, as a group, have been able to know, by such evidence as they require for credence, that man is instinct-dominated. Oblique evidence, however, had been accruing for a century. How many scientists, other than ethologists, now understand and accept this new fact, I cannot guess. One percent would be generous, among those pure researchers in all fields who have bothered to study and incorporated in their ideology the truth that man is as subject to instinctual fiat as a mouse, or a hawk, a skunk, bobcat, cobra, or amoeba.

The rest of the civilized population that has digested the knowledge amounts to about one man per ten thousand. And the number of men now trying effectively to deduce and express the rational implications of that knowledge could be carried in a jet or even, perhaps, a lifeboat.

If, however, we think, from the insights of ethology, about man's civilization and its fantastically sudden emergence, we can readily understand how the ancient (and, till now, true-seeming) concepts of man as against nature still prevail. And still dominate the main uses men have made of the new knowledge from the age of the steam engine into that of electricity, electronics, and atomics.

In the past three generations, however, the men becoming technological have also become increasingly skeptical of prior moral systems, especially those derived from religious and so-called philosophic systems. Today, even nominal believers in God generally disclose, by what they do with their time and energy if not by saying so, that they have a dwindling, or not any genuine faith in dogmatic religion. For if we Americans truly believed in doctrines of an afterlife, where reward or penalty would be based on earthly conduct, almost nothing we do would be done by us.

If (to translate our condition into my terms) to become modern we have, in effect, discarded or ignored right-wrong imperatives set forth to gain realms in postlife states, or in other dreamed fiefdoms, our residual moral quandary ought to appear as an intense want for an unknown ethos.

If we are scientists, users of reason for gaining knowledge but without prior or other aim, we will not want other ethics for our work. Unaware of ethology, we will not even imagine that our employment of reason, in our way, is still ordered by drives like tropisms and instincts, common to all other beings. We will presume instinct evaporated when man evolved logical powers. Instinct will seem an animal condition, one to be ruled out, even were it human, for purposes of research.

But all of us, or a huge majority of us, have kept part of our right-wrong guide, the old idea of vanquishing the evolution-long antagonist, or seeming antagonist, nature. Scientist or dogmatic believer, we retain that "ethical" standard, whatever added bits of an older "morality" we may doubt or drop.

I think the reader may now agree with that.

For all it means is that modern laymen see as "good" any application of a scientific finding, principle, law, or theory that leads to an immediate relief from what had been (and still seems) one more misery imposed by nature.

Good is all that cures diseases and heals ills of the flesh; it is all that prevents our helplessness before acts of what we oddly call God; it is all that enables us to raise more and more nourishing food in more and more sorts of land, with less and less effort of muscle and by less and less expenditure of time; it is easement, comfort, luxury, all mundane gain. Even those who still cling to no-longer-honestly-tenable religious dogmas prefer, with rare and sorry exceptions, to travel by car instead of doing so in buggies. They prefer to sit in upholstered chairs rather than on naked wooden benches. It's progress.

And the men who believe they are ruled by reason, the pure scientists, will obviously assume that everything we achieve for such patently practical ends is right, being the product of reason.

Both sorts of men, and they are the two main civilized sorts, are thus still occupied by the ancient (and long correct) endeavor to adapt by the only means men could employ till recently: the counterassault, as predator-slaughterer, on nature.

Such efforts are of ever-more expectable potency because improvements are assured, now that we've learned the basic trick.

But this form of our right-wrong code is real only in a present time, or in a short-term sense, since it relates only to technology, now known as open-ended.

Two genuine benefits accrued from our gains in the understanding of reality and from our special application of such understanding:

Men were able to do more work per individual—more and more, with every recent, swifter-moving decade. A minimal physical man-effort can now literally move mountains.

And with that increment of work capability much more could be undertaken, the second boon.

Mass production is only a half century old as an invention. When I was a boy, cars were put together by hand, one at a time. A house was built by hand, too, and nothing was pre-fabricated except bricks, cement, tiles, the few and simple gadgets of those days, and some other minor items. No food was precooked. Most of what we have now was inconceivable then, simply because it took so long to make each thing we could have. Locomotives moved materials about and other mechanical devices added to muscle power, but the cornucopia of mass production had not been opened.

So men have only recently learned how to save time enough to fabricate abundance. Saving time was the intrinsic value of the new technology. With it, men could increasingly possess so much, and achieve so much, that, to have an abundant life, one would need time in which to own, consume, use, or otherwise enjoy the abundance. Time-saving can be equated with, or seen as identical to, the aim of labor-saving, which was the paramount goal at the beginning of this century.

Once machines did the labor, saving time was the technological good; and time spent on work unnecessarily was sin—inefficiency, a waste of the one most precious benefit of technology. Each and every time-saving device or process was, thereafter, welcomed as the most noble product possible to man's imagination.

When I was ten, my grandfather used to thrill us with an account of speed. The fastest moving vehicle was the locomotive. Grandfather Edwards knew the length of a rail and used his big gold watch while on trains running at full throttle to calculate the speed by counting the clicks as car wheels crossed each rail interval. Grandpa had gone more than sixty miles an hour!

"Like sixty" was the term of choice, then and for many

years, to express the ultimate in speed. I can remember, too, when I first experienced that fabulous speed in a car. It was 1918, the streets were empty, and a chauffeur showed me what a Locomobile could do.

Speed as a main purpose had not yet become the end it is nowadays. But speed always fascinated man, perhaps, in part owing to its ability to extend, or seem to extend three-dimensional territory and by that, his sense of scope in the domain of time. (And speed potential also lessens a sense of crowd-oppression, of course.)

With accelerated mass production, a given labor force could turn out more goods at the same hourly wage.

Labor soon demanded shorter hours and higher wages for that reason. Men worked a twelve-hour day, for a dollar, millions of men in my youth. They talk now of a thirty-hour work week; and now they have, in millions, a forty-hour work week. Most of their time, then, is saved.

Relatively few men in America still work with their muscles alone. For time and money are deemed equivalents.

And to that end we have accelerated not only production and services but we have speeded up the worlds of communication and of calculation, of data processing, of record making and retrieval, in endless, once-tedious or even impossible chores. We have accelerated many such procedures by millions and billions of times: and we can add to such achievements without seeming limit.

How completely we are involved in saving time we do not generally realize; and if we did, we would see in it all only marvel and gain and a righteousness. The faster the better!

Of what item in our GNP, for reverse inference, do we say, "Make it slower. Take more time on it." What *one?*

It isn't enough that we can cook food without taking time to fell trees, saw them up, and split firewood. We must have food we can prepare faster, and we will lower standards to bare acceptability, for the sake of the time gained.

"Instant" is now the operational word, whether for coffee, a radiogram, or a daiquiri turned out in a blender.

The hope of nowadays for new products, their fabrication, transport, and consumption, is this:

Instant everything.

In pursuit of that goal, we have now "saved" most of the available time of most people.

That feat has given our majority the time (and the means) to possess, use, consume, or otherwise employ increasingly the products thus rendered possible of manufacture.

But we see that circumstance the other way around: Our technology has given the average man the chance to enjoy an abundance that was, till now, only somewhat accessible to a privileged few. Those among us who do not have the means to gain the general abundance make us feel we must find some way to supply them too—even, some people now maintain, if it is done by giving them the requisite money out of taxes.

That is the way we see greatness.

We have saved time, not to have time, but things.

And to have them now, or soon, and instantly, if possible.

The effect of that is very strange.

2 / Now People

The producers and consumers of "instant" artifacts, of precooked meals in disposable dishes, of gasoline-powered saws and lawn mowers, people who communicate by satellite around their planet, process a library full of data in minutes, and are spending billions on a passenger plane that will cross oceans at two thousand miles an hour, have an orientation toward time that is brand new.

They are saving so much time by such means and they are so deeply occupied in their working present by efforts toward means of improved or novel sorts that "now" has come to seem the only time of any importance or reality.

They even have begun to call themselves "now people."

We are a nation in which young people will soon be the majority and are so numerous at present as to exert massive influence on our production-consumption goals. They, also, participate as "now people." They borrowed the demanding slogan of their elders: *have now.* The historic distinction between the obligation to possess by earning and the idea of possessing as a right simply because of opportunity and abundance has thus been abandoned.

People over thirty, or over sixty, for that matter, in millions, actually do have, and now, a fantastic array of goods and services. Their unprecedented economic capability also permits them to supply and they do supply their offspring with mountains of the same or comparable baggage. And millions of these young people, under twenty-five, or in their teens, feel the situation is normal. Why should anybody be expected to earn, at sixteen or twenty, his or her own automobile? Or anything else? The idea is absurd.

And so it is, in the have-now philosophy of now-people. Our economic system supports the sub-adult demand for goods—for cause. A multibillion-dollar teen-age market exists and grows. The student-age market is probably greater. And industry reaches down to furnish the still younger boys and girls with a special, have-now cornucopia: miniature cars with real motors, clothing that is styled for fad and fast obsolescence, toys and games in such variety that now-kids have to have new things to play with as fast as a new "now" appears.

So, in a way, the have-now people are themselves products—to the degree that their objective and the mass production it necessitates regiments what they do and how they feel about that. The acceleration of any process, in other words, requires more standardization in the process, itself, and just because it then produces more, an increased number of consumers is necessary. It is as true in auto making as in education.

Many adults have long recognized that fact. Wordsworth was not saying anything new when he wrote about, "getting and spending" and "how little we have in Nature" as result. Joseph Wood Krutch has scathingly depicted us as, above all, "good little consumers." And it may surprise the now-people who are young to hear that their parents widely referred to business, long before they were born, as "the rat-race" or "merry-go-round."

Yet they kept racing with the other rats and spinning on the same nowhere-carousel that has now led to the avalanche of artifacts they possess and their youngsters assume they have a right to possess, and now and unearned. A sense of parental guilt may, then, sometimes enter into their lavish provision for their offspring. They indulge youth as a sort of ratty apology. Another motive is more evident: Adults bountifully outfit young America because in their own youth they were deprived. As, of course, they were, relatively if not in fact. No one my age or even a much younger adult, could get, in his teens, what multitudes of teenagers now take for granted. The stuff didn't exist, couldn't be imagined, and so, wasn't wanted.

But much of the immense, short-lived clutter now-people demand to have-now, is not even what they want, in any true sense of want. For, as Galbraith made clear in his recent book, *The New Industrial State,* we Americans have banished classical economic theory. Ours is not a buyer's market and the goods and services we consume are not those selected in a competitive market.

The nature of technology and industry make it essential that what will be for sale or hire in the future must be planned and pretested even before the machine tools for its mass manufacture are turned out and still longer before the product is put on the market. Each new and more "instant" commodity, luxury, or what-not requires the investment of large amounts of capital and takes a period of years to prepare for sale. Competition in such a system will plainly be too costly to be risked, providing means can be found to avoid it.

And the means have been found, of course. What ever-more-complex and apparently glamorous things the have-now people of the future will "want," they will be made to want. And though that is an oversimplification of Galbraith's thesis, it is lucid and complete enough, I think, to make the point I find relevant, here.

What we have in any "now" or in a next "now" is and will increasingly be what industry reckons we can be compelled to want, by advertising and other means. That is, and will more and more become, only such goods as industrial projection indicates it can spawn at a good profit attained by creatable wants.

Our abundance, then, and its future increment, has and will have no necessary relationship to what, as human beings, we are, and so, need. Rather, it currently provides, and will more bounteously supply, the on-going have-now people with what the machines need that the machine operators can make people think they want.

Galbraith's thesis aroused some erudite denial and it was very unwelcome to the Establishment. But I do not believe it can be refuted since what young people call our "scene" is its plain proof. What may be difficult for now-people to realize is, merely, that their have-now demands are being filled by a gross national product much of which they are consuming owing to delusion and illusion deliberately fabricated for that purpose and not even related to their own choices or to any other real, personal motive.

It is not surprising, then, that young America is in revolt against adult America, the "Establishment," and a world of people youth calls "straight" or "square." Our young people are feeling the pressures of the system far more keenly than their parents felt them. There are more young people, besides. The system, of course, demands a greatly expanded period for the education of young people, merely to enable them to enter and earn good livelihoods in its constantly more intricate configurations.

To man the means of production now requires technicians and skilled hands by millions whose training usually takes four college years and, for an ever-larger percentage, four more years of graduate study. The uneducated, even near-illiterate tycoon of the nineteenth century has vanished by default. And the idolized captain of industry of my own boyhood years, the "self-made man," isn't commonplace, now, because he cannot compete. So youth is under pressures to become as "highly educated" as possible which, till this era, did not act on young men and women in similar ways or to such a degree.

American educators have responded to the demand that technicians be supplied in enormous numbers by turning our secondary schools, colleges, universities, and graduate schools into factories for the mass production of specialists. Human stamp-mills.

The blanks fed into the educational assembly line consider they are human beings. But the farther they get along in the process, the clearer it is that their humanity, or, at least, their individual form of it, must fit the specifications. Their original composition, genetic and environmental, is assayed mathematically not for complete and intrinsic potential but only for amenability to machining. The brain-mill shoots them ahead or rejects them according to their grades in courses devised to meet specifications of the finished products. Parents consider the machine to be an end in itself for their offspring; rejection by it is tantamount to pre-failure in the rest of life.

Because the youths have become hordes, a certain amount of mechanization is essential to permit even the least automated educational jute mill to operate. Since most of them are not even attempting actual education but the fabrication of parts to fit specific places in the industrial state, the more the enterprise can be automated, computerized, and mechanized, the better its scholarly performance.

In a vast if dim way, the macerated raw material realizes this treatment is unfair and near to intolerable. So, recently, rather suddenly and to the horror of most adults, signs of mutiny have appeared in our youth. To understand the symptoms we must understand the spokesmen of the revolt.

The rebels have not been truly educated. That is the first and most flagrant aspect of what they do and say. They cannot think. They do not use logic. They are without reason. They are inconsistent. They are guilty, in most cases, of the very sins they protest. They are so now-fast as to have no idea that virtually every item in their bill of complaint has been presented before. And their violent claims, though true, are negative.

Even the most far-out of their numbers, the hippies, would be astonished to learn how repetitive, unoriginal, and dated their ideas and antics actually are. To a man of my age who, in the twenties, lived both in New York's Greenwich Village, or Bohemia, and also uptown, these self-made Jesuses of the anti-straight world sound and look like a rerun of an historic flop.

Artists and intellectuals of that ancient era were "long-hairs." They also were exponents and defenders of equal rights for women, woman's emancipation, and free love. Along with all classes of Americans, they defiantly protested

Prohibition by drinking to excess. This was the Jazz Age and that beat was as prevailing if not yet as loud as rock 'n' roll. Packed into ballrooms these people were showered with spots of colored light from huge, turning globes made of bits of multi-colored mirror glass—an unnamed but "psychedelic" effect.

Marijuana was known and smoked and other drugs were used. But then, as today, the outlawed intoxicant, booze, was the mind-blower of choice. Looking at and listening to a hippie family in drugged discourse or at a love-in is to behold and hear, again, the dragging-voiced, repetitive, giggling, rapt, or cockeyed mutilogue of any uptown or downtown drunken party "thrown" by self-righteous, silly, confused and emancipated young (and often older) people of the twenties.

Homosexuality was not unknown even then. For many females, promiscuity was mandatory as proof of liberation. Races mingled freely and it was what would now be called camp to go to Harlem where the jazz was loudest and drink with, dance with, or make love with Negroes. Oriental art and mysticism were in vogue. To Manhattan's Bohemia on weekends came the very young girls now known as teenyboppers.

Admittedly, LSD wasn't around in those ancient days. But everybody, pretty much, went on trips with the use of alcohol. And these people, waking with hideous headaches, depression, jitters, and a recollection of having spent their last cent and having then passed a bad check, of having engaged in sexual encounters now seen as bizarre and alarming, of having played the fool in the company of friends, of having likely contracted a venereal disease or of being ejected from parental home and care—of such things—would have agreed their binge was a bad trip. If they'd known the words, they would also, surely, have called their not rare episodes of delirium tremens "freaking out."

Not a few young men and women well known to me, while on such trips, drove cars into stone walls to end their anxiety. Others, high and feeling omnipotent, tried to walk across a street seven storys above it or to halt rushing traffic by stepping in front of it. Fatal. The hospitals were filled with trippers in post-alcoholic terror or idiot euphoria as well as the battered victims of foolish or mad drunken acts.

Far more adults, and more upper-class people, and far more professional people of the "smart set" sort engaged in hippie-like conduct in the twenties—and on into the thirties. In Manhattan, Los Angeles, and Miami, men and not a few women held paid love-ins under the auspices of such ladies as Polly Adler, Lee Francis, and Gertrude Walsh; and there were others in big cities who held home parties they called, simply, orgies.

Even before the twenties, rebellion-by-costume was undertaken. When, during World War I, a scarcity of fabric for uniforms led the President to request that all students wear old clothes, the reaction of my generally well-to-do high school classmates was opposite. The girls went out and bought new, summerlike wardrobes, the boys new white doeskin trousers. The presidental order was thereby doubly disobeyed. In protest to that, I dug out a tail-coat my father had worn as an undergraduate and wore that to school, with homemade pink satin trousers, and a monocle in silk ribbon —raiment as odd as mod, designed as protest-to-protest. The faculty kept their cool. Nobody ordered me to go home and change.

Anti-war spirit was widespread in the twenties. A war-opposing organization called "World Peaceways" advertised nationally.

Added parallels could easily be exhumed.

But there were certain differences between those who were young in that era and the have-now youths of the present.

Few of us had cars and of those who had, many earned them. If multitudes were turned on and tuned in then, not so many dropped out. And though, as university students, we were beginning to be aware of the cheating, thieving, and hypocrisy of the Establishment, we did not, ourselves, take to cheating with the feeble alibis of today. That because the grown-up world cheated we were entitled to; or that because we were obliged to take courses we judged of no value we had cause to cheat. We still knew that the cheat cheated himself more than others and by his act abdicated his own integrity.

So the majority, and perhaps even three quarters of college students, are said to cheat, nowadays. Yet their cheating, whether as retaliation or as a way of passing resented courses, is childish. For these are the same people who assert they cannot trust anyone over thirty. People over thirty, plainly and for certain, cannot trust most of them.

But people over thirty, though shocked at many aspects of youthful behavior, assume the great majority of students, not conspicuously rebellious, are going to graduate and quietly move into the Establishment. They may. Their have-now attitude and their cheatfulness ought to abet them, since it seems suitable for what they see as a straight but somehow cheatful world.

It is not possible to talk back much to these critical miscreants.

To begin with, most of their claims are valid. Their parents are, indeed, in a rat-race for material things—which, however, the kids demand, too.

The H-bomb is something older people both fabricated and proliferate. There are slums and riots. There is brutal segregation and inequality. American life grows more urban and more impersonal. Adults generally refrain from becoming involved and take care not to rock the boat. At the moment, the Vietnam conflict rages and young America considers it an immoral war, which in a way I believe it to be owing to its cause. But that, they neither know nor wish to learn. Yet some will not take part, while ignorant of causes.

They are judges of anything and everything that they find in error, inconvenient, or demanding. If they can determine a study course is without value before taking it, they evidently feel they can determine the "morality" of a war without bothering to learn its origin. They can cop out in empty-headed pretenses of righteousness. Their uninformed involvement with non-involvement reaches a zenith (or nadir) in the hippies who irrationally rely on the society that sustains them. Yet they have no substitute plan for what they would undermine and wreck, by "love"—a posture as silly as it is hostile.

They, and other now-people of all ages, have, however, one common, basic bond. They are engaged in a sex revolution. And, as a symptom, it merits special note. Young America's term for their part in the affair is sex-now. It has changed our scene. News of "wife-swapping" that shocked the middle-class public a dozen years ago no longer shocks anybody. Married couples and single people of both sexes, in growing millions, are joining swapping clubs to engage in what they term "group" or "social" sex.

Clubs formed for that purpose engage in the swapping for sex relations of all members with opposite sex members. The acts are ritualized, watched, and recorded on motion picture cameras for later exhibition and stimulus. Partners and performances are usually selected by lot. And not all activities are limited to heterosexual acts. Wives often perform with other females to furnish their spouses the same titillations favored for stag shows. Sadism and masochism are, however, generally taboo.

Members of swap clubs have even appeared on TV to argue the benefits of their behavior. It relieves the boredom of married fidelity, they say, and so, saves marriages. The divorce rate amongst swappers apparently is low and the group activity may heighten the married sex relationship—and inform it, too. The rules forbid emotional responses. Everything is done for kicks. There is no tenderness or love. Just sex. And, of course, the activities of the millions now engaged in social sex are concealed from their offspring.

One can imagine why. Tattletale tots might lead to police raids. But one wonders, at the same time, at what age the swappers would allow their sons and daughters to learn of and, logically, enter into the ritual orgies. In addition, of course, countless adults not engaged in such social relationships engage in outmoded extra-marital sex relations. But all of them try to maintain for their offspring the old "ideals" of chastity and fidelity.

Naturally, young Americans are not fooled. Their practice of sex-now is a reaction to the knowledge that adults are revolutionaries who have sex-now and are hypocrites, too. Since, in the fundamental matter of sexual manners and the concealed adult violation of what they preach, communication between adults and youths is impossible at the basic level of sex, all communication ceases.

One result is the ludicrous effort of parents to transfer what is called sex education to the schools. There, it becomes a farce, as it generally was, when a parental duty. I say farce simply because contemporary sex education offers little more than anatomical data together with an effort to support the old tenets about chastity and fidelity by such outrageous claims as that pre-marital sex will not be satisfactory, will diminish satisfaction in later marriage, that infidelity disrupts marriage, and so on. The venerable fortifiers of those caveats, risk of unmarried motherhood, and of venereal disease, are not valid, in fact, at least for young people with the knowledge and self-discipline needed for sex relations which avoid those risks.

But, far more farcically, so-called sex education ignores even the known truths about our sexuality.

Human beings of both sexes belong to the only species able to have and enjoy sex relations at any time and not just at periods of oestrus, or heat. They are also members of the only species that can, from birth, be stimulated to climax with the only difference an absence of ejaculation by pre-adolescent males. The latter fact, the innate craving that attends it, the ability for gratification and tension relief that follows the act, is ignored in teaching and would be the cause of outrage if even suggested as a normal, built-in physical and psychological condition.

Again, as Kinsey has shown, the sooner and oftener a male commences to engage in erotic acts, the greater his potency will be throughout life and the longer into old age it will continue. Other studies by scientists have proven that by specific exercises and with a sufficiently uninhibited attitude, the female is able to develop inner muscles and an attendant blood and nerve supply, enabling her to enjoy an orgasm of a sort measurelessly superior to the "clitoral" experience—still widely believed to be the only climax possible to the female.

These findings have not yet been published. The recent Masters-Johnson *Human Sexual Response* does not even mention all the anatomy involved. But among those aware of the facts it will be evident that the female, like the male, benefits sexually by specific practice and perhaps the earlier it begins the more effective it will become. It is also evident that Freud's claims for a "vaginal" orgasm and the superiority of that to the "clitoral," long flatly denied by medical men, and though neurologically and anatomically undefined by Freud, is essentially correct.

Any sex education deserving that name ought, of course, to be more than anatomy lessons and baleful warnings not to apply them. It ought to educate people in all that is known about sex and also in what the proper sexual behavior for mankind, birth to death, ought to be. Unfortunately, even with the knowledge we have, together with the unpublished information just noted, there is not and has never been a person with enough understanding of human sexuality to define the proper pattern for human sexual behavior.

Whether or not infants are entitled to erotic gratification is not known. Experiments in permissiveness for children such as those at Neill's Summerhill strongly suggest that our ruling attitudes about that are monstrous in design and disastrous in effect. But the most farcical corruption of truth in contemporary sex education rises from its effort to retain adherence to antiquated sex "morals" by evading and usually denying that sex is fun.

It is fun at any age. It is the greatest pleasure life offers in the view of most adults.

That is what the now-people have found out and what the swappers and sex-now youths are trying to have by their varied means: fun. It was apparent long ago that the fun aspect of sex would become dominant in man-woman relationships once control of venereal disease and effective measures for contraception became simple. I wrote a parable to point that out in a book published more than thirty years ago.

However, one notices that both the taboo, in social sex clubs, of all love and tenderness and the casual nature of the relationships of the sex-now generation tend to be depersonalizing. Their games doubtless furnish oceans of fun. But the rules forbid what seems to me, at least, the most important part of sexual intercourse. The act is the quintessence of interpersonal relations. So it ought to include more than a self-centered kick. For it is the best and most complete way by which a member of one sex can communicate an understanding, an appreciation, and an admiration of the other sex—and of the individual partner as its representative.

That may fall short of "love"; but sex-solely-for-kicks surely falls far short of *that*.

Some sociologists attribute our sex-now attitudes and our growing permissive promiscuity to our urban life. Their new sub-discipline is called, by Hall, "proxemics." He, with others, are seeking to find abnormalities among people, seen as territorial animals and presumably overcrowded. Some of those investigators report that the so-called sex revolution is, simply, the result of urban tensions and the mere proximity of sex partners in large numbers.

I would like to add to such thinking another step. Sexual intercourse responds to a drive as old in evolution as sex, itself. And it is the only drive left to which urban inhabitants can respond in a manner normal, unchanged, and natural. The more imperative drives are served by technological arrangements. City-dwellers do not carry the water that slakes their thirst. What they eat to satisfy their hunger they do not grow. All of it will have been transported to them for eating and most of it will have been transformed by technology. Urbanites do not dispose of their own feces. They do not even urinate outdoors since their outdoors is a street or lawn and it is illegal to micturate in such places.

The sexual drive and its gratification are the next most powerful individual imperatives to those listed, aside, probably, from the territorial. Gratification by the various means of the sex-now people may, in consequence, represent an attempt to use sexuality broadly in compensation for the absence of natural behavior in other areas of instinct. And it may have a second function, equally displaced:

The man who has access to the wives of his neighbors in exchange for their access to his wife and also the similarly exchanged wives may find in the situation a new sense of opened-territory, an unconscious feeling of relief from territorial overcrowding in other areas. Let me put the idea in another way. The spatial and time compression in an urban, technological society may increase, by some unknown factor, the sense that monogamy is boring. The restlessness set up by other and actual overcrowding may spill over into marriage, causing less limited sexual relationships to appear as relief or as a symbol of that. Sex-now amongst the young, and swapping for any age, may be seen as behavior similar to that of the owner-driver of an automobile who imagines he has enlarged his intolerable compression by that means.

If the idea is in any degree correct, the impersonality of all such behavior (even though it be a cancellation of real value) is accepted, unconsciously. Why? Because sex-now and so-cial sex, swapping and ritual orgies, could not occur under any aegis other than depersonalization.

Now-people, in sum, whatever their age, switched on and tuned in, and whether dropped out or most ardent supporters of our instant-everything world, have made themselves, by my definition, into non-people, or as near to it as they can get. Were they to attempt, successfully, my experiment in ruling our past and present to see themselves clear and whole in "now," they would fail. Their best efforts would, at most, approach a sense of themselves as wholly thing-related. Finding nothing beyond, they would assume an identification of self-now beyond attainment.

Their orientation is so very perverse that they cannot imagine the continuum of the species, let alone that process as an ethical criterion. The generation now so actively criticizing its parents never even mentions the generation it will birth and rear. Non-people: Q.E.D.

3 / The Hard Way

In our national treasury of mythical tenets there is one that is opposed by two others, as powerful, as idiot, and themselves antithetical.

The first postulate asserts that experience is the best, or even the only teacher. Learning by experience is called "the hard way."

If it were true that each generation must relearn by experience, the second asinine apothegm would not hold: that tradition can and should be learned and accepted without experience. You can, that is, become a convinced Christian without being crucified.

On the other hand, each young generation is busy at school and college soaking up proven beliefs and new ideas, often opposites of tradition. These are accepted, but not experienced, and used to the end of all man's progress. Thus the very cityscape is proof that neither tradition nor experience is necessary for the gain of knowledge.

What the now-people think of as their minds is a massive structure standing on such eroded props. And the young generation is proof, reviling what it would not learn and selecting what it would.

I have talked with hundreds and listened to as many young Americans. I have read hundreds of their reports of themselves and as many more by adults.

A personal confrontation with youth is shuddersome; but it bears out the general impression of the reports. And goes like this:

First comes the bit about the mistakes we made. This, I acknowledge to youth, and have acknowledged here.

Next comes a very nearly unanimous and resonant request, rather, demand: *Leave us alone.*

When a group of people is observed in agony, the humane tendency is to offer help, not to leave them in pain. One therefore asks why this generation wants no help.

Let us make our OWN mistakes.

They make that one response.

And it is a cod-dead giveaway. Consider:

These are people who want to make mistakes. Who intend to make mistakes. Who have no other expressed aim. Why?

The answer isn't as easy as the reader may think.

In fact, I'm not sure that anybody, except myself and now and here, has even wondered why the teen-agers, college students, and some under-thirties are so determined to be left alone by people over thirty so they can make mistakes, undesignated as to kind or magnitudes.

The first and best answer can be implied by another question:

Why doesn't any under-thirty male, female, or hermaphrodite ever say, *Leave us alone so we can figure out how to avoid or rectify the catastrophic blunders made by you people over thirty?*

Plainly, upon spotting that A-plus query and discerning its portent, a certain biggish number of the folk-rock, rock-folk set will instantly say, "That's what we *meant!*"

To which the condign response, at Berkeley or anywhere else, is "horse shit."

For that is exactly not what they said. And it is not really what they meant, either.

What they mean by this idiot passion to get out from under adult rule, law, logic, knowledge, wisdom, is other.

They may actually believe in the nitwit talisman about, to repeat, experience being the best teacher, involving trial and *error.* So they wish to try for a better answer by being allowed more widely to err even than they are, as is.

But I doubt one of the leave-us-alone-to-make-our-own-mistakes types in every thousand has ever penetrated their program that far; and certainly not half that percentage have carried it to that conclusion.

Not at all. The under-thirty now-people whom I have more or less assembled here as the have-now and sex-now division of the American wing of our species are sore. Very sore. They want adults to leave them alone, all right, but not out of worry lest meddlesome grownups corrupt them by that, but out of dread that mature people would expose them to themselves.

As what? Hypocrites and, very frequently, cowards, also. As ethical drop-outs. Cheaters. Infantile and spoiled.

They want, right now, and they get, in millions, everything the squares have, or its age-bracket equivalent. But they tearingly do not want to *be* squares. Yet they cannot wriggle out of the fact that all they have now was manufactured by the square techniques of the straight world, the only way possible.

So they make a sort of formula for ritual vengeance: leave us alone—to make our own mistakes. Actually, it should fool few cretins.

But it tends to fool most adults. It seems to indicate that the appalling (granted) fluffs of us older people are so gigantic we have lost all moral right to any authority over these (humble and less perfidious) people who admit freely they will err but thereby imply (think they do) that their cop-outs will be infinitely less stupid and terrifying than ours. For instance, they are going to *love*, maybe, which we didn't and don't. And they will be damned if they'll fight our immoral wars. Suppose we grant that, and accept, for argument's sake, their cowardice, or antipatriotism, or whatever they fake up even if it is but total selfishness. Do they or would they even then embark on an effort to find out how to out-love us? Or how we got into the repudiated-war-of-the-moment, and how to get out of it without some battle-readiness on their part?

No, as I said earlier.

They are brilliant students of our errors.

They are not interested in what we may have done right. No, no. They differ. Viz!

They have no intention of:

a) trying to figure out how we went off the rails or doing something about it if they have any success

b) missing out on any single item of the GNP that Pop can get, in his loathed, square way and world

c) giving up trying to get where they hope to without cheating

d) thinking about sex save as something to have-now with females only too eager to be had.

e) figuring out how to extend now-having into their future by the easiest means

f) making the slightest self-sacrifice—unless it involves full TV coverage

g) suffering

h) thinking

i) finding out what an education is and embarking on the lifelong trudge toward getting something perhaps near to one

j) considering the effects of their detested parents' and their own projected greedy program on their children, let alone on generations beyond

k) becoming honest

l) becoming logical

m) relating to other people in any manner for which the return might be smaller than the deed

n) trying to find out the truth insofar as it is known or can be discovered

o) being or becoming decent animals, e.g., moral

p) giving a good god damn for anybody but themselves and so,

q) being.

I am aware that those seventeen off-hand examples of what people-under-thirty have no intention of doing, of undertaking to do, of becoming, or of being are merely notes for an introduction to the fifty-foot shelf of books listing under-thirty shortcomings.

For the negations of youth are numberless. As they must be among have-now now-people. By saying all they have thus said, they have said what I mean: they are nothing and intend to proceed as ever-swelling cyphers.

Now, *wait* a minute, Junior!

Very well. Now, hold it.

Maybe, just maybe, not even one of the above faults applies to you. I said, though, didn't I, that there could be as many as one per two thousand living anti-dolls in your group? Okay. You may be among them.

But, admit it. I have pretty much followed your carefully drawn portrait of your dad, your mom, and their folks. And you're their kid, right? And I agreed that your description of them, though incomplete, was roughly and in large part apt—true? So how are you going to have what they have, and you have now or demand now, without being their spitting image? While, also, making your own mistakes—bound to be worse, since you don't know what their mistakes were because you won't learn how they happened?

Don't know, don't want to find out, couldn't imagine that their worst mistake might be you.

You're right about us. What proves it is . . . you.

And if I'm wrong about you, Junior, you will have to prove that by something better than protest.

Would to God you'd walked to school! You'd have such a better chance in such an attempt.

But I'll give you a start.

It's neither what you think about us, or we about you, that matters. Our mistake was this: we loved you some; we loved things more; it's catching and fatal. Neither we nor you can do much about each other, now.

All that can be done that's worth doing is what you could do for your kids.

That's the only way to have it made—sometime, maybe in ten or a hundred thousand years.

I'm trying to tell you what I tried to be—personally, not an over thirty, or a parent, a grandparent, or a square!

Not, a now-man.

A *tomorrow man*.

I love you still; and I loved your parents and your grandparents who are or were my pals. Still, they worried me. And you worry hell out of me.

For being a tomorrow-man commits me not to them but to you. And as a Grade A, on-the-record, certified prophet (which is an avocation of tomorrow-people), your future looks terrifying to me and that of your kids seems almost unbearable even to imagine—at least it does and will so long as you remain a now-man, Junior.

It's all really that simple, life—and about a million times tougher to have a real one than you believe.

Now, I mean.

Chapter
Eleven

THE
MAGIC
ANIMAL

FOR THREE billion years or so, nature conducted the long story on this earth, life's evolution.

The means were patently statistical. One small but useful event in each thousand random mutations of a gene led all the way from our microscopic first ancestor to ourselves. In us evolved access to time by our imagination that no prior creature had possessed and nature had used three thousand million years for the giving.

Our term of ownership, some two million years, is short as the span of a species has usually been measured. We are a young experiment. Primitives, who have misused our gift, till now, to create illusions of grandeur. To see ourselves as images of imagined gods and God. As intended potentates of the planet. As reasoning, yet as irresponsible for the employment of our reasoned images of reality.

Today as deists or materialists, we continue the perversion. To do so, we were and are compelled to imagine we are not the animals we were, and are. And that compulsion has cut us off from the old morality, the law of specific right and specific wrong for every living being. Our images of our grandeur can be sustained by that one means only—by an assumption of aggression as the support of our perverted righteousnesses. With that grim half of truth, we had, of course, to repress all whisper and any inkling of the opposite, the law that limits aggression to define what is right.

It now is evident that any man who dreams he will live eternally when he dies, cannot accept a limit, and has rejected limitation by such a belief. Similarly, one whose image of himself is that of master of all living things, and all things unalive, as well, and ordained to do as he wishes with them, cannot acknowledge a restriction and still service such vainglory. And even a man who makes an image of himself and his breed as without meaning has declared a comparable irresponsibility.

In that mistaken way man has continued to this day his serial endeavors to achieve a stable civilization. He has always failed.

That he is still animal he just learned and has not yet much accepted. That he is ruled by instinct is a newer finding. That he is a territorial being and subject to the instinctual laws of that kind of creature he discovered yesterday.

But he has not yet seen how the arrogant descriptions he invented for himself became territory in his view. Realms in time only, and there, fantasies. So he has not yet discovered why he holds those dreamlands with an aggression impossible to other animals. Madness, alone, could turn other creatures into such a state. But it is man's. A beast with rabies, depraved, mindless, sick, snapping at all before it, and lost to recollection of restraint to keep its place in the scheme of being. A maniac that even ravages its own kind in the terrible attempt to prove it is not animal.

The disastrous effects of that lunatic looting are manifest. But not the cause. Man sees his kind as menaced but does not see mankind. His special territory is, to man, more precious than the whole.

What man whose image of righteousness is America, or California, and the provincial values such words project in his head, will consider a need for universal morals? Which one of that kind will open up his ideological borders of "Christendom," or the "free world," to attempt intercourse with Communist provinces that are even more tightly shut?

In such mad prisons and in ten thousand such, men were and are made into unrestricted predators. God the idol or objective reason, either legend a lie.

As Jung said, "All men live by a myth."

The myth of each is his inner territory, held to be true and, as truth, defining his physical domains and his sense of the right, the very duty of infinite aggression against other men because their different myth is seen, now, manifestly wrong. Evil; wherefore dangerous.

(And offense, of course, is the best defense.)

Yet even here, perhaps, exists an overlooked opportunity for a strange understanding.

Men have gathered the myths of mankind, adducing them from artifacts in prehistoric graves, translating them from dead languages, copying them from the storytellers of primitive tribes and adding those of civilized peoples. Comparison reveals that they contain parallel or identical meanings.

In them man sees himself as godlike. The hero of "a thousand faces" has the same face and miraculous history. He appears by virgin birth or other unearthly beginning. He proceeds to sacrificial or transcendent death. His struggle is against the thousand-faced, one devil in mankind. And his days are a tale of tragedy, even though, as he dies (to save us, or as sacrifice to virtue, or to love) he becomes our means of redemption and salvation.

The Jesus-myth was muttered to Olduvai Gorge a thousand times earlier than two thousand years ago.

Sometimes, where a genius found what he presumed a truer image of man, but found no myth to sustain it, he invented a legend. Freud did so, in his fable of the primordial son who killed his father to get his woman, his mother. The oedipal myth, which was for a while so persuasive a parable, but is no longer credible.

To such great minds as the mind of Carl Jung, and to many others, the historic-prehistoric myths seemed archetypal. They were regarded as correct representations of the human, conscious-unconscious struggles in man's moral predicament.

But here, an apt question went unspoken.

This question:

Do these "myths men live by," which are presumed to embody a universal formulation of man's reality, achieve that intent? Or do they, to deepen the query, represent only how man and his moral struggle seems and has always seemed to man—owing to some fallacy in his original and continuing view of himself?

I think that question can be asked, now, and should be; for I think it can be answered. And though I have no inclination to examine numbers of the legends to elicit my response, let me consider one, to illustrate my method.

I shall choose the legend of Eden.

The lovely fable of man's Fall. The story of Original Sin and how it became man's eternal penalty, from which he could be redeemed only by magical acceptance and necromantic means. The account of the first man, as well, and also, the first woman.

The Garden of Eden is a beautiful vision, one that seems to be like my image, in this book, of time and moral order in the world before there was man. What then happened, in my revision of the story, or is the sort of thing that happened then, in Eden happening now?

Man ate the fruit of the Tree of Knowledge, Genesis reports, tempted by woman, who was made temptress by a serpent. Having eaten the forbidden fruit, Adam gained his knowledge, that of time, I call it. He entered the new "territory" and was punished by God for the wickedness, scripture avers.

What was the penalty Adam and Eve paid in the archetypal fable? That they would be mortal! And ashamed of their sexuality!

So it has seemed to men, in that analogue, and myriads like it, ever since the Beginning.

But is it a fit analogue or just one for our seeming of the human condition?

Is fate, kismet, the built-in tragedy of a Shakespeare, doom of old Athens, real and innate? And is sexuality shameful? Are we, alone among living beings, born foul and accursed?

Not all cultures consider sex inherently vile. But in all, sexuality has led to special arrangements, taboos, rituals, and rules. Violators of every local sex code are punished.

So, to all, sex has that risk and limitation even where the codes are not buttressed, as in Judaic law, by profanation. Even so, the ancient Hebrews were not as viciously intent on making sex vile as were early Christians, Paul and Augustine, the most ferocious. They and their followers in the Reformation, together with the Roman priesthood, helped to make sex bestial, and beast-related, for Christians, which was, in one more hideous case, the attribution to animals of untruth —for the old end of the separation of man from them.

Is any image among all that are but suggested here, valid? Are the universal myths of afterlife and their companion mythology of sex rules sound archetypes as is assumed by scholars?

Nature invented sex to speed evolution, remember, and then had to invent individual death as a balance. Since all groups of myths are allegories for ways to afterlife, were their makers not forced by them to compensate for that illusion about death, by destroying the value of its biological companion, sexuality? Are we not also obliged, however unconsciously, to alter our modern concept of sexuality as we control death—by a fable and ritual and doctrine of mercy and a right to live? Is that but a myth we install in men as if a truth? Have we no mercy on posterity?

Let us return to Eden, a place where Adam and Eve had found "every prospect pleases," but not yet that "only man is vile." Nature, seen before the conquering hero arrived. The eternal-now world of moral animals.

If the fruit on the Tree of Knowledge was an apple (or almost any other), Eve, being a woman and perhaps more observant in certain ways than males, might have noticed that the butterflies and birds and herbivores relished fallen apples and seen how, when these had rotted a bit and fermented considerably, the apple-eaters lost all their fear. Butterflies calmly faced birds that would normally devour them while the intoxicated birds failed to react, and seemed, in their bland state, above so mean a deed. The fermented fruit brought restless little animals a dreamy-eyed and peaceful pleasure; and it made stodgy bugs start dancing.

Some predators who fed on the alcohol-filled insects,

though only some, no longer menaced their prey and appeared to smile at them in occult happiness.

So Eve suggested Adam try the windfall—of the (nottaboo) Tree of Knowledge. He did and she did. Drunk, then, they enjoyed a sense of omnipotence, of their own wonder and splendor—that heightening of reality sought today in pot and LSD. They felt so great they decided they must be super-animals, and the knowledge of death (which came with Knowledge) seemed no dark and tragic thing but the opportunity to imagine, in that condition, an afterlife, an Eden beyond death, and so the first myth burgeoned in a glorious binge.

Came the morrow and hangover. Came, then, the creeping fears that are its nervous response. Death looked terrible now. Frightening. The drunk dream of escape to Paradise was hard to recall clearly, and harder to believe. Something was the matter. In their elevated yesterday they had, of course, made lavish love and invented erotic antics when, in the preknowledgeable time, they had not perceived how to invent. They'd done as animals do; but now they were scared, shaky, and upset. The jag that made them feel omnipotent, superior to reality, and eternally alive had somehow produced this worrisome state. They felt they'd done wrong, in consequence. Seemed guilty of error. But, if there was any truth in their wild dream of eternal life, some penalty must clearly be paid, now, to atone for this sense of wrongdoing that had ensued.

The fruit showed them the dream of heaven which they were determined to retain. What they did that animals did, but did while drunk, was not suitable for a super-being. Plainly, a sin, shameful. Sex must be ritualized, controlled, and not, as previously, the uninhibited pleasure of animals. That must have been their sin, not the image of Paradise.

They became self-conscious in this mistaken view of those two experiences; their new but misinterpreted consciousness erred. They grabbed fig leaves, being naked and convinced sex was shameful for people.

That slightly outrageous parody of the old myth will do to make my point. Knowledge wasn't forbidden to man. He misused it to heighten his vanity, by self-intoxication, and paid for that in his erroneous assay of his morning-after anxieties. The Fall of Man, then, was owing to his initial eating of fallen fruit—fruit that had fermented and made him drunk. Such ripe fruit of knowledge as he has subsequently plucked from the Tree has been interpreted, ever after, according to the original mistake occasioned by the first sampling. The dream that gave rise to was too bewitching to reject: and the false guilt it cost was equally self-designed and then self-imposed, as the willingly paid price. Original Sin was born of original cider.

By a serious reassessment of our myths, however, we might come to perceive they represent no proper analogue for ourselves. We might realize how it is that all the myths, however nobly intended, produce as effect such dreadful opposites of their stated aim.

Christians, for example, insist their great Jesus legend is the path to truth and the way of love. They even claim that, out of its wide adoption, came all the knowledge and science and technology of our era. One can doubt them. One can say, for instance, that science was repressed for a thousand, or nearly two thousand, years, by Christians, and might have reached its present state centuries ago in a world devoted to a more real and truer myth.

But if we accept any part of the claim as worth considering, we must ask why the symbol of Christianity is not Light. A beacon, to represent the "way, the truth, and the life." Why is it, instead, that ghastliest of emblems, a crucifix, a device for imposing death by torture? And why have the acts of Christians made all the world a hell, for the long ages in which men have used the Jesus-myth to justify their unspeakable aggressions against all others?

Why is the myth of dialectical materialism, or of our own economic dream, venting menace and threatening all people trapped with us on earth? Progress by technology under whatever political aegis points to the same general fate.

That myth must be in error. It must represent, again, not what men are but what they always imagined themselves to be. The language of it is somehow mistaken. How? Well, the pioneers of America did not conquer the wilderness. They annihilated it. And the culture raised up—when the trees

were gone, the stumps burned, the semi-desert of civilization spread forth—is starting to pay the forfeit. For to open
up new lands in our fashion is to shut down their steady
state.

It is aggression, then, defined as progress, performed as
destruction, regarded as a human good because of man's
images of himself, in his head, that are false and without
limits he accepts, wherefore, arrogant beyond earth's capacity to support.

It is the arrogance of believers in these myths that leads
them into the way of aggression and hides from them the
law that they may not kill others to seize their dominions,
nor one another to establish pecking orders.

Arrogance. Which breeds supererogation. Which imagines my faith, my nation, my kind of people, my fellow
citizens have the right myth, which entitles us, yea, binds
us, to the duty of evangelizing the rest of man. Our region
and the dotted line we draw on paper maps to describe it
are holy; we must kill, before even a suspected killer crosses
into our homeland. We must prohibit him from speaking his
(obvious) myth, to keep pure and intact our beloved American myth and the fifty states it has set up and owns, is and
embodies, our "free, Christian nation." What arrogance!
What a route to aggression! What a way to run a species!

Alas, we only see error in beliefs unlike our own, erroneous image.

Faith that allows no doubt is the way that night is brought
down upon us. And the schoolhouse assists in its way, its
like way.

To make our image as near to real as we can we must
first recover faith in a self, already lost beyond retrieve,
for most.

Reality! To see it as false image in time, as artifact or as
pure reason, is not to see it at all, as both image and act,
both being and doing.

Old myths (though I've said they must have been disoriented from the start) are not without casual treasures.
People used to say, for example, that madmen were possessed
of devils. A statement very near to territorial perception.
But we laugh at it now. We are hardly able to imagine that

to possess a belief is to be possessed by it—and, in result, moved into crazed aggression for its support, whenever and wherever it is questioned or fails to define reality. We describe insanity, however, as the loss of contact with reality; but we do not extend that accurate description to mythical possession of and by either religious or "rational" beliefs.

A man with a phobia, a fear of height, for example, is plainly seen by us to be out of touch with a certain reality. He is neurotic, mentally ill in a certain degree. His belief, in that area, is unreal.

He cannot spend a night in a high hotel room. To lean from a window so far above the streets that the cars on it seem beetles terrifies him. And he can project his fear, so that a glimpse of other men at work on the girders of a rising skyscraper appalls him, though he is on the ground, and they are not distressed. His life has to be arranged to prevent any accident of transport to a lofty place. But all who do not share his acrophobia are aware it is unsound, imaginary, a myth he somehow believes.

Its cause is probably its invention as a symbol for a deeper and greater image error or a conflict in his inner mythology. It can sometimes be found and revealed to him and he may then no longer need to act in ritual fashion so as to evade facing his true but intolerable, wherefore repressed, fear image.

What, then, was his myth about himself, in a high room? A fearful myth, but its image a fear of self. So frightening that to prevent the perception of this terrible, hidden fear he made an image as its whipping boy and so, its cover.

While he clung to his phobia it was useless to tell him he but imagined height to be a threat. Height is not animate, malicious, itself a risk. What is there to fear? His answer would be, falling. On a lofty balcony he is terrified lest he might cast himself to death, he explains. Why? He could not say. He would admit, however, the image possessing him to be unreal, and no truth in his interpretation. But the admission would never cure the delusion. Yet, to his mind, beyond reach of logic, that territorial delusion and displacement would prevail over all else. He could not be made to doubt it by any offering of sense, truth, or actuality. It is as if faith-originated and faith-serviced.

That description shows how man creates territorial images which are not real, but seem so, once the image-maker is trapped by them.

Yet will my reader see that all his beliefs are precisely such, unless they are founded on reality? Unless they lead him to evaluate himself as meaningful by portraying himself as an animal and one morally guided by the value system of good and evil, right and wrong, as measured only for the posterity of all mankind? No other image is real. No other, sane. All other visions of meaning, purpose, and the physical body of man are phobias, maniac dreams, as unrelated to reality as the horrors of schizophrenics and the compulsive acts of paranoids.

There is only one useful or even hopeful myth: man as becoming.

Not long ago, the scores of millions of Roman Catholics in our land were permitted by the Vicar-of-God to give up a dogmatic rite. They were allowed meat on Fridays, as if they were infants in highchairs, finally permitted a lollipop every day instead of just six days a week. I wondered if they felt as embarrassed by that as I did? Or as concerned?

The same Vatican had not yet let them manage their own sexual love, or whether or not they choose to breed by it, or merely to commune that way—man with woman, woman with man. Perhaps, I mused, the Friday lollipop was compensation for the maintenance of that other grim, ruinous, and evil continuation of a Dark Age violence. And its arrogance. And its territorial grasp of man's very power to imagine, truly, and so dispense with holy hocus-pocus.

But I was not very hopeful of dispensation soon. The State and Church are not separate in America. The many images of the Christians, and other godly mythologists, prevail over our land.

The right of a man to believe by faith is indisputable. If he then believes bodily ill is the penalty of evil or wrong-thinking, and biology is myth, let him, and let him die of plague. If he believes his special society of deities and saints is faith-certified and holds other Christians, with some variant in their cosmic pecking order, are deluded, and will not be saved, let him have such solace as that mean sanctity affords him, while he lives, and smile in knowing he will not learn his folly. He will but be dead at the expectant time.

The right to self-mystification, even by faith that eschews doubt, stands. One can be sorry for those who pervert half their magical powers to deny the power in the rest. They will have missed existence in this age, being unable to take part in the contemporary adventure.

But what moral right have they in whatsoever a big aggregate to act from their conglomerate and indigestible ideas and compel others to obey their derived rituals, or prohibit others from doing what their incantations forbid? Why must all people, the so-called free, shut shop on their holy day? Or why must the believers wrestle with one another with similar aggression? Why do those for whom Saturday is holy have to revere the Sabbath of contrary-claiming Christians? Why are these pre-Christian and the Dark Age people, these leftovers from bitter centuries of Reformation and Puritanism, accorded any right to jail hundreds of thousands of their fellow Americans for acts they, alone, fantasy as obscene, or lewd, immoral or bestial?

I have said obscenity is like beauty; it occurs in the eye of the beholder. These godly aggressors, then, impose visions of their vile nightmare, as law, on all of us, not the free, then, but their slaves. They are less than bestial. For men cannot be noble to the beast's degree. But why should they be allowed to impound clean minds in their erotic privy where they must remain, beneath the defecation of these self-sanctified defilers of nature?

What right have they to poison the general morality? What legal permission can decently be given them, to keep all mankind vile, as a means to clamp their Jehovah and Jesus on all?

Who are they?

Freedom on their lips is mockery!

Let them believe, however. Have their mind-splitting, half-brain faith. But let us, as the first step in our aim toward a moral species, stop their abuse of liberty and their illicit use of power to inhibit reason. They are heretics to each other! How, then, can they lay heresy on all who do not pay lip service to them, accept mental blockade where they set it up, and conduct their confused, arbitrary rituals against the willingness of others to use reason, use doubt, to learn, be, grow, change, become, and find new meanings, to love, abandon all such aggression, and be free?

How can they be allowed, especially, to indoctrinate their helpless own children in medleys of Mysteries, prisons from which escape is made all but impossible? In it, young victims will have had their heads boarded and feet bound to be tormented into freaks the parents will call beautiful and good, monstrosities God wants molded out of babies and tots—that all the world with eyes will afterward perceive as different; a crippling that prevents the grown mind from walking well or far, a flat-headedness that has deformed brains and made their sad owners forever stupefied.

What right have any of us to force others, and our own offspring among the lot, into such mangled freaks?

In the present state of our culture we cannot hope to achieve the morality I have discussed. Our images that we call tradition prevent that. And we have not yet learned truth enough to proceed in proper acts. We have not even found, or yet tried to find, a minimal criterion for an adequate man. We do not know what genes of our races will best be preserved and mixed together to attain the known advantage of variation in the gene mixture. All we can now attempt is an understanding of our purpose, the moral truth found in ethology, and—eyes open, potential perceived —communicate the fact while striving to enlarge freedom for our next generation so it will be able to gather the knowledge necessary for beginning the act.

We must take charge, then, of tradition. We are the animals with imagination equal to that deed. We need now to recognize it is the different individual, that one, perhaps, in a thousand unconventional persons, who has the genius to move us forward. That, or we shall continue to hold the individual with old fetters, failing to understand any better than those before us whose myths raised great cities that archaeologists dig out of the layered dusts of time.

Old boundaries must be thrown open to gain even a little more territory for truer images.

Yet, as I have said, and said again, the one true inner territory for man is his species, mankind.

Not according to one image of salvation and survival in eternity. Not to any idol's alleged infinite being or omnipotence. And not to the control of Nature.

It may seem easy to assent to that. Of course, you may be saying, man and his future is "all": goal and the meaning.

But if, beloved reader, you assent that way, then ask this of yourself:

Has my life been designed to that one end? Is my inner territory, the image of mankind as one, and my right-wrong standard what I can see as the most good and greatest value of myself for posterity? And is evil, for me, whatsoever I believe, or do, that diminishes or blemishes the opportunity of generations to come, in all the earth, to extend that ideal and act more and more in accordance with that law of nature?

(How infamous, here, to follow rules invented by ancient ignoramuses, who knew nothing of nature, but called their cruel and mindless inventions "natural law!")

Let me put this great question in yet another way.

Man is the magic animal. He can make images of himself (and himself in time-future) that are not magical but demonic. He can employ his imagination to assert he is not animal, but more and other, the ruler of reality, owing to the ordinances pertaining to his dreamed-up, unreal eternity, infinity, omnipotence. He can. He can presume, with such absolute arrogance, and thereby will lose touch with all reality and its limits for life forms, seen then as not to include his own.

But he could, if he would, recover the great and necessary half of man and culture, of civilization and compassion, which he sank beneath the sea to allow his vanity its untrammeled aggressiveness.

For what man should become is what the gift of imagination surely was intended to allow: meaningful.

What, then, is man, as that allowed being?

Man is a creative artist.

He is that, anyhow, willed or not, though now confined in imagined and anti-creative realms of heaven, of progress by technology or of whatever anti-dream he takes for a specious seeming of self-aggrandizement.

Each man is minimally the artist of himself. Each paints that masterpiece, or blotch, that smeared picture of a thug, obscene etching of the holy inventor of obscenity, that portrait of the reasoning being, the humanist, the objective man —unaware he has but engraved himself on a pinhead.

Each man also composes the symphony of himself, or the dissonant noise he is, the song or the croak, concerto of affirmation, or mutter in his chosen dungeon.

Each is the author of his tale, as well—his saga, epic poem, vulgar joke, illiterate gabble.

Each is his own scientist, too. His laboratory may be on Palomar and his work to watch the outward thrust of galaxies and interpret that. Or his laboratory may be confined to the chambers of some "Nicaean Evangelical Church of Jesus," where the equipment is useless for fruitful research since all truth and immutable law is thought to have been revealed to, and set forth, by louse-infested, unclean, burlap-robed old men a millennium and a half ago, who had never heard of galaxies, or even of biology, and yet contrived to make the image of God a Monad, but Threefold, in Nicaea, by huggermugger.

Each scientist can work in a vacuum, a space unoccupied by any whole human being, for gains he can call pure, which men may then exploit while he remains indifferent yet claiming he has virtue, is reasonable, and uses logic.

Each scientist-as-self can accept truer truths as similarly engaged men announce them; or he can ignore all but those in his rooms (for studying tissue-immunity) and if he decides to do this, he can assent by that chicane to the territory of Baptists, or Orthodox Jews, and presume his workrooms and their fruits lie in a different territory.

As that scientist he can be quack, on the side, alchemist, astrologer, patron of fortunetellers, a numerologist, or Rosicrucian—whatever anti-scientist he would split his mind to allow.

So, then, is man—a creative artist of himself, always.

And there is more.

Each usual man, with any like woman, can procreate others. Together, they have that magic capability. And when a pair select each other for that end, they can do so as procreative artists, with the most splendid and just hopes for their bodily creativity, or they can choose one another for some other and alien image in the mind, status, say, outward looks, the need of someone to screw with, legally —the innumerable criteria that, as images of right-wrong obligation, are, in fact, irrelevant to the art of making better people. Criteria that relate to the alleged intentions of God, or to the dowry of the bride, the income of the groom, the mere ecstasy, discovered or expected, of fucking.

But such are our false dreams of man as divinely ruled and as subject to redemption or salvation, by fancied and evil ideas of love, that we have no art of reproduction. Few men and women, nowadays, could even imagine procreative acts as art and as a way we could, were our images truer, take charge of the improvement of posterity and its heritage of body and being, as our two-sexed masterpiece for all men in their forever that is our only eternity, also.

We cannot even imagine what a splendor would burst upon us, males and females, if we reared both to be artists of the species by their loving—and loving used for creating people only when unions were intent on that tremendous and beautiful purpose. Love among two sexes with that understanding would be free and open and proud and as meaningful as sex—made as valuable exactly as death is made necessary by sex. Love for loving, and loving to procreate, only when the ecstasy also was used for that gain and value and wonder.

Man as a procreative artist has barely glimpsed his possibility—the necessity, indeed, of becoming the artist of himself.

How shall we move toward that moral glory?

We shall first have to re-evaluate the Old Books men live by, in their heads, and act from, with their vicious rage.

The Bible must be put away in libraries where it belongs. Filed to gather dust beneath appropriate labels: Mythology, Ancient History, Superstition, Folklore, Prescientific Philosophy, and so on. All the Holy Books, ancient or recent, must be taken there, not left in homes to corrupt children, or in hotel rooms, and on altars, to close minds and devastate the hope of different and greater images for mankind.

We must cease calling such founts of barbarity springs of wisdom. Six words in the Old Testament have led a billion men to regard twenty times their number, down the ages, as lower than their arrogant selves. The words?

"Hewers of wood" and "drawers of water."

A book that has been employed to degrade so many by inflaming such genocidal vanity needs to be banished to the archives.

And with that Scripture we should put away the rest, Apocrypha, Talmud, Koran, Book of Mormon, Mary Baker Eddy's dangerous drivel, the variegated literature of those who rewrote and bastardized the original texts, St. Augustine, St. Paul, Calvin, Knox, Luther, Wesley, the vast store of writ that sets up images of man, for man, and calls it God's truth, or the truth of Lao-tse or Buddha, even when mangled.

Curiosities, scholarly mines, worth keeping when rightly catalogued, that is, when examined, then read less to discern the integrity and true vision of ancient men and recent men and women than to remember their terrible vanity and the hideous behavior of all men who assumed it righteous. Beside these works, of course, will stand those of Marx, Engels, Lenin, Stalin, and Mao, all the saints of materialist religions.

In another and huge wing of that needed repository will be stored the texts and treatises men have composed to assert the species is above nature, and meant to manage and exploit it, no part of the chain-of-life but the chain-breaker.

The old territorial images must be yielded up before the true image of mankind and of morality can be seen, or, when seen, adopted.

The inner image of men they call "race" must be abandoned. Every honest scrutiny has shown no difference of any meaningful sort amongst our species. White, black, red, brown, and yellow are not definitions of otherness but only of skin pigment and slight variations in contour. We are of one kind, and white-tailed deer, or honeybees, are more various but identical, still, in species. Anthropology, psychology, biological scrutiny, make that evident and if any gene of racial advantage be found it should become prized for all of us.

The only meaning in that dreamed-up term "miscegenation" is the meaning given the condition of its offspring by men who try to climb to an imaginary height on their cruelly used backs.

To be a man in mankind with the moral image of that estate is to see a nation as a group that must not be permitted to impose its images or its will on any other. And this must be seen by all, for any one to act ideally.

A government of man founded to ascertain and order what is valuable to do, and outlaw what is greedy and destructive in relation to men yet to come is not envisaged now. The best that the best of us see there is some world government that will end national murder of masses in the prosecution of national images of truth. But even that is, at least, a beginning, an inkling of the need to halt aggression at physical boundaries, if not to stop savagery in the area of its origin, the territorial beliefs men hold and exploit to seem right, that make others seem wrong, or lesser, and enemy.

These carved-up, invented domains in human heads and hearts, I think, must first be routed from their boundaries and cleared of their artifacts, the tax-free, tremendous trappings of despotic landlords, before anything can be done about the national insecurity that such men call security.

Perhaps this effort, to restore man to nature and morality, will not be made, or even much envisioned, now, or for centuries to come.

Perhaps, nature has not lent us all of its imaginative powers and still operates with a part withheld. Perhaps, that is, "the hard way" is, still, man's self-blinded route.

In such a case, it is I who have dreamed, dreamed of you, myself, and now as able to become more gifted and potentially freer, more moral and self-determined than evolution has as yet allowed. If so, I hope that exaggeration can be forgiven, since its intent was but to draw that scene and say that hope.

For though I am convinced my concept of our error cannot be disputed but only made clearer or modified, I cannot say it will be understood, applied, and prevail. The misuse of imagination in the ways I have set forth may have stranded too many of us in egocentricity so that not enough will have the imaginative valor or integrity to escape our state.

We may not have evolved far enough to own sufficient imagination for continuum. We may not be able to grasp the truth that our meaning is defined by the opportunity for meaning we bequeath to future men. And we even see that, in a way—half of it.

We see that our heirs may starve amid slag heaps on the desert we are preparing. We know they may smother in the smoldering, spent air we leave to them. And some of us realize how easily we might erase ourselves any day in radioactive proof of local rectitudes and of our allegedly reasoned use of reason. Even we, or more likely our living children may perish in such a self-annihilation, wondering why, in a last flare of cleansing light. Nature may thus discard man as unworthy of his one distinction and man will then be the agent of his discard owing to his belief that his inner, invented territory is more real than territory itself. Then it cannot be known (unless or until a better animal evolves to restore the planet we ruined) whether man, a self-made fossil, misused imagination or lacked enough of it. Only man's future will show which one was cause. But no man will then exist for such archaeological determination.

Man, then, will have been but a futile effort of evolution, not important, and not missed, another dead end among myriads here and probably decillions elsewhere. A wondrous invention of nature that would not or maybe could not go along with the Greater Design.

But there will have been a unique cast to his failure, in a sense. He will have failed at least semi-consciously, to adapt to himself or his environ. He will have applied his powerful imagination to other ends than adaptation. Nature's time and means for the ascent of life—trial and error in mutant individuals, where one in a thousand such perhaps took part in the magnificent process—was turned over to man as his option, to perceive, comprehend, and take into his charge. But he will not, then, have picked up the option.

The idea that he must take command of his evolution is contemplated by few civilized men. Most meet it with shock, if at all, with resistance, fear, and holy hate. Man belongs to their images of God, they say, and must not tamper with life. (Oh, no?) Adapt the environment to man's present wants, he declaims, and his commercially forced wants, even though supplying them will soon render the environment unlivable. But don't touch life! Life is sacred.

In its human manifestation, life is sacred. Every pushing gobbet of meat extruded from a human womb must be kept alive. Baptized. A hundred able lives must be sacrificed to maintain half as many monsters and all, idiots. A thousand skilled brains must bend their days to find more means to salvage protoplasmic rubbish. And ten thousand as rare, in each generation, or ten times the number, must devote their "scientific" careers to seeking improved techniques for the maintenance of genetic mistakes up to and beyond their breeding point. Life is sacred according to Christians. Such acts demonstrate the strength and infamy of their beliefs. In their view all men must—and we are—bound by law to this sin, even though the gene-pool of men yet to be is daily weakened by the act and the seed of such salvaged contaminators.

Life now is sacred because of its immortal soul. The very biology of man that promises what real or relative immortality he may truly have is not even deemed relevant. Let posterity become a deformed rabble but save the souls of blubber-parodies of man, now and forevermore.

Keep the senile living, too, though demented, and at whatever waste of able lives. It is but Christian love and mercy to do so. And this, besides:

Forbid mercy to those that implore it owing to, say, their cancer—the millions tied for a year on anthills, passing two years as on an Inquisitional rack, or their three, like people floundering in fuming acid. For them, being crucified or burned at the stake would be as many times more merciful as are such short releases, compared to the hundred or thousand longer times we make them bear their agonies. Because of Christian love and mercy. Written in our laws of a *free* people.

I could tell you what I, alone, have watched, till you vomited. But I forbear because, once you caught your breath, you would probably resume your cant about the sacredness of life. And I do not want to vomit. Yet, as that animal best able to imagine agony in another, you *could* be merciful.

Can you not, at least, let go of your vicious imprinting so your heirs will be free to make less obscene designs for love and mercy and sanctity? They will make others, anyhow, and far worse, if you bind them to your present and hateful hypocrisy concerning life and your gods, and the bastard of your technology, that combine to make earth everyman's gas chamber?

Man was meant to be a creative artist. He must accept the role before he attempts to be a moral arbiter. He has the genius if he will cease exploiting genius and allow geniuses then-to-be-expected their being and a voice.

Now, we ignore or segregate our intended form and limit the function. Art is put in a small territory and genius not even understood. What is it?

Genius becomes potential when a man searches within himself, among the images there, to find some clearer figure of them, as they represent images of all that is found within and seen without the man. When and if the man finds, by that search, some clearer vision, the possibility for genius becomes actual. But to be a genius, he must find, still, some medium or means to give his new, inner image an outward expression others will understand.

Then if he succeeds, he is a genius. He has thus added to his species a value, a work of art, an idea, theory, a newly discovered territory that man did not notice till he revealed it. He has become a creative artist.

His music, his painting, his mathematics, his insight into living cells, whatever his new image may be is cherished as a treasure of all, and as a value added to mankind. Yet, often, and perhaps usually, the artist himself is not appreciated. In America, his kind is widely scorned.

To make his contribution he will have had to question, rearrange, or even discard traditional images: to violate a current taboo, then. He is like the valuable mutant in every thousand such, all, rarities in the horde, he alone beyond price. Yet he seems a threat to most men, for being untraditional, unconventional, a breaker of taboo, or reshaper of belief. That is all men notice about him, usually, and it but disturbs them.

They treasure his contribution, in time, but tend to mock him while he lives, denying what he expresses, even letting him starve. Then he will not be present to humble a general tradition and thus show a humble man can do so. His contribution can be incorporated inchmeal and tactfully, and given superhuman luster to keep the living from seeing how genius is but a human being and normal. All contributions to man occur in one man, alone, first. Clever collaborations are possible. But no team and no committee ever had a new idea.

To be sure, a great artist has occasionally been given his due before his death and without spooking his fixed, conservative contemporaries. But, in our so-called civilization, the artist usually is misnamed or invisible. People prefer pandering to their low taste, or anti-artists, to express their emptiness. The necessity to be in some way unconventional in order to add to convention is still felt to be alarming, as circumstance. All incidental behavior, human but imperfect, is usually held to be the resentful act of the resented genius, outrageous, lawless, wanton, heretical, rebellious, obscene, irreverent, and the sad rest of that—projection that indicts mankind, not artists.

Creative scientists rarely think of themselves as artists. Their disciplines rest on logic: art does not. If they employ the term at all, they generally do so in a self-deprecatory way. We cannot do this, or do not understand that, they say, "in the present state of the art."

Yet the pure scientist who makes each of the quantum jumps that keep knowledge expanding into new areas and by new ways and in new dimensions will have performed the act I tried to define as art and the art of a genius. Such a man's objective concepts of reality must also be logically explicable and susceptible of confirmation. So that kind of image-maker tends to flinch from the idea of himself as artist. Aesthetics have nothing to do with his effort. He isn't allowed to involve himself with beauty. (Unless the Universe and Nature and Life and Evolution, mayhap, are deemed [or are truly] beautiful.) Order and law, relationships, actions and reactions of constant sorts concern him—not disorder; not the deliberate and arbitrary means artists, who even use distorted relationships and senseless actions, exaggeration and unproven fancy for their results.

But the searching scientist must go through the inner equivalent of such efforts for success. He is trying, as do the artists in other media, to rearrange his established and logical concepts and re-perceive them in new-structured manners. He must often turn from or upturn present logics. Indeed, his claim as genius and scientist will arise only if he abandons "fact" and "theory," in an arbitrary and undisciplined effort to get beyond the conventional and stated, to a description new of "truth" that will be other and cause a mutation in the status quo of science. Genius, then . . . magician and artist.

Man is potentially that magical an animal.

He will be that only if he sees it means he must recover all the truth of his animal that he has so massively set aside and denied, and he must also use his magic to make him a creative artist instead of a self-bewitched fiend and biological idiot.

Scientists must perceive that requirement in this time and all time to come, and in this style. For the route to the real but unknowable goal is their path and they should explain it to all. Moreover, they should provide the information that determines where, next, they, as humanity's first credible explorers, should search and also, what searches ought to be given less effort, or postponed, as well, obviously, as what results of their past endeavors should be applied, and how, and what others ought to be deferred for further study before application, or, as in nuclear physics, limited to sane applications, if such there be, in the present state of that art.

Some scientists I am acquainted with, Bentley Glass, Barry Commoner, and Ralph Lapp among more, are beginning to talk of scientists as men and therefore under human obligation. Others whom I would enjoy meeting, like the great Konrad Lorenz and the eloquent Loren Eiseley, are also speaking in that way. But, as Lapp has said, the people in the disciplines often speak of "the community of science" although there is no such thing. The super-city of Ivory Tower has no government. Nor sense of duty as a human abode.

Science seeks weapons the Pentagon wants, or whatever business hopes may lead to profitable goods; science engages in an attempt to race other nations for mere lunatic status or undertakes some investigation that scientifically brainless Congress has been led to think important, by special pleaders. What frightens ordinary people as alleged national lag (that then alters the educational curriculum) also sets science to work. Such are the present and nitwit standards for priorities in "science." The pious public fears that some proposed projects might turn up knowledge of an unwanted sort act conversely, as a mighty (though often invisible and unconscious) inhibitor of research. Industry, furthermore, doesn't want anybody to find facts that would expose its sham or the menaces of its products. Christians in millions don't care to have their tax dollar subsidize investigations that reveal the "higher truths" of their dogma as mere rubbish.

Woodrow Wilson was, perhaps, the first president to express dread of government by specialists; by scientists, he meant. But that is not what I here imply. For we already have what Wilson feared, and in a worse form. We have a government by representatives too ignorant of science to be able to judge the merits of any scientific intent. They therefore are dependent upon the slanted say-so of hired lobbyists, or upon superstitious fears or, mainly on what they can see, in a given effort, as lucrative for their constituents. Of such things is their index for appropriations for research composed. We are, then, greatly misgoverned, by ignoramuses to whom scientists defer, often without demur.

That "community of science" is the plain need. But its first requisite is a new and majestic discipline, that of a science of sciences. Not many men at this time would be eligible even as amateur members in groups trying merely to define that super-discipline. The hundred sorts of physicists are now getting the greatest precedence and with it the multibillions. To reach the moon and the planets. To build costly particle accelerators in an effort to find out everything about the ultimate bits of matter and their states, atoms and their structure—energy, then, and electromagnetic radiation propagation, together with gravity, cosmogony, and cosmology. Pure knowledge and needful, admittedly.

Meanwhile, however, the hundreds of different sorts of biologists are fiscally starved. In my opinion, which I have tried to make clear, they should have both the precedence and the money for equipment as well as the most funds for education. For what will it boot us, if we come to understand atoms near absolutely, and lack understanding of the species with that knowledge.

Since ethology provides the clues used here to elucidate our errors and suggest how to rectify them, it is the most important branch of biology, I believe. Ecology is second. Few could even define the term. But unless all soon learn and apply its meaning, man's dead. Psychology, though now seen mostly as an uncertain subdivision of medicine, or an academic fiddling with pigs, ducks, or people (as "subjects") needs a vast opportunity. For it, too, is a little-explored branch of the life science, biology.

But where is the court of appraisal for scientific research? Nowhere. Nor in science nor government.

In my years as a consultant on matters related to nuclear weapons I have seen innumerable acts of physicists and engineers executed in an appalling ignorance of biological fact, even and often without any awareness that life and its single chain were involved in what they did.

I stand witness that science, in its so-called purest form, is often corrupt, mindless, ignorant and without direction even from within, where rational direction, alone, could originate. Science follows fads, is opportunist, can be bought, and has forsaken discipline, reason, logic . . . and always, man.

More money went into the search for a polio cure than into an effort to remedy childhood ills of a greater and more devastating sort. Men will gladly subsidize an attempt to find a cancer remedy but turn away from contributing funds to support studies of their own conduct and their inner state.

The art of science, then, is still practiced in the main by artisans and their apprentices, its skills for sale for the sake of commercial gain, or subject to repression from the fear of bigots.

In a way, that unscholarly state of scholarship is another analogue for the general disaster called man's "condition." Consider:

From our first accession to the time realm by our first use of imagination, we have predicated ends and then developed means to seem to attain them.

The Christian catechism begins with the command:

"What is the chief end of man?"

Answer: "To love and glorify God."

God, then, is the concept of our end, as loved and glorified.

In science, the error persists as overriding rule, too:

What end have we in view? To get to Mars. Cure cancer. Control weather. Mine the ocean. Even the proclaimed end of seeking knowledge "for its own sake," is just as mythical, as I've tried to show, and as irrational. It yields but a concept of man and universe which existentialists would call "absurd"—and by that pronounce their own absurdity. It is a religious postulate, too, but in opposite form. Such an end of science is faith-in-faithlessness and no more relevant to reality than godly faith.

The "chief end of man" cannot be adoration or glorification of idols that he invented to inflate synthetic images of himself. That but led to our long history of serial failures. But neither can man's chief end be to seek and gather knowledge for no other purpose than the ridiculous one of Everest-climbers: because it is there.

Faith as method perpetuates false images of man and nature. The scientific method, skepticism of the present "known," honest testing, the use of imagination to find truer truths, if used for its own sake, is then a negative use of faith to create new inner territory as artificial, unreal, empty of value and unhuman as the kingdoms of the faithful.

It is not even self-perpetuating. It has no more reality

than Hell, Heaven, Valhalla, or Happy Hunting Grounds. It is abiological in a parallel way. For the principle demands that pure scientists concern themselves with "now" and people-now, acting on that proposition without concern for people-to-be or if they will be destroyed, whether by the images of individual immortality, or by the artifacts that such knowledge-finders enabled men to make. Neither "ideal" admits obligation to the human future and its absolute value to all of us.

Both the pious and the scientific purists are but now-people, and therefore non-people. The creeds of both are opposite sides of one act, abdication of man. The inner territory of both is false in the same way. And for causes that only seem opposite. Each, however, is an effort to put man-now into a mythical realm where he can imagine he is not responsible for his reality or for nature and so, perversely, greater than either. Perhaps the fact that ninety percent of all scientists are living today makes them peculiarly liable to their illusion. But not one priest or cleric or shaman in a million of that lot lives now. Most living scientists can see that the beliefs of the living specimens are nutty. And all can see the ancient ones were kook, and crooked, besides. It ought to scare hell out of them.

Still, scientists, rather, one here, one there, have discovered the very truths that should now be used to make men abandon all such fraudulent territories. What truths? That we are animals. That animals have moralities they must abide by, each kind for each, to live onward. And that we are the only one to try to escape the requirement. Magic animals, given nature's art by our gift of imagination, which, now, we must employ morally for our continuum, if we are to have any. Abandoning, thereby, our displaced clutch on and our mad defense of the inner territories in which we are lost since they do not exist outside our heads.

So I shall say to you these things:

If you imagine you can do more than that, you have not yet much used imagination, or used it honestly, at all.

When you tell me of God, I hear you talking about yourself, and nothing else, and boastfully and meanly, besides.

When I observe your prayers, I see a child writing letters to Santa Claus.

When you set forth on the mission of enlightening others with your deprivation, I am ashamed of us, you for the vanity, me for the failure to expose it more lucidly.

When your statements of your God and your prayers generously include the welfare of mankind, I shudder, since it is your idea of welfare-as-end you offer.

And when your faith, your drug and your addiction, lead you to act out your inevitable fears as vengeance on "lesser breeds," or the "wrong-thinking," the enemy you feel imperils your small domain whom you therefore propose to subdue, I weep for them, and you, and for me.

When you describe right-thinking people, your arrogance has blazed forth another time. They are those who hold images identical with your own. And neither you nor they can think or will try to, since you and they will have jettisoned that magical ability, to seem righteous, but to be repellently wrong.

If it is un-American to disagree with your image of Americanism, there is no such nation, for you have, by such an assertion, destroyed its freedom and rewritten the Constitution in your terms as a tyranny.

If you tell me about life beyond the grave, you are talking about all who will be alive when you are dead, and nothing else.

When you mention eternity, you have but brought up the possibility of an indefinite future existence for man, providing he finds the way toward that unknowable territory. Your immortality is but that hope.

When you say you are seeking knowledge for its own sake, objectively, even by imagined but rational logics, you are but boasting, too, and not as a human being, so I think back at you, "We have no use for you, at all, being men, which you have refused to be. Go away! Go away! Go, die! Or all of us will, for your idiot presumption and your alienation from reality imposed on us by your default."

When you are sure of technology as means for progress to some end you call a Great Society, or whatever name you happen at any time to have for that, I count your dead from the progress you've made already by that delusion.

To say you seek honest answers, and then admit you cheat as reprisal for being cheated, floods me with anger, too. For you have lost touch with the means to any answers but those cheatful ones we have forever tried to live by, and forever perished on account of.

When you mention love, I have some immediate expectation. I listen to find what images you cherish so I can measure what you will fear and, by that, discover if you even know it is fear you have, for your love, and not just hate, as you probably presume. For what you despise, or rob of value by trickery, gives the weight of what you really love, know that or not.

And when you talk of conquering nature or controlling it, I am sick again, and bewildered, because your nature exists within the whole, and you have therefore said you do not know who you are.

When you attribute to life forms that are not human attributes of mankind alone, aspects that are mad, irrational, wild, brutal, savage, wanton, parasitical, headless, red in tooth and fang, bestial, and the rest, I am reduced to despair, for they are moral and you are what you say of them. To pretend to a lie so great it cannot long sustain man is your measure of your lack of worth.

Tell me you are a now-person, bent upon having, instantly or as near it as possible, all things and enjoyments and, even, all that you deem knowledge, and you become invisible to my eyes, a non-person, a nobody-there. For what you said you were, a moment ago, is without future being, intent, and meaning; your words will have been spoken in what is now my present, your terminated past, and the result, your near-zero presence and absolute non-future.

Life arose when conditions on this planet made the phenomenon inevitable. That date was long ago even as time's reckoned for the present universe. Earth made some thousands of millions of star circuits as life forms multiplied, evolved, and grew complex. Your date appeared on that calendar and so, you. Now, you have persisted for a part of the era of life, less than one thousandth of its whole.

You are different from other animals only in one way and that but an order of magnitude: the extent of your imaginative capacity. Darwin was only half right, though. The history of your physical evolution is a truth. But who has contemplated the subjective half to see if it developed in keeping with the object? Who asks that question in its right form? What would the answer be?

Man did not develop subjectively according to the ethological imperative of other beings. He exploited his newevolved capability to aggrandize his self-image and to invent artificial territories as escapes from the truths his power disclosed. Images of these areas were validated, he imagined, by the territory he then took and "defended." Islam, Holy Roman Empire, Christendom, the Red madlands. Dream, earthly correlative, aggression.

Finally and recently, however, some men began a search for knowledge with a new end, its own sake. They agreed to imagine honestly in their fields and communicate openly all truths discovered by appraising cause and effect, by careful measurement, and by inventing theoretical images for experimental check. It will seem ironical to most, if they think at all, that a non-motivated labor by non-people for no-end could be fruitful. Yet even that was a great step forward in the employment of imagination.

The means of science swiftly banished the old fiefdoms of fantasy. But it did not reveal the territorial anti-fantasy it usurped. In their irresponsible vacuum scientists merely issued bulletins and washed their hands of consequence.

The usual consequences. New truths were exploited for whatever end man desired in his imaginary domains. *Homo habilis*, or *sapiens*, renamed himself (and his new gods by inference). He is *homo technicus.*

The efficacy of the scientific method led jealous academicians, intellectuals, educators (and their victims, the educated) to new inventions of territory.

"Economics" is one, for example. There is not any such thing but only ecology.

Sociology and its ersatz outlands is another specious province.

We are, to be sure, social animals. Our brains and bodies

are principally designed for what the architects of non-landscape call "interpersonal relations." But I do not believe we can claim sociology in view of such interpersonal relations as I have seen in World War I, World War II, Korea, Vietnam, the Red tyranny-by-terror, the hot summer riots in our own cities, the Christian collaborators with Hitler, Gasser-of-Jews, or even in the roaring sewer we call "news."

To sustain any ego at all in this age men have abdicated themselves as human and even as animals. With Kafka their scene is befuddlement. With Sartre, their thing is an absurd universe and shows their own absurdity. In some final effort to justify materialism many say man is a machine. Automaton of cybernetics. All abiological images, religious, mechanistic, or nihilist are designed to permit infinite predation of biology itself and nature.

Man has "machines" like the "computer" I used as symbol for one such. He has never programmed that one sanely. But no machine can be programmed with the data of a microbe and print out specifications for a man. Man himself lacks that information, owing to willful preferences. So the lunacies increase with "progress." *The medium is the message,* I'm informed. Orwell could not have dreamed up a neater perversion.

Man is the medium and his acts the message.

All his contraptions have communicated the same sad word, too. I daresay readers of this book may now be disappointed. I agreed to state here what I am for. And then I told what you are not that you imagine you are.

Man's only "power," I said, is his imagination. All other "power" is illusory. He has the potential to become a magic animal. But to achieve that he must abandon all the dreamed territory he thinks he occupies. The same cost was asked for less: an invented soul with its presumed end of entering the Kingdom of Heaven. The myths by which we have lived were synthesized to define ends.

There is none we can know or should invent.

Man is but means to unknowable and other means of future men.

What I am "for" is that moral means which alone could lead toward a myth which any image would destroy. A single vision of human relations among magic animals or what marvels they would build and enjoy would be treason.

I cannot offer a utopia. Only an opportunity for meaningful existence and only that as you, not I, might find it by mythic morals.

Our present rape of life and matter and man for a proliferation of mere toys is visible as error, to you, perhaps. You may further see that the terrible toys of the same men, fabricated to defend their territory, have an adequate caliber for a Malthusian act in a world overpeopled by such technology.

If you have seen that equation, you have gone a long way toward mine.

And I feel the rest of the journey warrants the offer of this sure benefit:

I am not a stranger, here, any longer.

Are you?

Thus endeth the reading of the lesson.

89 leading doctors tell you how they lose weight and keep it off— without crash diets, diet pills or "special" foods!

It's all here, in a remarkable new book designed to help you adjust your eating and exercise habits for a healthier, happier, longer life.

FREE 30-day trial

Send for your copy of HOW THE DOCTORS DIET. When it arrives, read through it . . . apply some of the doctors' techniques to your own eating and exercise habits. If you're not completely convinced that this book can make a difference in your life, return it within 30 days and owe nothing. If you decide to keep the book, we will bill you only $4.95 plus a small mailing charge. You have nothing to lose—but some excess weight! At all bookstores or mail the coupon to Trident Press, Dept. TP-4, 630 Fifth Avenue, New York, N.Y. 10020.

77066